MORAL VISION

MORAL VISION

Seeing the World with Love and Justice

David Matzko McCarthy & James M. Donohue, CR

WILLIAM B. EERDMANS PUBLISHING COMPANY
GRAND RAPIDS, MICHIGAN

Wm. B. Eerdmans Publishing Co.
4035 Park East Court SE, Grand Rapids, Michigan 49546
www.eerdmans.com

ISBN 978-0-8028-7487-0

Library of Congress Cataloging-in-Publication Data

Names: McCarthy, David Matzko, author.
Title: Moral vision : seeing the world with love and justice / David Matzko McCarthy
    and James M. Donohue, CR.
Description: Grand Rapids : Eerdmans Publishing Co., 2018. |
    Includes bibliographical references and index.
Identifiers: LCCN 2018020962 | ISBN 9780802874870 (pbk. : alk. paper)
Subjects: LCSH: Christian ethics. | Ethics. | Values. | Prejudices—Religious aspects—
    Christianity. | Prejudices.
Classification: LCC BJ1275 .M39 2018 | DDC 241—dc23
    LC record available at https://lccn.loc.gov/2018020962

For the Congregation of the Resurrection, Ontario-Kentucky Province,

"called . . . to be a community which is a living sign
of the gospel . . . of justice, truth, and love."

RESURRECTION PRAYER:
O Risen Lord, the way, the truth, and the life,
make us faithful followers of the spirit of your resurrection.
Grant that we may be inwardly renewed; dying to ourselves
in order that you may live in us.
May our lives serve as signs of the transforming power of your love.
Use us as your instruments for the renewal of society,
bringing your life and love to all people and leading them to your Church.
This we ask of you, Lord Jesus,
living and reigning with the Father, in the unity of the Holy Spirit,
God forever. Amen.

Congregation of the Resurrection,
Ontario-Kentucky Province
(https://resurrectionists.ca/)

Contents

Foreword

It is not too large an exaggeration to say that the history of moral philosophy and theology has been dominated by the question of the relationship between the true and the good. Put differently, is the virtuous moral life primarily a matter of knowledge or of choice? In modern times, we might ask whether it is primarily a matter of reason or of will. Socrates famously thought that virtue is knowledge, and therefore vice is ignorance. Aristotle attempted to describe an intricate nexus between desire and reason. The development of the notion of what we now call "the will" helped tilt that balance away from knowledge, perhaps most obviously in the voluntarists of the fourteenth century. In the post-Enlightenment or modern period, we can say that reason is clearly losing to will and desire. Hume famously described reason as slave to passion, and Kant based his grounding of morality on an affirmation that the only truly good thing without qualification is a good will. Twentieth-century debates in moral philosophy have fixated on the relationship between reason and will (or desire), between the "is" and "ought," and in particular how to jump the assumed gap between them. The regnant model of practical reasoning today—from policy and economic discussions to the focus in philosophy on "instrumentalism"—is that human desires provide us with the ends we seek, and practical reasoning entails the use of reason in securing those given ends through choices we make. In this model, reason never "reaches back" to the ends we possess, but rather is "instrumental" in helping to secure them.

In this context, a book on morality entitled *Moral Vision* is a radically countercultural endeavor. McCarthy and Donohue claim their book "will address seeing, becoming, and doing, but seeing—moral vision—is our main concern" (11). They address the last century's imbalance by focusing on the true and not only the good. Rather than seeking to establish reason as some abstract foundation of morality, they turn to the everyday and describe the ways in which how we see is a moral activity. Relying on Aristotle and Thomas Aquinas, their book is a reflection on that intricate interpenetration of reason and will. It thus dislodges the modern assumption that reason is uninfluenced by character and morality. It explains that how we see is a moral endeavor. Their goal is not to further entrench the hegemony of will and desire to overwhelm reason even in our particular choices. Rather, their portrayal of this interpenetration "reaches back," so that not only our assessment of what is true may be shaped by our grasp of the good, but also our grasp of what is true might be a source of what we recognize as good. "In sum, a source of our good and bad actions, when freely done, is our knowledge and vision of what is good" (14). How we see shapes how we act and who we become. And in turn, who we are shapes how we see. *Moral Vision* is a beautiful guide to the lifelong journey of growing in the "disciplined attention" (18) that is "seeing the world with love and justice."

One of the most obvious ways we connect reason and will is through personal encounters. Relationships with people help us to "see" certain things as true. At times we are unable to see clearly the matter at hand for a variety of reasons, and people help us to do so. Perhaps the matter at hand is not inherently unseeable but beyond our expertise, as when we are advised by a car mechanic or lawyer. Perhaps the matter at hand does entail mystery, as when we discern marriage or a career choice, and in these cases mentors and friends help us see the most life-giving path. The Christian tradition affirms that faith in Christ is a sort of knowledge that is possible only through encounters with persons. Since there is something not ultimately provable (either way) about the reality that "Jesus is Lord," it is only through encountering persons that we are drawn to "see" truths such as this. In fact, the "seeing" that is faith is only possible through an encounter with the person of Christ, for most of us through his body the church. In his encyclical *Lumen fidei*, Pope Francis describes faith as hearing, and he claims that "knowledge linked to a word is always personal knowledge." It is "knowledge bound to the passage of time," and "can thus help to bring out more clearly the bond between knowledge and love" (no. 29). He recounts the lament of Jean Jacques Rousseau that God relies on the mediation of personal encounter and on salvation history to reveal himself to us. "Is it really so simple and natural that God would have sought out Moses in order to speak to Jean Jacques Rousseau?" (no. 14)! Pope Francis decries Rousseau's "individualistic and narrow conception of knowledge" and says he fails to "appreciate the significance of mediation, this capacity to participate in the vision of another, this shared knowledge which is the knowledge proper to love" (no. 14). Personal encounters and the stories that are their medium are not at all merely incidental to moral vision. Through personal encounters we are able to see more clearly, since we affirm the truth by being drawn to it as good.

Unsurprisingly, then, *Moral Vision* is a deeply *personal* book, one that is full of stories. It is true of the authors themselves, who are present in this book in a way that is hospitable and illuminating. They write from the first person at times and share stories from their own histories. Readers will long remember the different reactions of David and his wife to found money, or the exchanges between Fr. Jim's mother and father when it comes to lighting a grill! The authors also incorporate stories from literature, such as the powerful account of Fr. Brown from a story by G. K. Chesterton, or the many narratives to which they direct readers at the ends of chapters (addressed below). These personal narratives are not merely ornamental. They model for readers how people come to see things, and they guide readers in how they themselves will come to "see" things in their own lives.

There is another way this book makes a striking, if subtle, contribution to the importance of personal encounters and narratives. As Pope Francis notes above, God has chosen to reveal himself to and relate to his people through the story of salvation history. *Moral Vision* subtly but masterfully invites readers, who are usually less than familiar with the Scriptures, into the biblical narrative of salvation history. Teachers of theology today commonly lament that students do not know the basics about the Bible and salvation history. It has long been recognized that an account of God's history with his people is central to passing on the good news. From Peter's and Stephen's first speeches in the earliest days of the church (Acts 2 and 7), to Augustine's catechetical guide (*De catechizandis rudibus*), it has always been regarded as central to share the "story" of God's relationship with his people. Yet contemporary teachers know how easy it is to do this poorly, in a way students regard as heavy-handed or irrelevant. McCarthy and Donohue manage to incorporate nearly all the central features of biblical history into their book in a manner that is seamlessly interwoven. They address creation, the fall, Abraham, the exodus, the kingdom, the prophets, the gospels, and the early church. It was not until toward the end of the book that I realized how carefully and comprehensively they achieved this. This is far more than a subversive way to "sneak" into their book a basic education in salvation history. It is a continuation of the book's emphasis on personal encounters and narrative. It is through relationships and stories with people that we come to see truthfully. It is true of the moral life, as it is true of God's history and relationship with his people.

With its subtle incorporation of salvation history, as well as its attention to central theological topics (such as providence, incarnation, and church), *Moral Vision* can serve as an introduction to theology. It can also be accurately described as an introduction to morality. It "covers" the main topics in moral theology, such as intentionality, virtue, law, and conscience. It even has chapters that could fit into a moral philosophy course, since they contrast the authors' approach to those of Hume and Kant. But in another sense it would be unfair to call this book an introduction, if by "introduction" one means presenting a comprehensive overview of a field. The book is not primarily about "presenting," and it succeeds in resisting the temptation to first and foremost attempt to "cover it all." Instead, it is an *active* book. The moral vision it depicts is very active, something that one does attentively and that even requires discipline. And so, appropriately enough, the book models a very engaged and participatory type of teaching.

This is most obvious in the "For Reflection and Further Study" sections at the end of each chapter. Far from mere lists of source texts or questions for summarization, these sections at times approach the main text in length. Yet rather than opportunities to present more material, they serve as the authors' guidance to readers in how to actively engage texts and topics for further reflection, as individual readers or as a class. The chapters do indeed teach material to the readers. These closing sections then propel readers to deepen that knowledge through inquiry-based learning. This method makes the text superb for classroom use and models the vision of the moral life it presents. The moral life is constituted by activity, the activity of seeing—or perhaps even better, "looking"—as well as doing. This text guides its readers in looking, and thus helps initiate them into the very life it commends.

In this text, McCarthy and Donohue offer a powerfully countercultural account of the moral life that is nonetheless accessible, hospitable, even personal. They model the very account of moral vision their book offers. They exude the friendship that is so central to the good life; they evidence deep friendship with one another and others in the text; they guide their readers as generous hosts; and they point their readers toward that ultimate goal of any Christian account of morality: friendship with God.

WILLIAM C. MATTISON III

Introduction

The book focuses primarily on "vision" as an issue and problem, but from this point of departure, it provides opportunity for a broad treatment of moral theology. The chapters are short and thematic, intent on orienting the reader to elements of moral investigation, vision, and inquiry, such as the nature of practical reason and the passions. Following the treatment of a theme, we provide exercises for reflection and further study. It is possible, even likely, that a reader or class would spend longer on these questions and exercises than the chapter itself. This is our intent. Our chapters provide a framework to undertake broader questions. The book could be used as an introduction to moral theology; or, with the use of the questions for reflection and discussion, it can provide the framework for an entire course. To facilitate further inquiry, we cite and direct the reader to texts that are in the public domain and readily available online, such as Plato's *Republic*, Aristotle's *Nicomachean Ethics*, Thomas Aquinas's *Summa theologica*, and the New American translation of the Bible (see usccb.org/bible).

Our attention to moral vision comes from long years of teaching about the moral life and, of course, working to become better people ourselves. Between moral principles like "Do not bear false witness," and deliberation about a course of action, there is a need—and certainly the need for an ability—to see people, events, and ourselves more truthfully, justly, and lovingly. This very problem of bearing false witness is treated in chapter 7, when we discuss a detective story by G. K. Chesterton, "The Man in the Passage." Honorable characters in the short story, an aristocrat and a decorated officer, are unable to see truthfully (they actually see with anger and jealousy) because of ingrained habits of seeing. The main character of the story, Father Brown, sees what is going on plainly and clearly because he is far less self-centered.

This kind of vision is the topic of *Moral Vision* as a whole. How do we learn to see and, because we see, to love and to draw near what is good? We find that this question is a useful and interesting vantage point from which to consider various other topics in moral theology.

Moral Vision attends to philosophical and theological questions, and in this sense, it is unmistakably a work in moral theology. Our goal is to cultivate a theological vision with the help of and in terms of ancient and modern philosophical questions. With a quick look at the table of contents, you will see chapters on passions, moral reason, and prudence, as well as faith, providence, and prayer. We give opportunity for the reader to give closer attention to the writings and thought of Plato and Aristotle, David Hume and Immanuel Kant, and of course, Thomas Aquinas. Following the long and broad tradition of moral theology—a tradition renewed and enlivened (for Catholics) at Vatican II—our treatment of moral vision in the first part of the book leads in the second part to a discussion of Scripture, liturgy, and ecclesiology. The Bible is, for Christians, the fundamental source for a theological vision of God's love, goodness, justice, and mercy. We have found that studying Scripture and pondering deep questions in moral theology can be life-giving and transformative. We hope that *Moral Vision* communicates these experiences to you.

PART 1

Vision

CHAPTER 1

Moral Vision

W hen going from a set of residence halls to various other buildings—the academic center, library, dining hall, and student center—students at Mount St. Mary's University walk across a broad lawn. The lawn is crossed throughout the day and evening. It is on a gently sloping hillside that is crisscrossed with walkways. During the day, especially between classes, the hillside walkways are busy streets. In the twilight and more so during nighttime, the experience is much different. One is likely to be and to feel very much alone and isolated. It is on this hillside that we would like to consider a kind of experiment in "seeing." The main point of the exercise is to make a connection between how we see the world around us and how we feel, choose, and act. The main goal of this chapter is to understand "seeing" as a moral task. We begin with the simple point that different people see situations and events differently. From there, we consider that some people see things in an immature way (like a nine-year-old's perspective), some admirable, others thoughtless, and even some in a selfish way. These descriptions—immature, praiseworthy, and thoughtless—are moral evaluations; underlying the evaluations is the conviction that we are responsible for how we see.

Seeing What Is Happening

Imagine that a student walks across our hillside in the dim of evening, and she sees a small dark object on the concrete walkway. You might have had a similar experience driving on a highway. From a distance, you see an unknown object in the middle of the road, and only as you draw near do

5

you discover that it is simply a chunk of truck tire or a piece of cardboard. Imagine that our Mount St. Mary's student, when nearing an object on the ground, discovers that the object is a clip full of bills. What does she see? She would see money certainly. But to describe this act of seeing properly, we have to extend the description further. Does she see money that has been lost? Or does she see money that has been found? When she reaches her campus apartment, how will she describe the event to her roommates? What will it be? "I just found $100!" Or, "Someone lost $100!"

The exclamation points have been added so that we might hear in the student's voice her own certainty about what she has seen and experienced. If she declares with clarity and certainty that someone has lost $100, then her set of choices and course of action have already taken shape. If someone has lost $100, then her declaration to her roommates implies questions about how to return it. Does she contact Public Safety? Does she ask around to find out who uses a money clip? Does she put up signs? What is the extent of her responsibility? You—the reader—might be thinking that this set of questions might not be asked at all. It might be that a student declares, "Someone has lost $100," and then asks, "How should we spend it?" Also, you might have an objection that a person will be using the word *found* ("I found this money") but clearly means and emphasizes that the money has been lost. Grant us some leeway on how our student uses her words. If our student is rushing back to her apartment thinking about spending the money, the first words that pop out of her mouth will be, "I found $100!" She has already "seen" something that she owns. If she says, "I found $100 . . . someone must have dropped it on the way back from the bank machine," she has seen something that belongs to someone else. Whatever the exact words, our point in the example is that, morally speaking, two people might see different things.

I (David) have a clear memory of both experiences—of "someone has lost!" and "we have found!" First, I will recount the tunnel vision of finding something great. When I was about nine years old, I was walking home from baseball practice with Gerry, my neighbor and friend. We were passing through a neighborhood not our own when we found $5 on the sidewalk. It is interesting how images form in memories. Three images are fixed in my mind. I will offer them in reverse order. Third: I am staring at my own green glass quart bottle of ginger ale. I feel the heat as I sit on the concrete curb outside a Cumberland Farms convenience store. Second, I am staring at a candy bar display at the grocery store across the street. I should add that a candy bar in the mid-1970s was about 25¢, so that $5 went a long way. This fact about 25¢ candy bars leads to the first and most important image, the five-dollar bill on the sidewalk. In my memory, the only thing that I see is a five-dollar bill on concrete. I have no memory of more than about a ten-inch square of walkway—no street, no lawns, no houses, no people, not even Gerry. Every so often, as the years passed, we would share the memory so that I am relatively certain he was there. But in truth, I only remember the five-dollar bill, the candy, and the ginger ale.

The clarity of what Gerry and I were able to see translated into a feeling of delight, a set of choices (what to buy and where) and a set of actions (the change of route to the stores and our purchases).[1] Our common vision shaped our experiences. Without question or doubt, Gerry and I were convinced that we had found the money for ourselves. We had absolutely no concern or even passing thought of the fact that someone had lost it. In theory, if we saw $5 as a great boon for us, we should have been able to imagine that it was a great loss to another. But our moral imagination did not extend beyond our own fortune. There could have been someone walking ten yards ahead of us, who might have been the original owner. There could have been, but we didn't notice and have no memory of such a person. Once our eyes were on the five-dollar bill, our vision narrowed. What we saw determined how we felt, what we thought, and what we did.

But the same relationship between seeing, feeling, choices, and action can be shown when someone finds what another has lost. Recently, David's wife, Bridget, found a wallet near the stadium on campus—at Mount St. Mary's. By the same evening (with the help of Google), she had identified and contacted the owner and then driven ten miles to deliver the lost wallet. We asked Bridget what she saw. We received an interesting answer: "That woman's whole life was in that wallet—insurance cards, credit cards, everything." Seeing Bridget's face when she gave this answer made her experience even clearer to us. We saw her worry and compassion. We saw empathy. In contrast, David and Gerry saw something that produced immediate delight. It never occurred to them that some other nine-year-old might be absolutely heartbroken. Their faces, no doubt, radiated the joy of their own fortune. Bridget, in contrast, saw something that produced immediate worry for another. Her expression of feeling confirms the connection

1. The experience reminds us of the parable in Matthew 13:45-46, which is sometimes titled "The Pearl of Great Price." "Again, the kingdom of heaven is like a merchant searching for fine pearls. When he finds a pearl of great price, he goes and sells all that he has and buys it." The parable puts emphasis on seeing. Once someone sees the kingdom, what else can he or she do but to live for it above all things (Matt. 6:33)?

between seeing, experiencing, and choosing. Bridget saw and experienced someone's loss.

We have yet to deal with the hard cases. Our examples so far are relatively easy to manage. The experiences are clear and certain. But the clarity and certainty imply a difficulty that has troubled philosophers, theologians, moral psychologists, political thinkers, and others for at least 2,400 years. In Plato's dialogue *Meno*, Socrates asks, "Can virtue be taught?" Can or how does one change from seeing money as found! (with no care for the original owner) to seeing money as lost! (with immediate concern for another)? Our examples suggest moral maturation, from the tunnel vision of a nine-year-old to an adult concern for others. However, the appeal to moral maturation does not settle the problem. Some nine-year-olds would immediately knock on a door or find someone to ask about the lost five-dollar bill. Why and how do they come to have this response (while Gerry and David did not)? In contrast to the virtuous nine-year-old, plenty of adults would immediately pocket found money or shift responsibility to another. Some might see a wallet on the ground, say "Oh, that's too bad," and continue on their way. What is the difference between them and Bridget? What happened or did not happen to her and them, what was learned or not learned by her and them?

Besides the hard case of changing one's moral vision, there is a difficult middle ground inhabited by many who see the money bound within the money clip. We see a good bit of money, but we cannot be certain of the details and the full description. The uncertainty is similar to when a parent hears a crash and crying in another room of the house, walks into the room and sees a child crying, another child looking surprised, and a broken lamp. The parent will ask, "What is going on?" The crying child could have knocked it over. Or it could have been the other child. Or they could have broken the lamp together and are just reacting differently. What we see, at first glance, is not always clear and easy to understand. Likewise, when we come across a money clip with a wad of cash, we are likely to ask, "What happened?" David and Gerry did not ask this question. They knew that they had found money. Bridget did not ask this question. She was certain of one basic fact—obvious to her—that money had been lost. However, often we are not so certain of what we see (in a moral sense).

Imagine that our student who finds $100 on the walkway uses both the words "found" and "lost" when explaining the event to her roommate. She says something like, "I found some money; I guess someone lost it." In a moral sense, she might be uncertain as to what she has seen, and she hopes that the conversation with her friend will help clarify the meaning of the experience. These types of conversations are at the heart of a good friendship. Our student holds up the money clip and says, "Look what I found on the sidewalk. What do you think I should do?" The discussion that follows will be about how best to describe the experience of coming across the money. The question, "What should I do?," will turn back to a proper description of what has happened. The money was lost, no doubt, but what kinds of rights and responsibilities are given and imposed on a person who finds it? What are the conditions of its loss? Under what conditions was it found? For example: finding $100 on the walkway of a relatively small campus (one that refers to itself as a community) is different than finding $100 in a stadium parking lot, full of cars and empty of people. In the second case, we arrive at the game late, and on our way from parking lot to stadium, we find scattered twenty-dollar bills tumbling in the breeze. How we describe these events, morally speaking, is going to be different. Different elements of the "finding" are going to come into focus.

Seeing as a Moral Task

Our point is that the description of what happened—the responsibility of seeing what is going on—is in itself a moral task. Consider our original examples: nine-year-old David and adult Bridget do not see the same thing when they see cash on the ground. We can call the difference a matter of maturity and wisdom. We might not blame the nine-year-old for his tunnel vision, but we certainly should praise Bridget for her vision. She saw, not merely a wallet, but also the suffering of another person. Our other examples are less clear: somewhere between the certainties of "found!" and "lost!," our uncertain student and her roommate will work their way through a moral task of description. The student will have a chance to articulate the details, and her roommate will respond to them in a way that helps our uncertain student figure out what she has experienced. How much money? Where? Was anyone else around? What's going on at the McGowan Center? When all is said, will her roommate see that what she has in her hand is something owned by someone else? Does the roommate see money that has put someone else in a terrible state of worry? Does her roommate see something trivial or grave? (For example, if it were $1 rather than $100, the matter would be more trivial. The possibility of discovering the owner of a stray dollar is far more remote, and if by chance the owner were found, she could dig into her pocket and deliver the dollar on the spot.) Through a series of questions and descriptions, the two friends will figure out what to do by first articulating what has happened.

The moral importance of description is underlined by the possibility, which we noted above, that it is conceivable that our student states, "Someone has lost $100," and then asks, "How should we spend it?" The case of recognizing that the money is lost by another, but immediately claiming it as one's own—without some good-faith effort to find the owner—seems to present us with thoughtlessness and/or greed. Both amount to an inability to see the "lost" from someone else's point of view. They amount to a self-centeredness that is at least moral immaturity if not callousness. Imagine the roommate saying, "We have to try to find who lost it. Someone needs that $100." Imagine the response, "Who cares?" Here we have a deeply immature or callous vision of the world. It is certainly a self-centered, and most likely an inconsistent view. "That's tough; it's mine now." People like this often claim the opposite when *they* lose the money. In this way, how we see a moral problem is deeply set within how we see ourselves in relationship to others and to what is good.

Allow us to string the example out further. Imagine that we hear that Joseph had lost $100 and that it had been found and spent by Andy. A group of us discuss the events. We will hold Andy responsible for his actions. Yes, Andy could have found out that Joe lost the money. We did; he could have. He now knows. We wonder why on earth Andy made no effort to find the owner. Did he just not think that someone was suffering a loss? That is, was he thoughtless and immature? Or did he realize that someone had suffered a considerable loss, but did not want to try to find the owner because he wanted to keep the money? That is, was he callous and greedy? Certainly, Andy does not want to be called cold-hearted and greedy. He might say, "How was I supposed to know?" But honestly, is his claim of ignorance and thoughtlessness any better? If someone is twenty years old, shouldn't he know that his "find" was someone else's "loss"? When he argues, "How was I supposed to know?," won't someone respond, "What, are you nine years old?" Because he is responsible for his actions, Andy is also responsible for how he sees the situation in the first place. His inability to see what was going on is a moral failure—of a different sort than scheming greed—but a moral failure nonetheless. We should expect anyone on campus to "see" the situation properly: money found in a clip on campus is lost money. We should expect—especially on a campus that calls itself a community—that there will be avenues for discovering who uses a money clip and who has lost one holding $100.

We have been teaching long enough to know that people get anxious when we start to describe (and therefore to judge) moral behavior. But it is unavoidable. Someone is going to want to defend Andy by citing some element of the situation or knowledge available to him at the time. We will be told that we have left out an important detail or that we have misinterpreted his acts. In each case, Andy's advocate will be offering an alternative description of his acts. So if the alternative description is convincing, we can say we are wrong about Andy and come to the same point about "seeing." In other words, someone can give us a reason why Andy saw the money as his find rather than someone's loss. The reasons might be convincing. Given the reasons, we would see that—morally speaking—Andy's vision was appropriate. And this "reason giving" supports our point. How we see makes a difference to how we act. And there are better and worse ways to see things. On one hand we can see with compassion, or on the other with selfishness. Lost or found: these kinds of descriptions of acts, experiences, and events are shared, and as shared, they are fundamental to how we live—to how we inhabit the world—indeed, to who we are and our view of life.

Conclusion

Moral vision is the foundation of good choices and actions, and good actions form the foundation of becoming good. Likewise, this book is about moral vision, but it will also attend to what we do and who we are called to be. The book will address seeing, becoming, and doing, but seeing—moral vision— is our main concern. This chapter, as an introduction to moral vison, has made a few basic points. First, how and what we see shapes what we do. Second, how and what we see is itself a moral activity, and this activity is a responsiveness to the goodness of people and things in the world. Third, then, we are responsible for our moral vision. We hope that last example—about Andy finding Joe's money—was convincing. Circumstances were such that Andy should have seen that the owner of the $100 would be greatly troubled by his loss and that Andy had avenues for discovering who the person might be. But what Andy actually saw was his own good fortune. If we hold Andy responsible for his lack of vision and thoughtlessness, then moral vision is, indeed, a moral task.

For Reflection and Further Study

1. Playboy to Iron Man

The importance of moral vision is displayed well by the film *Iron Man* (dir. Jon Favreau, 2008). In the film, we see how the main character, Tony Stark, becomes Iron Man. He changes from a classic "playboy," who is concerned only with his own pleasure, to a classic hero, who is willing to sacrifice his own good for the good of others. Fundamental to this transformation is a change in his vision of his work and his role in the world. Watch the film and think about the experiences that Tony goes through, how these experiences change his vision, and how his vision changes his actions and who he begins to become.

Consider, also, that Tony has the same basic personality both before and after his transformation. He is inventive, bold, brave, intelligent, and self-assured. Throughout the film, his personality does not change. But his change in moral vision alters his character—how he is a moral agent in the world.

2. Prejudice

Mother Teresa is remembered as saying, "There is only one God and He is God to all; therefore it is important that everyone is seen as equal before God." For Mother Teresa, this vision of others is the beginning of love. In contrast, seeing others as not equal, as somehow deficient, is at the heart of racism, sexism, and other forms of discrimination.

You might know examples of how minorities in the United States, specifically African Americans, have been seen as not the same kind of human as Caucasian persons. In the eighteenth and nineteenth centuries, those who defended slavery viewed Africans as different—as lower in the order of things—than white people. For example, some justified slavery by identifying Africans with the "Sons of Ham" who were cursed by Noah to be slaves of the sons of Shem and Japheth (Gen. 9:20-27). In contrast, those who rejected slavery had a different vision of the enslaved Africans. Abolitionists, whether white or black, were able to see slaves as human beings—sons of Adam like all human beings.

For example, in his autobiography, the *Narrative of the Life of Frederick Douglass*, Frederick Douglass describes changes that occur in how he views himself. One key change starts to occur when he begins to learn to read. He comes to see himself differently—as destined to be a free man. Read chapter 8 of the *Narrative of the Life of Frederick Douglass*. It is about four pages long and can be found online (some editions are in the public domain). In chapter 6, Douglass describes how a new owner, Mrs. Auld, saw him differently than he was used to being seen by white people. She had not owned slaves before. She had not been trained in the vision and habits of slaveownership. Her way of seeing him (as an ordinary person) helps him to see himself differently. Unfortunately, she changes her view. She starts to see him through the eyes of her husband. Douglass also describes how he starts to see himself differently when he moves from life on a plantation to the city of Baltimore. The chapter is full of shifts in moral vision. Consider the shifts and their moral implications.

Consider, also, the Nazis' view of Jews. Can you think of other examples? The common element of these examples is not just what people did, but also how they viewed others.

3. When and how are we responsible?
We have proposed that people are responsible for their moral vision. Certainly, responsibility varies in degree and gravity according to circumstances and other factors pertaining to the who, the what, and the where.

- We are not likely to ascribe fault to David and Gerry because they were nine years old. But their parents would likely help them widen their vision. "David, don't you think you might have tried to find out who had lost the money?" Their parents may have rightly called them to responsibility.
- We will praise someone like Bridget who goes the extra mile (ten miles actually) to return a lost wallet. Not only did she see someone else's property, but also she saw another's pain and worry. She immediately saw (in her moral imagination) someone for whom she was concerned and wanted to help.
- In reference to slavery in the ante-bellum South, we might give a "reluctant" and "compassionate" slaveholder (such as Thomas Jefferson?) a bit of moral latitude, saying, perhaps the slaveholding mindset was simply part of the culture. We might, but certainly, we may not. We could cite the fact that clear arguments against slavery were stated strongly by abolitionists (and Jefferson himself). Slaveholders could have made a choice to see slavery as a wrong that could not be tolerated.

With these three examples, we see various questions that are raised and judgments that have to be made in understanding our responsibility for moral vision.

The issue of moral vision arises in Aristotle's *Nicomachean Ethics*, when he is discussing voluntary and involuntary action in book 3, chapter 1. For Aristotle (and Plato before him), we go wrong and do wrong, for the most part, because we misunderstand or disorder what is good. In other words, we do not aim at bad things, but mistake them for good. We are able to act well and live well when we have made an effort to gain wisdom and understanding about the good things in life and particular human goods. In sum, a source of our good and bad actions, when freely done, is our knowledge and vision of what is good. Our moral vision is operative both in the abstract (in the conviction that giving to those in need is good) and in the particular (my ability to recognize that a particular person is in need). When discussing these matters, Aristotle makes a distinction between "actions *due* to ignorance and acting *in* ignorance."[2] Actions due to ignorance are inadvertent (and therefore do not carry responsibility) and acting in ignorance is a result of our choices (which of course make us responsible for our moral vision).

Acting in ignorance involves a lack of understanding and wisdom about the basics of human goods. For example, imagine that you complain, "I lost $100," and a friend responds, "Wow, too bad, I found it yesterday. Finders keepers; losers weepers." In this case, the "friend" lacks what we think is basic knowledge about transferring ownership, not to mention the basics of friendship. If he is two years old we will not blame him; if he is twenty, we know that something is wrong. Barring some medical condition or trauma, he is responsible for his view of the events. Acting in ignorance also occurs when a person refuses (or lacks the ability) to deliberate on a course of action. You complain, "I lost $100," and a friend responds, "Wow, I found it yesterday, but I spent it. I didn't think it was a big deal." It was a big deal to you of course, but your friend is telling you that she didn't deliberate on the matter at all. Again, shouldn't a twenty-year-old have the ability to think it through? Actions due to ignorance are much different. They pertain to particulars. Aristotle notes that when we become aware of our ignorance in retrospect, we will express regret. "You think you lost it between here and the Academic Center? Oh, I might have seen it in the distance. I thought it

2. Aristotle, *Nicomachean Ethics*, trans. Martin Ostwald (New York: Macmillan, 1962), 1110b, lines 25–26.

was trash, but didn't get close enough to see. I'm sorry. If I had taken a little detour you might have your $100 right now."

We have given a quick review of Aristotle's account of the responsibility that we have for our moral vision in *Nicomachean Ethics*, book 3, chapter 1. We recommend that you consider chapter 5 of book 3, where he discusses our responsibility for our character.[3] Toward the end of the chapter he answers a contrary view. "All men seek what appears good to them, but they have no control over how things appear to them" (1114a, lines 34-35). Consider the issue, "Are we responsible for our moral vision?" Consider Aristotle's answer to the question.

---

3. Aristotle's *Nicomachean Ethics* can be found online, for example, at Internet Classics, http://classics.mit.edu/Aristotle/nicomachaen.html.

CHAPTER 2

Attentiveness

The previous chapter on moral vision is encapsulated by the following statement: "I can only choose within the world I can see, in the moral sense of 'see' which implies that clear vision is a result of moral imagination and moral effort."[1] We see the good, and we seek to become the kind of people who participate in that good. These insights about moral vision are made by Iris Murdoch (1919–1999), an Anglo-Irish novelist and philosopher.[2] As a novelist, Murdoch was interested in drawing out "the connection, if there is any, between our inner lives and our actions and utterances in the social world."[3] As a philosopher, she argued that the moral life requires slow and painstaking attention to the transcendent, unified, and not fully graspable good. The moral life is continual movement outside of ourselves toward this higher good. Murdoch did not expect that the good or the good of persons or the moral life could be encapsulated and fully understood. Instead, she hoped that moral philosophy could provide "conceptual schemes which help us reflect upon the nature of moral progress and moral failure."[4] The good is not fully grasped, not because it is vague or unintelligible, but because the

---

1. Iris Murdoch, *The Sovereignty of Good* (New York: Routledge & Kegan Paul, 1986), 37.

2. Murdoch's ancestry was Scottish/Presbyterian. She was born in Dublin. Her family moved to London when she was a year old, but they visited Ireland often and maintained their Irish identity. She attended and was later a lecturer at Oxford University. See Peter J. Conradi, *Iris Murdoch: A Life* (New York: W. W. Norton, 2001).

3. Alasdair MacIntyre, "Which World Do You See?," *The New York Times Book Review*, January 3, 1993, 9.

4. Murdoch, *The Sovereignty of Good*, 45. Of the moral life and art, Murdoch says that "our moral experience shares in the peculiar density of art, and in its imaginative cognitive activity." *Metaphysics as a Guide to Morals* (New York: Penguin, 1992), 341.

good is abundant. It has a depth and a reach that we cannot capture fully in a concept, argument, or idea. In this sense, Murdoch's idea of "moral vision" points to our capacity to see clearly the good in the everyday matters of life and to make progress—to attain deeper vision and sensitivity to people, relationships, difficulties, and joys, all in terms of a real, transcendent, and enduring good.

In this chapter, we will discuss moral vision and the moral life as a pathway. Along the path, we learn to see signposts that help us know which way we are able to go. The chapter will discuss the relationship between knowing and choosing (between knowledge and freedom, intellect and will). Our main point might seem obvious: when we see the good, we act accordingly; when we act accordingly, we begin to see more clearly. The chapter's focus on moral vision will provide a contrast to our modern inclinations to master and manage morality rather than to surrender to an all-encompassing good that is not fully within our grasp. The moral life is not a process of creating and possessing our own good; it is not about me and having my own personal ethics. The moral life is seeing a good outside of ourselves and desiring to become the kind of person who is able to participate in that good.

Disciplined Attention

In this book on morality, our emphasis on moral vision might strike the reader as a bit off topic. People tend to think about morality as doing something at some decisive moment. If action is required, we moderns trust proof and clear results far more than insight and little steps forward. We prefer taking hold rather than being grasped. In this regard, Iris Murdoch's focus on how we "see" the world offers a corrective to reducing the moral life to a few key actions or decisions. Highlighting the importance of "seeing" puts meditative, contemplative, and prayerful habits at the center of the moral life. This concern for our contemplative side is ages old. Aristotle, for example, balances virtuous activity and contemplation throughout his *Nicomachean Ethics*.[5] Contemplative "activities" might not look, at first glance, to be related to moral activities. In fact, they do not look like "doing" anything at

---

5. Aristotle develops the relationship between contemplation and action in book 10 of his *Nicomachean Ethics*. Note also chapter 7 of book 1, where Aristotle is discussing the function of the human being. Here he suggests (1098a) that contemplative knowledge of the good should not be subordinated to the practical use of the good.

all. However, a good portion of our moral efforts and goals is constituted by learning to pay close attention, to see what is really going on, to know things as they really are. A good bit of the moral life is in listening well rather than talking and in seeing rightly rather than demanding to be seen.

Attention is the task, but the principal metaphor is the eye—vision. Bodily metaphors are used readily in our language about the moral life. Consider a few examples. If someone implores others to be courageous and take personal risks, we might wonder if he himself can "walk the talk." In moral terms, we think of life as a journey—walking a path. St. Paul uses the parts of the body to speak about relationships and the unity of common life (Romans 12; 1 Corinthians 12). Jesus, in the Gospel of Mark, commands, "If your hand causes you to sin, cut it off" (9:43). In each case, the hearers of these biblical commands would not have understood them literally. Each term is figurative and best understood in its context.[6] We also are using figurative language when we speak of moral vision. Moral vision is "the just and loving gaze directed upon an individual reality."[7] It is "a refined and honest perception of what is really the case, a patient and just discernment and exploration of what confronts one, which is the result not simply of opening one's eyes but of a certain perfectly familiar kind of moral discipline."[8]

Moral vision is disciplined attention. It requires an intention to improve how we see; we put our mind to it. We are self-critical, thinking about everyday encounters, seeking to see situations and relationships better the next time. We hope to see the right things—what matters—and in the right way. Moral vision also carries the implication that what we see rightly is attractive; we start to see moral beauty and desire it. The good is attractive, and what is attractive draws our attention. With this connection to "attention," vision is a useful metaphor because our eyes are open almost all of our waking moments. However, in this regard, it might help to explain this "seeing" or "attention" by shifting metaphors. Quinlan McCarthy (David's son) has a friend on the high school swim team, James, who has been blind since birth. James is a remarkable person (friendly, self-confident, and interesting) regardless of whether or not he has use of his eyes. But lacking eyesight, his attention to his surroundings is impressive. He always knows the who, what,

6. The "hand" of Mark 9 "could apply to a range of forbidden actions," and the command to cut it off—obviously—shocks us into paying attention to the gravity of evildoing. See Adela Yarbro Collins, *Mark: A Commentary*, Hermeneia: A Critical and Historical Commentary on the Bible (Minneapolis: Fortress, 2007), 452.

7. Murdoch, *The Sovereignty of Good*, 34.

8. Murdoch, *The Sovereignty of Good*, 28.

where, and when of his surroundings . . . a claim that cannot be made for Quin. (Sorry Quin, but it's true.)

For James, attention is a way of life. From the pool to our town, there is a fifteen-mile drive with plenty of turns and winding country roads. Among the seven teenagers who might be in the McCarthy van, it is James (and probably only James) who knows the route. After a turn and a little stretch of road, he will say, "Oh, the McAteers live over there to the right." If you introduce yourself to James once, he will recognize you the next time you say a simple "hello." He is sure to know your name and recall your previous conversation. This recall is impressive, not because he identifies a person by her voice, but because he is attentive to each person and what she has to say. Many other examples can be given. But the best thing to say, in sum, is that James does not rush. He is patient. He focuses on the little things about people and his surroundings. Think of all the things we are likely to miss as we rush from one thing to another. We might say that James's lack of sight has put him in a situation where he has learned to take notice of what most of us miss. But it is not a lack of sight that produced his capacity for attention. It is his desire to know what is important and his discipline in undertaking an attentive way of life. This desire and discipline of attention are what we mean by moral vision.

James's capacity for moral vision challenges how many of us think about morality. It is not uncommon to think about morality as a set of big issues that we encounter from time to time (such as war or euthanasia). According to this "big issue" view, most of life is morally neutral; only occasionally do we confront a problem. Consider a few examples: Is it okay to lie to my boss in order to avoid an unreasonable and unfair reprimand? Is it okay to cheat on a test if the teaching has been terrible, and I don't know what is going on?

With these examples, the reprimand or test is an issue to be confronted, but the crisis of each represents a lack of attention. Questions of lying and cheating don't come upon us all of a sudden. They come from a lack of attention to relationships and common tasks—with boss and coworkers at work and teachers and fellow students at school. If a student contemplates cheating on a test, he knows that there has been a problem for a good while. But he has not given proper attention to it. That is, the real moral problem or set of problems existed long before the "examination" (whether in the form of workplace evaluation or classroom test). We feel we have to lie or cheat because it is the best option, perhaps the only option, given our lack of attention to the fact that there has been an ongoing problem with the teaching, or our lack of investment in the class. Moral vision or, in these cases, a lack of vision accounts for how we see the options.

In these cases, moral indifference or inattention leads to a moral issue that cannot be ignored (fail or cheat). In other words, we have a crisis because we have ignored the ongoing moral issues. Most of the moral life comes between the "issues," through growth in attentiveness to people, situations, and relationships in everyday life. If an employee had attended to strained relationships with coworkers and the boss, the crisis that might lead to a severe reprimand for some might be seen as an entirely different situation for the attentive employee. She might find the crisis as a catalyst for change in the workplace. A student who communicates with the teacher about the failure of communication might not encounter the question, "Should I cheat?" The teacher may not know there is a problem. In this regard, the student might be able to see the impending test as an avenue to engage the teacher in a new, more helpful way.

Take euthanasia as a more newsworthy and less everyday issue (for most of us). For the purposes of this brief treatment of a broad topic, we will narrow our concerns. Euthanasia is sometimes (wrongly) considered any form of care that is directly or indirectly related to a person's death. For example, in this definition, refusing or withholding futile treatment would be considered "passive" euthanasia. In the Catholic tradition, a withdrawal of useless treatment is not euthanasia but simply allowing a person to die. To be against euthanasia does not mean "to keep alive at all costs." On the contrary, often end-of-life care is a matter of keeping a person as comfortable as possible on his or her way to death. With "keeping alive at all costs" off the table, the issue of euthanasia is important for several other reasons. People fear the helplessness of death. They don't want to be a burden. End-of-life care is costly. A dying person might be alone, lonely, and depressed. A person might be enduring great pain. These reasons are legitimate, and they call us to see our lives (not just the issue of euthanasia) through a moral lens.

Each of the issues (for example, pain, loneliness, and cost) is not an end-of-life issue per se; each requires that we attend to how we live day-to-day in relationship to the dying. In effect, the issue of euthanasia requires attention to issues of suffering, loneliness, and healthcare costs long before we see a person on a hospital bed. Long before we imagine ourselves in hospital beds with tubes and machines, we need to attend to how we live together, how we keep company with the sick, and how we intend to support others financially. The issue of euthanasia is about how our lives together are structured.

Do we avoid mutual dependence in our everyday lives? Do we segregate the sick and elderly from community and social systems? Do we support hospice care as an integral part of common life? Are doctors and nurses trained in pain management and hospice care? Rushing from one thing to another and one stage of life to another, we often fail to see how our habits of life will shape how we die. The common desire to die quickly and painlessly might reveal a common desire to ignore death and its implications for how we are living together. In this sense, euthanasia is an "issue" long before the hospital bed. In between the crises of death, we ought to attend to basic moral questions about how we share our lives day-to-day.

The task of this chapter is to describe the importance of moral vision. The danger of using euthanasia as an example is that it is a controversial issue and may lead us astray by its own gravity. In using the example, our point is to shift our vision onto points on which opponents and proponents of euthanasia can agree—that we fear dying alone, bankrupt, and in pain. If the "issue" of euthanasia is about our lives together long before situations of dying, then we have to imagine that, because people have lived differently, they might see death from different perspectives and, morally speaking, might be in different situations when dying. The point, then, with issues of euthanasia is to live well and care for others so that they will not be in a situation where they see death as an escape—as a solution to the problem of life. This approach will not resolve all issues of euthanasia, but it certainly will head us in the right direction and give us a pathway to help others die with hope rather than despair.

Seeing and Choosing

The task of moral vision is to make progress in attention and sensitivity to a real good—ultimately to the Good. To note that individuals might encounter a difficult test and poor teaching differently, or a job crisis and a surly boss differently, is not to argue for moral relativism—at least not in the approach we are describing. The difference is that one person's attention to moral matters has situated him in a better or worse way to deal with the problem at hand. We do not approach life or moral problems as neutral observers. In a dispute, we might consult someone who is impartial to one side or another, who does not have a horse in the race, as it were. But we don't want neutral observers in the sense that they do not have cares or concerns about what is good; rather, we should hope for loving and wise counsel.

Here, under the heading of "attention," we are shifting to Iris Murdoch's critique of what she calls moral neutrality. A call for moral neutrality would require that we set aside our hopes and loves and our convictions about what is good in order to make a disinterested decision. In contrast, Murdoch argues that the moral life is hardly neutral, but requires investment and love. Everyone (as a human being) comes to issues and decisions with biases; we should learn, not to avoid them, but to aspire to good ones. In the neutral and anonymous framework of approaching moral issues, the moral growth of persons makes no difference to how the issue is encountered and how the decisions are made. In contrast, in the framework of moral vision, good choices are made when we learn to look to and to love the good beyond ourselves.

Consider the problem of moral choices in terms of a shopping analogy. Murdoch uses a shopping analogy when she criticizes a theory of neutrality, a view that disregards moral vision and considers moral problems in terms of an anonymous actor (any person X) and an abstract (nameless) will and its choices.[9] In the shopping framework, the consumer views the same products as everyone else in an imagined "John Q. Customer" position of neutrality and abstract freedom of choice. The consumer then wills herself to take one product rather than another, the one that is most useful and appealing to her. In effect, the objects on the shelf have value only in terms of what she prefers. Back to our example of cheating, the options might be to cheat and get a good grade or to be honest and fail. The option will hinge, perhaps, on the guilt and shame in cheating, or the risk of getting caught, or the benefit of cheating. The customer weighs the options.

But in real life, the situation is not usually experienced as this neutral weighing of options. A person who cheats typically will say, "I had to; I had no choice." As teachers we have heard this sentiment (if not the exact words) often enough. On the other hand, a person who does not cheat and does fail a test is likely to have never considered cheating as a real option. He might be offended by the question, "Why didn't you cheat?" Or he simply might not have an answer because he never actually considered the option in earnest. We choose within the world that we see. You might ask a person who bought a car, "Why didn't you buy a Hummer?" But if someone buys a compact hybrid, she probably did not consider buying a Hummer. The Hummer was not considered a viable choice. It wasn't an option. Similarly, it might be that our attentive student is as likely to fail the test as the

9. Murdoch, *The Sovereignty of Good*, 8.

inattentive student, but she simply does not see "cheating" as an option on the shelf. However, and this is the interesting consideration, she might see other options that the "cheater" does not. The attentive student will probably face problems sooner and broach the issues with her professor. There are a multitude of options between "to cheat" and "to fail." In terms of the shopping analogy, it is not the case that every John Q. Customer sees the same things on the moral shelf.

We have used the shopping analogy to criticize an approach that ignores the importance of moral vision, but now we will alter the shopping analogy to our purposes. We will make the shopkeeper a wine dealer and imagine the different perspectives (moral visions) of the wine connoisseur and amateur drinker. The expert will see the range of wines differently—deeper, more nuanced, and more sophisticated choices. The amateur might see only prices and reds and whites. He is likely to choose poorly; he is likely to assume that a high price is equivalent to excellence. He has no other standard by which to judge. In sum, the connoisseur and leisure drinker will encounter the shop with entirely different eyes and sets of options. The shortcoming of the analogy is that their differences can be reduced to information that the expert has and the non-expert does not. For the analogy to work, we have to look, not to information (for instance, if the amateur was able to google wines while in the shop), but to the wine lover's appreciation and sensitivity to wine. Even if the casual drinker had the right information about what to buy, he still may not appreciate good wine. He is likely, perhaps, to not appreciate the beauty and goodness of what he is drinking. He may prefer what wine-people would agree, without a doubt, to be an objectively inferior wine. Or he may choose what he is told is better wine, but he will not appreciate it as a connoisseur would.

Seeing and choosing the objectively better (wine) are central to the example. But the quality of wine does not carry great moral significance, so the analogy falters when we reach the conclusion about enjoying objectively inferior or superior wine. Who cares? We know who cares . . . people who care about wine. And we are sure that they can tell us why we should care. But for most of us, the analogy might work better when health comes into the picture. Imagine a "snack shop" where fresh vegetables are set alongside a variety of candies. Please set aside issues of price and the implausibility of Brussels sprouts being displayed next to Snickers bars and lollipops. We could say that a customer with appreciation and sensitivity to garden-grown (not hot-house) tomatoes and green beans has an objectively better as well as a healthier vision than someone who goes into the shop and sees nothing but heaps of candy.[10] This sensitivity and appreciation, as with wine, is acquired and cultivated—through disciplined attention to food. It is imaginable, for example, that our vegetable lover is also a gardener. The customer that is overwhelmed by the choices of candy might wish that she could see and desire the good in vegetables if she is able to notice them at all. The reverse is not likely to be the case. People who truly enjoy healthy food seldom say, "I wish I were attracted to junk food."

Moral vision—seeing things as they really are—is key to the example. But like the wine analogy, the case of vegetables and candy can lead to a misunderstanding. The example might encourage us to think only in terms of the force of the will rather than the vision that opens us to good choices. We can imagine our candy lover restraining herself and willing herself to purchase the green beans that she knows she *should* like more than candy but, in fact, does not. This is a case in which our customer is on the way to appreciating vegetables but has not yet attained this way of seeing. It is easy enough to picture a parent saying to her daughter (a nine-year-old), "We *should* buy some of these *wonderful* tomatoes." Or in the case of an adult, "I should buy these lower-calorie but hardly enjoyable tomatoes." She is her own parent. Here, in a kind of leap of faith, she is acting on what she is able to see only dimly or not at all. She is attempting to exercise disciplined attention to how things really are, and with some day-to-day attention, day in and day out, she may be on her way to a vision of an objective good. When she does reach the point where she appreciates a good tomato or cucumber for what it is, a whole new world of choices will open up to her.

Before we begin our final example, recall Iris Murdoch's description of moral vision: "the just and loving gaze directed upon an individual reality . . . a refined and honest perception of what is really the case . . . which is the result not simply of opening one's eyes but of a certain perfectly familiar kind of moral discipline." Here we offer the familiar case of friendship. Over the years, we (Jim and David) have developed the habit of discussing everyday struggles and joys concerning students, colleagues, and superiors (deans and the provost of the university).[11] The main outcome of the discussions is a proper view of the person in question (say a recalcitrant student), and the proper view is that this person is someone who is to be loved—in whom we can learn to see

10. We imagine some readers have objections. They will point out that some candies, chocolates in particular, can be refined. We grant the point: some sweets are objectively better than others.

11. In *The Sovereignty of Good*, Murdoch uses the inner struggle of mother-in-law M with daughter-in-law D (17–23).

the good and for whom we are able to give what is good. We do not, at first, ask for advice or advise each other about what to do. We simply describe a set of encounters and experiences and ask, "What do you think is going on?"

Central to friendship is a common vision. For us—David and Jim—our friendship began with a similar understanding of our vocation of teaching, but through the years, we have developed and clarified that vision together. Our conversations about students are usually not high-minded. Sometimes we complain and express frustration. On occasion, one of us comes to the other with what he *thinks* he would like to do—sometimes something rash or unreasonable. This uncharitable feeling is not always the case. But if it is, one or both of us will come around to the reality of who we are and what we are about. In so many words, we get around to the facts. We are teachers who are called to the good of our students; our students have their own struggles. They often feel overwhelmed. In any case, we *want to* work for their good. Once we have articulated these facts, we are able to imagine the best thing to do. In this way, friendship is a practice in moral vision—of seeing the good in everyday matters of life.

Conclusion

We began this chapter with Murdoch's insight that "I can only choose within the world I can see, in the moral sense of 'see' which implies that clear vision is a result of moral imagination and moral effort."[12] We have used a variety of examples to help you see her point. There are better and worse ways to "attend" to the world and the people in our lives, and we learn to grow in moral vision when we desire to know and to love. Moral vision opens up choices and imaginative ways of living.

For Reflection and Further Study

1. Priggishness and generosity
You, the reader, are likely to raise objections to our shopping example. To many, our appeal to a connoisseur—whether of wine or the goodness of life—will seem to recommend a judgmental and intolerant attitude toward others.

---

12. Murdoch, *The Sovereignty of Good*, 37.

Wine connoisseurs are sometimes caricatured as prigs and snobs. We agree that priggishness is a danger. But if a person goes this direction, we propose that he or she is not a real connoisseur.

A connoisseur of wine or of "a life well lived" will not care about labels and other external images. She will not make her judgments on reputation or popularity. She will see goodness where others overlook it. She will have a subtle sense of goodness, so that she will be able to sense it and articulate its presence, when others with less refined taste will entirely miss the nuance of good things. If someone were to say, "I don't care what I drink," he has already stated indifference to the goodness of the wine. Perhaps he just wants to get alcohol into his system. In any case, his tolerance for terrible taste is a result of his disregard for wine. In effect, it is the connoisseur who is able to see more goodness (rather than less). It is the connoisseur who is able to see beauty, goodness, and joy in living with the poor, the sick, and the outcast. Consider this proposal offered by Pope Francis:

> God is in every person's life. God is in everyone's life. Even if the life of a person has been a disaster, even if it is destroyed by vices, drugs or anything else—God is in this person's life. You can, you must try to seek God in every human life. Although the life of a person is a land full of thorns and weeds, there is always a space in which the good seed can grow. You have to trust God.[13]

Consider now our basic point. If a person loves and desires what is good, she will learn to seek it and see it everywhere she can. Rather than being indifferent, she will be open and responsive to outsiders, outcasts, and generally people who are overlooked.

2. What is ethics all about?

In answering the question, "What is ethics all about?," Herbert McCabe, OP, draws an analogy with literary criticism, which is similar to our analogy of the connoisseur. McCabe points out that if you wrote a paper or gave a presentation on T. S. Eliot's *The Waste Land*, you would not have said very much (and certainly would not have said much interesting or worthwhile) if your

---

13. Antonio Spadaro, SJ, "A Big Heart Open to God: An Interview with Pope Francis," *America: The National Catholic Review* 209, no. 38 (September 30, 2013). For the interview in its entirety, see http://americamagazine.org/pope-interview.

purpose was to show that the poem is good or bad. More than one disinterested student has called this work bad, even hideous. In contrast, many students have filled their presentations with superlatives—masterful, awesome—but they have not said much worthwhile either. McCabe grants that the literary critic will have to make judgments about good and bad, better and worse. But these judgments do not get to the purpose of literary criticism. "Its purpose," McCabe explains, "is to enable us to enjoy the poems more by responding to them more sensitively, by entering more deeply into their significance."[14]

By analogy, this sensitivity and depth is what McCabe proposes that ethics is all about. "Now the purpose of ethics is similarly to enable us to enjoy life more by responding to it more sensitively, by entering into the significance of human action."[15] Again, this approach does not dispense with judgments of good and bad. But it does make the task more interesting. We will begin to see the good things in something considered bad, and failures in things universally thought of as good. The point of each of these approaches is to understand and enjoy what is good and possibly better.

Consider these other parallels between ethics and literary criticism:

- McCabe reflects on his own statement, "the purpose of ethics is similarly to enable us to enjoy life more by responding to it more sensitively," and focuses on the word "enjoy." He asserts, "it is impossible to appreciate the significance of human behavior unless one is to some extent involved in it." One cannot be a mere spectator.
- Like literary criticism, ethics does not come to an end. McCabe explains, "I mean that, except in the case of something that can be fairly quickly dismissed as atrocious, you would not claim to have said the last word about a poem." Likewise, "Moral judgment does not consist in seeing something at 'the moral level' or 'in light of morality'; it consists in the process of trying to see things always at a yet deeper level."[16]

3. Knowing led by desiring

When Iris Murdoch develops her account of "attention" (moral vision), she notes the influence upon her of the work of Simone Weil (1909-1943).[17] Weil

14. Herbert McCabe, *What Is Ethics All About?* (Washington, DC: Corpus Books, 1969), 95.

15. McCabe, *What Is Ethics All About?*, 95.

16. McCabe, *What Is Ethics All About?*, 96, 97.

17. See Murdoch, *The Sovereignty of Good*, 34.

was a philosopher, activist, and mystic. From a Jewish family, she fled from the Nazi occupation in France. She died of tuberculosis in England in 1943. The excerpt below is from Weil's "Reflections on the Right Use of School Studies with a View to the Love of God."[18] The essay was written as a letter to her friend Fr. Joseph-Marie Perrin. We propose that the process of knowing that Weil describes can be readily applied to knowledge of the good. In any case, Murdoch makes this connection. Consider Weil's claim that desire plays a vital role in knowing.

> Willpower, the kind that, if need be, makes us grit our teeth and endure suffering, is the principal weapon of the apprentice engaged in manual work. But, contrary to the usual belief, it has practically no place in study. The intelligence can only be led by desire. For there to be desire, there must be pleasure and joy in the work. The intelligence only grows and bears fruit in joy. The joy of learning is as indispensable in study as breathing is in running. Where it is lacking there are no real students, but only caricatures of apprentices who, at the end of their apprenticeship, will not even have a trade.[19]

Consider the implications of Weil's proposal and Murdoch's use of it. It may be that the study of ethics, to be fruitful, requires that the students desire and love the good. How can this love be present in a classroom?

18. Simone Weil, *Waiting for God*, trans. Emma Craufurd (New York: Putnam, 1951), 105-16.

19. Weil, *Waiting for God*, 110.

CHAPTER 3

Seeing the Good

We are not very far into the moral task of "seeing," and we already have a problem. If moral vision is a "just and loving gaze" upon reality, then what is real is not indeterminate or neutral but good and lovable. The implication is that when we see goodness in the world, when we love others and desire justice, we have started to see how things really are. But we have a problem. When we state what we love, we usually assume that we are merely giving our own opinions, likes, and dislikes. Our claim—and a claim made from Plato to Pope Francis—is that when we truly seek to love, we begin to see and know what is good. But how can this claim be something other than personal opinion? When we say "truly" seek to love and know, who defines "truly"? How can we really know what is good?

In this chapter, we hope to point you in the right direction. Actual answers to such questions are not settled by reading a book, but are experienced by living for the good of people in our lives, for the good things that we share, and ultimately for our own good too. Nonetheless, reading and study can set us upon a pathway. When getting the right directions (like on Google maps), we must first know where we want to go. In the moral life, the destination is harder to pinpoint. Rather than a simple journey to a known destination, the moral life is a quest. As a quest, it is a journey to find where we are going, and through the search, we are transformed. It is a quest, not to faraway lands, but to seek the good in the little things day-to-day. In our lives, over the days, weeks, months, and years, we will find that we have traveled a long way. The journey begins and continues on with the question, "What is good?" This simple yet very difficult question is the topic of this chapter. Rather than attempting a simple answer, we will attend to difficulties and problems. In gaining a clearer view of the struggles, we may get nearer to answering the question, "How do we know what is good?" We propose that the first step in answering the question with our lives is to start to see our lives as a moral journey.

What Is Good?

"What is good?" is an age-old question. How do we know when we see it? You might be familiar with the allegory of the cave in Plato's *Republic*.[1] According to the allegory, we see only shadows of the true reality. In *The Republic*, the allegory of the cave is introduced when Plato describes a dialogue between Socrates and Plato's brother Glaucon. Socrates asks Glaucon to imagine prisoners in a cave. They are positioned and tied up so that they can face only one direction. With a fire and real things behind them, they see only shadows of things cast upon a wall. They are unable to see the source of the shadows. They are unable to see the real things and the fire behind them. We miss the key points of the allegory if we take the spatial metaphor literally, that is, if we dwell on realms of shadows and reality as different places. In the context of *The Republic*, the allegory points to the aim of education and the role of philosophers in Greek society. Philosophers—lovers of wisdom—are those whose lives, day-to-day, are dedicated to the question, "What is good?" The message of the allegory is that, if we devote our lives to the question, we may well move past mere "appearances" to get to what is true and good.

In the modern world, the message remains apt. We suggest that you consider the allegory of the cave figuratively—that is, allegorically—the spatial metaphor suggesting that we have to learn to see a different world amid the world of appearances. People, today, often say that appearances are not the true measure of who we are. Yet we tend to trust material facts. When we start talking about less tangible matters, like the depth of what life means, we tend to back away and say things like, "Well, that's just how I feel; it may be different for you." In this chapter, we will call this backing away the relativist response: There is no real good; each individual merely has feelings and preferences. In this relativist view, the "good" is equivalent to things that we like. The good is relative to the person.

In contrast, the allegory of the cave recommends that we be self-critical of our preferences and comfort zones. By pushing against a relativist view,

1. Plato, *The Republic*, trans. Robin Waterfield (New York: Oxford University Press, 1993), 514a–518b.

we are not recommending intolerance.[2] Our worry is stagnation and self-satisfaction. Through the allegory, Plato suggests that our world is a reflection of what is true and good, but that seeing the true and good requires risk and transformation. He notes the pain and confusion that we have to go through when our eyes adjust to the light. According to the allegory of the cave, people are accustomed to the shadows. We could imagine that the prisoners, in the process of adjusting to the light, might argue that the shadows are real and that the real things are artificial. Liberated from the cave, they might think they have entered an artificial world.[3] Again, we miss the point if we take the different places of the cave and Plato's world of ideal forms literally. The point is that, when the prisoners enter the light of day, they would still trust the shadows. They are comfortable with their own view. They resist transformation. For this reason, in the context of *The Republic*, Plato encourages people to trust the lover of wisdom—the person whose life is dedicated to knowing the true and good.[4]

In the previous chapter, we offered our own allegory of this problem of perspective: we suggested a way forward through the analogy between shopping and moral choice. The typical shopping image, you might recall, gives no attention to the process of knowing. Things are just "there." Products are there to see on the shelves, and we choose to have one rather than another. Our judgment is based on our preferences rather than the products. One choice is as good as another. We modified the example by inserting a wine connoisseur and tomato lover. The connoisseur spends her days studying, focusing on, experiencing, appreciating, understanding, and celebrating

2. Defending the idea that there is no "real" good and that everyone has their own version of what is good does not encourage tolerance. Tolerance develops when we think that differences between us (persons and peoples) matter, but the fact that differences and disagreements matter does not mean that we suppress or revile the other point of view. In such a situation, we learn tolerance. When we say that different views of the good don't matter (because there is no real good), we do not have to develop tolerance. We replace it with indifference. Indifference is certainly better than hate, violence, and oppression. But indifference is not better than real tolerance (you are different, and I will listen to what you have to say because it matters).

3. Socrates says that prisoners still in the cave would not believe the tales of a prisoner who had seen the light and then had returned. They "would grab hold of anyone who tried to set them free and take them up there and kill him" (Plato, *The Republic*, 517a).

4. The implication, for Plato, is that ordinary citizens trust appearances rather than the vision of the lover of wisdom, that is, the philosopher. This conflict between society and the lover of wisdom is the source of Socrates's execution by an Athenian court in 399 BCE. The opposition to Socrates might be extreme, but not unusual. Like the question "What is real?," the question about what is good can lead to grave disagreements.

good wine. Through this way of life, the connoisseur begins to embody the wisdom required to judge one wine as better than another. Likewise, through the effort of growing, caring for, and loving tomatoes, the gardener is able to see tomatoes with more nuance and depth than the average shopper.

The examples of the wine connoisseur and tomato lover are attempts to include and move beyond knowledge as mere information. In the moral life, knowing is a process of formation—of transformation. This transformation is basic to our examples of wine and tomato lovers, but it is excluded from the standard shopping analogy, which assumes that the value of a product is simply private preference. The wine connoisseur will convince us that there is really such a thing as a better wine. To this degree, our examples (wine and tomato) move knowledge toward appreciation, sensitivity, and love. The examples move beyond thinking about moral knowledge as neutral. Certainly, the tomato is meant to be eaten, but there is a way of life in relationship to the vegetable that draws a person to love and appreciate an excellent tomato for its own sake. A "perfect" tomato is one that fulfills all that a tomato should be; it is simply admirable and good. The perfect tomato is a product of human ingenuity in cooperation with nature, and this cooperation is also admirable and good. Life in the garden is a good life. In sum, the "how" of knowing the good will look less like downloading information from a website about wine or tomatoes and more like a way of life and a relationship to—a participation in—the thing to be known.

Put simply, we can become "connoisseurs" of goodness. We can learn to see with depth the good in things and people, a subtle goodness that many might miss. We will begin to take joy in it. And unlike the wine connoisseur, gardener, or Plato's philosopher, we can seek, love, and begin to understand the good amid countless different things that we do. The connoisseur's attention, time, energy, and resources put to gardening will take away time and attention given to something else—say, reading American history. One cannot read a history book and garden at the same time. But the love of the good has the opposite effect. The love of the good will encourage deeper participation in the tasks, relationships, and ways of life with which we are already engaged.

Let's call this "participation" an ordinary way of knowing, where a person has a relationship to what is known well. Plato's allegory of the cave might seem, at first, to mean that knowledge of the good is extraordinary. But the point is the opposite: to know something well means we have to make our relationship to it part of our ordinary life. By ordinary, we mean a regular and everyday relationship. For example, tax codes leave most of us in shadows, but an accountant will know them as a regular part of life. When looking at the numbers, she will see possibilities and options that most of us would not see. In Plato's *Republic*, the philosopher is educated and formed to have this kind of ordinary relationship to the good. In effect, a relationship to the good is the philosopher's structure of life. For Plato, this way of life seems to exclude other forms of life. Our claim (or we could simply say a modern claim) is that one can become a lover of wisdom amid various walks of life. Moral vision is grounded in our everyday life because everyday life is grounded in a real good.

Participation in the Good

Up to this point, we have been dealing with the problem of relativism and morality as mere preference. At this juncture, we turn to the flipside of the problem. On one side, morality is merely personal; on the other side, it is totally impersonal. Although they seem to be opposites, both views assume the typical modern picture of knowing what is "good." Like the typical shopper, the knower is a universal knower, not situated in any particular way to what is known. In this kind of framework, either morality is personal preference because the individual is the only judge, or, on the flipside, we need a perspective that is detached and disengaged—impersonal. Our contrasting term to both is "participation" in the good, and participation means an ongoing life of attention to the good—to become a connoisseur of goodness.

In diagnosing the modern flip-flop between mere personal preference and impersonal detachment, Iris Murdoch notes that, in the modern era, theories of morality go through a Copernican revolution.[5] This revolution initiates great progress in understanding the natural world. But a comparable revolution in moral theory is unfortunate for how we think about the moral life. Different things in life require different ways of knowing. For example, it is not advisable to apply geometry to understanding disagreements and problems of communication with a coworker or friend. Likewise, applying the way of knowing in physics or chemistry is not an advisable way to undertake the moral life. In the modern era, the unfortunate shift

5. Iris Murdoch, *The Sovereignty of Good* (New York: Routledge & Kegan Paul, 1986), 24. Immanuel Kant refers to Copernicus in the Preface to the 2nd edition of his *Critique of Pure Reason*, trans. Paul Guyer (New York: Cambridge University Press, 1999), 113. Kant's analogy to Copernicus is used to say that reason now centers on the human knower rather than the thing to be known.

in moral thinking is that various moral theories start to disregard what we are calling participation and moral vision. Morality begins to be *reduced* to impersonal calculations—to applying an abstract formula to determine what we should do.[6] This statement may sound odd. The reader may ask, "What is morality if not deciding what we should do?" Our claim is that it is also—and even primarily—what we see and who we become. While knowing in natural and social sciences comes from following a method, knowing in the moral life comes from who a person is and how she is able to see the world.

One effect of the Copernican revolution in knowing is that it becomes far more difficult to see life as a common journey—as a shared moral life.[7] The new scientific way of knowing starts with parts rather than wholes, with atoms rather than whole systems. In order to achieve or at least point to a common moral standard, we moderns become more inclined to speak of "morality," "moral issues," and "moral law" as separate from other parts of life. The belief—clearly motivated by a concern for doing the right thing—is that we need a way to determine moral issues without depending upon people. People disagree; technology is more trustworthy. The challenge of modern moral philosophers (at least since the eighteenth century) is how to convince people to agree on calculations and facts that don't depend upon people. Gravity is just a fact. Likewise, it is believed that the basis of morality must be detached from any of us in order to avoid a relativist claim that all views are relative to the person or group. One typically modern point of view is that we need to clean our fingerprints and personal DNA off the test tubes and crucibles before we can make accurate and objective claims. In this regard—apropos of the shopping example—"moral vision," "the loving gaze," and "attention" are assumed to be unnecessary or even a detriment or just one relativist position among others. The wine connoisseur would tell

6. See Charles Taylor, *A Secular Age* (Cambridge, MA: Belknap, 2007), 221-34.

7. The phrase "Copernican revolution," as it is used today, represents far more than Copernicus. Nicolaus Copernicus (1473-1543) offered arguments and evidence that the earth was not a fixed point above which the sun, stars, and planets traveled. He was able to figure out that the earth and planets revolved around the sun. However, the symbol of Copernicus goes far beyond the thought and history of the sixteenth-century thinker. The changes brought by modern scientific methods span about four hundred years, but the Copernican revolution is an image of decisive and fundamental change in how people see and know our world. New methods in natural science led the way, and because of the indisputable success of the scientific method and its technological advances, all ways of knowing had to keep up with the changes: political theory, economics, philosophy, theology, and so on. The world had changed. Moral philosophy and theology (among other disciplines) had to understand the new contours of this modern world and how the human being fit within it.

us that to "know" wine we will have to follow a way of life in relationship to wine. In the impersonal framework, to know the wine, we put it in a sterilized beaker.

As we outline effects of the Copernican revolutions in ethics, we will stay with the metaphor of vision and ask you to picture our place in the world in two different ways. The first is biblical and also part of ancient and medieval philosophy. It is aligned, ordered, and united through spatial metaphors. People often say that they have a "standpoint." Think of looking up and out from where you stand to where you hope to go as the basic metaphor for how to look for what is real and true. We look up and out to a future in this life and the next. We hope to make progress in improving our abilities, our lives, and relationships—to being "in a good place." We have a place where we are standing, and there is a place where we are going. According to this first set of images, life is a journey. We use the metaphors of a path and road, and we hope that we are making progress. We hope that we don't get stuck and stagnant, with our lives going nowhere.

The second set of images is modern and tends not to have a spatial orientation. Where we are going becomes less relevant. If we hold to the relativist option (that morality is merely the preference of persons or groups), then where we already are determines everything. Morally speaking, there is no place to go. Likewise, if we want an objective point of view, we try to disregard where we stand. We want to make our personal perspective and standpoint irrelevant to how we know. We are looking for principles of operation. We hope to take off the back of the timepiece or laptop to look at the mechanism or circuitry to see what makes it work. The first set of images is the point of view of a pilgrim on the way. The second is the point of view of an observer of the pilgrim wanting to know how his legs work and how he keeps a sense of direction. This kind of observation is best done in a laboratory or classroom.

In modern theory, there is—metaphorically speaking—an emphasis on mechanisms over metaphysics. Metaphysics asks, "What is life? What is existence? What is the meaning of life?" In mechanics, we look at matter and investigate how it works. "What are the principles of its operation?" Metaphysics seeks to imagine the whole of things and how the parts fit into the whole. It asks about the purpose of things. What are they for? Where do they belong? Mechanics, in contrast, begins with the parts and then makes generalizations about the whole. Both the relativist and the detached views focus on mechanisms. The relativist points to a mechanism that is cultural or personal (morality is relative to these). The contrasting view points to a mechanism

35

that is impersonal, such as a "selfish gene" or a "purely rational" calculation.[8] The basic difference between the two approaches is that a journey-formed approach is concerned not merely with existence and life itself but also with the primary questions—the questions to be asked first. In contrast, modern moral theory is inclined to replace "How does my life fit in the scheme of things" with "What part of us is the moral part and how does it work?"

Our concern here is philosophical. The change in orientation from the first to the second picture, from pilgrim's landscape to laboratory, represents a dislocation of the human being in the course of things. With these contrasting pictures, we recognize that we are simplifying a long history of developments. We recognize that we risk misinterpretation. We want to emphasize, at this juncture, that we are not being anti-scientific. We are concerned with a form of detachment in ethics that leads, ironically, to a relativist view of how we come to know what is good. (There is no conflict between science and religion or science and morality. Each coordinates with the other in understanding our world.) The problem is that, in moral questions, we often flip-flop between "objective" detachment (borrowed from modern science) and private subjectivity (of modern opinion making). One view encourages the other. Each disregards the wisdom and insight that comes from a life of engagement and attention to goodness, beauty, and truth.

One of our main points is that these moral theories do not account accurately for how we actually live and think. We have called "participation" an ordinary way of knowing. From Plato's philosopher, we moved to the examples of accountants and wine connoisseurs, who spend their ordinary days attending to some good to be known. From there, we suggested that participation in the good is not a single, specific way of life, but a particular way of living amid a variety of walks of life. In day-to-day life, the true, good, and beautiful are known only through loving and just attention to people, places, and things.

Consider the life of the artist, for example. Words like "art" and evaluations like "artistic excellence" cannot be quantified by detached observation. If detachment is required, then an evaluation of art is either reduced to technique or mere popularity (what sells), or it becomes a matter of in-

8. The term "selfish gene" is developed by evolutionary biologist/ethologist Richard Dawkins in *The Selfish Gene* (New York: Oxford University Press, 1990). Dawkins, in some fundamental ways, is heir to Scottish philosopher David Hume (1711-1776), whose theory of morality is treated in our chapter 5, on the passions. The view of morality as a kind of calculation is treated in our chapter 6, on moral reason, and chapter 7, on art, virtue, and the law.

dividual preference. In this framework, beauty is not really "there," but only in the eyes of the beholder. However, an artist will hope that beauty is really "there" if he has spent his life perfecting his talents. If his art were to be judged at a show, he wouldn't want the judge to be guided by individual preference. Imagine an art critic exclaiming, "What? No kittens? I love kittens." The artist looks to the judge/critic who is fully immersed in the world of art, who knows the history of art, its periods and struggles and contemporary schools, who has appreciation and sensitivity that has been formed within an artistic tradition. In other words, an objective evaluation of art (moving beyond individual preference) requires the disciplines and ways of knowing that have developed within the world of art. What is to be known (here art)—if it is really "there"—gives shape to how we learn to know it, and learning to know it requires what Iris Murdoch (in our chapter 2) calls "attention."

Likewise, in the framework of a moral pilgrimage, the personal and shared come together when we trust the vision of people who live a good life—the vision of the loving, just, and wise. We ought to trust and learn from the vision of good people. Certainly, answers to the big questions are often merely a person's preference, and we find ways to make such judgments. "Take his view with a grain of salt." For good judgments about friendship, family, and effectively feeding the poor, we do well to seek out those with experience, a good track record, praiseworthy intentions, and wisdom. But the goal is not to parrot someone else. The moral journey is about our own participation in a life of goodness and developing our capacities for moral vision. The context for developing our moral vision is a moral landscape where we see ourselves on a journey (up and out) toward nearness to what is good. Our guides are the lives of people who live well and show us the way. The task is to undertake the day-to-day discipline of attention to what is good. Plato's *Republic* had its philosophers to guide the people. We have each other.

Conclusion

We hear you now saying, "Is that it? Is that all you have for truly knowing what is good?" As we predicted at the beginning of the chapter, we have not managed to define goodness. Our intention has been to consider the problem of knowing the good and, in doing so, suggest a way forward. We deliberately began by citing Plato's allegory of the cave. If you were to read the context of the allegory in books 6 and 7 of *The Republic*, you would find an interesting overall point. In Plato's *Republic*, Socrates argues that goodness is not a quality of a thing, like heavy or green. It is not a value that we assign to something that we think important. Goodness is a reality that makes it possible to know things as they really are, to see them, as it were, in the light of day.[9] This is an astounding claim. The good is not a thing, but the source for knowing all things as good.

The good is not a quality that we ascribe; it is not even a "thing" to be known. It is the source of the knowable. We do not see it directly, but it is the one good that is the unity of all the good that we see. In Plato's *Republic*, Socrates admits that he cannot delineate goodness. But fully explaining and seeing/recognizing are not the same. In Plato's dialogues, Socrates does his best to persuade his listeners—by analogy, argument, and insight—that goodness is reality in its highest form. Living by this conviction, a person can know and, in this sense of know, also love the good. This claim will be developed in the following chapters. If the moral life requires moral vision, this seeing begins with convictions that shape a way of life. To quote St. Augustine, "Therefore do not seek to understand in order to believe, but believe that thou mayest understand."[10] We encourage you to set out on a moral journey with the conviction that life is good.

For Reflection and Further Study

1. Formative practices
Moral vision—as participation and a way of life—can be understood through analogies to training in music, sports, academics, and various occupations. Friendship provides another set of examples if you grant that we learn to be friends, and friendship changes how we see the world. Often this change is difficult, taxing, and even painful. Select a "way of life" (like playing the piano) that you have experienced. After describing the experiences, develop analogies between the "training" and "formation" in this area and the jour-

9. See the sun analogy in 507a–509c: "And it isn't only the known-ness of the things we know which is conferred upon them by goodness, but also their reality and their being, although goodness isn't actually the state of being, but surpasses being in majesty and might."

10. Augustine, *Ten Homilies on the First Epistle of John*, tractate 29 on John 7:14–18, no. 6, in *A Select Library of the Nicene and Post-Nicene Fathers of the Christian Church*, vol. 7, ed. Philip Schaff (New York: Scribner's, 1903).

ney of the moral life. We put training and formation in quotation marks because we have found that people don't like the idea that friendships and other relationships form who we are. We encourage you, however, to think about life as "training," as "working out," and as "developing" who we are becoming.

2. The moral journey (out of the cave)

Read and discuss the allegory of the cave in Plato's *Republic*. You may have a copy of the book. If not, it is offered by a number of websites and can be found easily on the internet. The standard numbering is not by page but is found in the margin. The allegory of the cave starts at 514a. Consider the allegory in terms of its metaphors for the difficulty of seeing the true and good. Also note the context. Plato outlines the way of life required to see the good. His concern is education. We are interested in Plato's metaphors of vision, but we depart from his precise framework for education and the superior role of philosophers.

We would, however, like you to consider the following statement made by Socrates. "That is what education should be . . . the art of orientation. Educators should devise the simplest and most effective methods of turning minds around. It shouldn't be the art of implanting sight in the organ, but should proceed on the understanding that the organ already has the capacity, but is improperly aligned and isn't facing the right way."[11] Our interest in Socrates's proposal does not pertain specifically to education. Our interest is in thinking about moral vision in terms of a journey.

The book that you are reading right now certainly has the purpose of education. In this regard, this chapter has been mainly about your orientation to the very topic of moral theory. At this point, our goal has been to inspire a way of seeing "morality" rather than give you methods to calculate actions and outcomes. Along this line, we ask you to consider where you hope your life is going (graduation, job advancement, marriage, parenthood, etc.). Can this same journey be characterized as a moral journey? If so, what are its goals? What might be the main struggles? How do we know we are making progress?

11. Plato, *The Republic*, 518d.

3. Seeing what we want to see

A young adult series of novels by Rick Riordan, *Percy Jackson and the Olympians*, is set in contemporary America, but it is populated also by gods and demi-gods, satyrs and centaurs, cyclopses and furies. We learn that there is a hidden world within our world. In the first book, *The Lightning Thief*, this hidden world is revealed to us through the experiences of the main character, Percy, who is in the process of discovering that he is a demi-god, a son of Poseidon. At one point, his teacher, Chiron, gives him a magic sword. Percy is worried that people will see it if he actually tries to use it. Chiron's answer is that humans will see, not a sword, but something else, something mistaken, something they would expect to see a twelve-year-old boy carrying. Chiron concludes, "Remarkable really, the lengths to which humans will go to fit things into their version of reality."[12]

Our tendency to see what we want to see is both the challenge and the vulnerability of moral vision. We might trust too much in how we see others and even ourselves. For this reason, Plato's allegory of the cave is interesting and useful. When Socrates explains the allegory to Glaucon, he puts the philosopher (himself) in the position of the one who has been liberated and now sees things as they are. We, however, have assumed that we (we two and the larger we) are in the position of those in the cave who have to change in order to see rightly. We do not assume that a philosopher-king will guide us. We will need guides for sure. But the moral journey is personal. We, together, will have to stumble and get up again, stumble again and slowly make our way, certainly with the help of others, but ultimately through our own engagement and participation in the question "What is good?"

The problem of moral vision is also the concern of a remarkable essay by Robert Sokolowski, "What Is Natural Law?"[13] Sokolowski notes that we are not issued a blueprint for seeing the good of things (people, places, institutions) in themselves. Moral vision is not about reading a blueprint and then subsequently applying the knowledge. It is about seeing the good amid the complications of life. We have to think through the meaning of things (we develop the blueprint) as we are engaged with the ordinary matters of life. Moral vision requires that we sort through our own wishes and intentions, that we learn to see through (by means of) what we desire but also beyond.

---

12. Rick Riordan, *The Lightning Thief* (New York: Hyperion Books, 2005), 155.

13. Robert Sokolowski, "What Is Natural Law?," *The Thomist* 68, no. 4 (October 2004): 507-29. The full text can be found through the website of the Philosophy Department at the Catholic University of America: http://philosophy.cua.edu/res/docs/faculty/rss/What%20 is%20Natural%20Law.pdf.

For example, if I become a physician to make a good living, I will have to learn to distinguish my own desires from the good of medicine itself, which is to care for the health of my patients. I will have to learn to think beyond myself, to subordinate my desires, if need be, to what medicine really is. If I see medicine *as* a way to make money, I will cut corners on my care for patients in order to achieve that end. If I understand that medicine *is* care for health, I will welcome the income, but subordinate it to the proper good of medicine.

In his essay, Sokolowski outlines some ways that our vision can be inhibited. For example, it might be that I resist the idea that there is a real good at all. When a colleague criticizes me for putting money before my patients, I give a classic juvenile response, "So what?" To my "so what," she responds that we are doctors and that the doctor is called to care for the health of patients. I respond, "Well, that is just your opinion. You have your view, and I have mine." Sokolowski's worry about this response is, not simply that I am self-centered, but also that I refuse to entertain that there is a good of medicine beyond my opinion and interests. The problem is not precisely that I disagree with my colleague on an important point, but that I refuse to engage her on the question "What is the good of medicine?"

The interesting point that we want to draw out from Sokolowski's article is this: my refusal to engage my colleague is not merely a theoretical problem, but also a moral problem. We can try to name the various moral failings in my defensive statement, "Well, that is just your opinion." Is it pride? Is it a kind of apathy—a "carelessness"—a refusal to care too deeply about anything? Whatever the case, the problem connects the issues of knowing (moral vision) with moral growth and transformation. If I desire to be better, I might very well have the desire, courage, and compassion to see better. Our claim here goes in the opposite direction from an example given in chapter 1. In the movie *Iron Man*, Tony Stark is confronted with a shocking vision of what his work as a weapons inventor and supplier has done. Then he changes. It is worth thinking about the process in reverse. We seek to act, live, and be better, and in the process we start to see people, events, and ourselves in a new way. Consider this question: "What is the relationship between moral vision and the development of our character?"

CHAPTER 4

A Journey

This chapter presents a time-honored understanding of life as a journey to a moral destination or end. "End," in this sense, does not mean a terminal point, but an activity that realizes the fullness of something. For example, the end for a carrot peeler is realized as carrots are being peeled (not when it becomes dull and useless and, in a sense, dies). Here, the terminus of the carrot peeler is the opposite of its end (in the philosophical sense that we are using the term). In the moral life, we seek ends that are good in themselves, and in the process, we are becoming good human beings. A good carrot peeler has a limited purpose; it is easy to define. But the moral life is directed ultimately to what is fully good, and this good is notoriously difficult to define. In this chapter, we will draw on traditional ways of understanding the human end—that is, who human beings are meant to be. Who we are meant to be—as human beings and as individuals—usually takes a lifetime to start to clearly see. This process of discovery is the journey of moral vision.

A Good End

We are, in a sense, introducing what is called Aristotle's function argument, found in *Nicomachean Ethics*, book 1, chapter 7. We say "in a sense," because if you were to google "Aristotle's function argument," you would likely arrive at descriptions that we find inadequate. You might find explanations like "what is distinctively human is reason" or "to have a function means that things have a purpose" (as if in answer to the question "What are human beings for?"). Each of these answers fits within the function argument, but there is more to it. We want to add that the appeal to function suggests a way of functioning. The carrot peeler has things that it does and is suited to do. (It will probably break if you use it to pry out a nail.) Its very makeup (thing that it is) has capacities for functioning. It has a way of being what it is that transcends any given carrot peelers (some are ill made or have been misused).[1] When these capacities are put to actuality we call them excellent. They fulfill what it means to be a carrot peeler.

When the function argument is applied to human beings, the account of who we are (the kind of thing that we are) is obviously going to be much more complicated and variable. We are different and have quite different roles and relationships, etc. The answer to the function argument about human beings cannot be put in the same framework as understanding the function of a carrot peeler. Perhaps Aristotle points to our rational nature because unlike a carrot peeler, our function includes discovering and shaping our function. Up to this point in the book, we have already outlined a picture of a person on a moral journey. Recall the spatial analogies of the previous chapter or the image of the connoisseur in chapter 2. Imagine our connoisseur of living well. She is convinced that there is good in the world. She believes that there is a real good, independent of her perspectives or feelings, and she seeks it out in the ordinary people and matters of life. Over time and through concerted attention, she learns to see, love, and appreciate goodness—like a connoisseur of fine wine or a gardener in relationship to roses. Imagine what her coworkers might say about her. "Great person" might be the common refrain. (Excellent carrot peeler.)

But chances are, when asked to say more, her colleagues will describe her moral fiber in contrary ways. One will talk about her personal ethics in a therapeutic mode. This colleague will notice that she has developed a way to express herself in positive and life-giving ways. She is a happy person. Another colleague, in contrast, will talk about her selflessness. He will notice that she doesn't think of herself, but puts others first. One view emphasizes self-expression, the other self-denial. The first focuses on rewarding experiences, the second on her ability to act regardless of personal gratification. Neither description points to where she is going, to a moral journey and a good to which she strives. And it is the journey that pulls the seemingly opposite views together.

---

1. Aristotle calls the thing that it is its form. So we could have carrot peelers made of various materials (wood, plastic, metal). But insofar as they are carrot peelers, they have the form of a carrot peeler.

For this reason, both views are partly right. They are right to point to her self-expression and other-directed actions, but each is wrong to neglect the other. Both are right to look within her character (feelings and force of will); they are wrong to stop there. They look entirely within her (self-expression or self-denial), but she sets her life in relationship to the good and sees the people, roles, callings, and activities of her life as real goods (in themselves). As real goods, they form the landscape of her relationship to the good. Her relationship to the good differs from her coworkers' misinterpretations of her actions. This disjunction represents the contrast, noted in the last chapter, between looking outward to where one is going (morally speaking) and looking inside for a moral mechanism or circuitry. Although her colleagues disagree with each other, both are looking for a mechanism inside her, like feelings or her willful self-denial. In contrast, she looks within herself *and* outward to others. She looks both inward and outward in relationship to a transcendent good—to a pathway to becoming a better person.[2]

As we have noted, this chapter will focus on thinking about the moral life in terms of an "end" and "ends" that are good in themselves. In relationship to "seeing" and "moral vision," we have been attempting to show that the first task of the moral life is to envision what is good in our lives and, throughout our lives and in every part of our lives, to keep this "end" in view. In moral philosophy and theology, the term "end" refers to the various goods toward which we aim. This end is not a termination point like retirement or death. It is not when a buzzer sounds at the end of a game. The end, even as we draw near, is an ongoing experience of fulfillment. It is a fulfillment that gets ever "fuller" as we carry on.

A carpenter attains the "end" of carpentry when he shows repeatedly that he has mastered the excellences of his craft, when it is clear that he is a skilled carpenter. His mastery is complete in a sense, but in another sense it is not. His fulfillment of the craft opens up his vision to greater fullness. The end is not a stopping point, but a fullness of activity. In various activities of life, humans are drawn to this kind of good end and transformed by it. In being drawn and drawing near to the good, we become good people—or at least better than we were before. In becoming better, we gain a clear vision of a good end.

---

2. In developing the contrast between "mechanism/circuitry" and "journey," we rely on the framework provided by Alasdair MacIntyre in his *After Virtue*, 2nd edition (Notre Dame: University of Notre Dame Press, 1984), 36-61, and Julius Kovesi, *Moral Notions* (London: Routledge & Kegan Paul, 1967), 92-143.

This concept of an "end" is found in the very first lines of Aristotle's *Nicomachean Ethics*:

> Every art or applied science and every systematic investigation, and similarly every action and choice, seem to aim at some good; the good, therefore, has been well defined as that at which all things aim. . . . Since there are many activities, arts, and sciences, the number of ends is correspondingly large: of medicine the end is health, of shipbuilding a vessel.[3]

Aristotle's reference to the ends of such things as shipbuilding (and later horsemanship) breaks the ice, as it were, in his discussion of the moral life and virtue. Quickly, he moves from the general idea of an aim to the purpose and the point of life.

The aim and point of life is "the good for the human being," which Aristotle will call "human flourishing" or "happiness."[4] These terms do not tell us much. They do not tell us what is good or what constitutes flourishing. But they do outline an area of inquiry and an order of "goods." Aristotle orders goods by distinguishing two kinds of aims. On the one hand, we aim at goods that are good for something else, like money for what it can buy, such as a home, education, or healthcare. On the other hand, we aim at goods that are good in themselves, for their own sake, such as friendship. Friends are certainly useful, but they are not merely useful. Money does us no good unless it is used (even as "saved" it is set aside for future use). Friends are not used in this way, or set aside for future use. If a person is used merely in a functional way (even if a good way, like an insurance agent), she would not be a friend, by the very definition of "friend."[5]

---

3. Aristotle, *Nicomachean Ethics*, trans. Martin Ostwald (New York: Macmillan, 1962), 1094a (p. 3).

4. The Greek word *eudaimonia* literally means "good spirit," and is usually translated as happiness. However, modern conceptions of happiness tend to focus on pleasure. The modern concept of pleasure is much different than Aristotle's focus on becoming a virtuous person. For this reason, many translate *eudaimonia* as "human flourishing."

5. It is common for us to use other persons and not in a bad way. For example, we use insurance agents and electricians for their services. So, to be clear, we do not actually use insurance agents *as persons*; we use them *as insurance agents*. To use an insurance agent is not bad, but it is not friendship. Our insurance agent could be our friend also, but this would mean that we do not merely use her as an insurance agent.

The point, for Aristotle, is that some goods like friendship are pursued for their own sake. At this juncture, he proposes that—among all the things that are good in themselves, which like friendship are good for something else too—there must be some good "which we desire for its own sake, an end which determines our other desires."[6] This is "the highest good," which Aristotle calls "the good for man."[7]

Various questions and philosophical problems go along with this conception of the "good." For example, Plato makes the "form of the good" central to his thought. Yet his explanations of it are difficult to understand. His very explanations seem to create irresolvable problems. In a famous passage in *The Republic* (508a-e), Plato offers an analogy of the sun, which "is not to be identified with sight, but is responsible for sight and is itself within the visible realm."[8] By analogy, the form of the good cannot be grasped in itself; the "good" cannot be seen as a separate and distinct thing. Yet it is what makes knowledge possible, and therefore is "within" the visible realm in a sense.

Insofar as Plato's view of the good is difficult to interpret, Aristotle attributes any confusion to Plato's mistaken attempt to posit a transcendent good that is "universal, common to all cases, and single."[9] Aristotle thinks, not in terms of this transcendent good, but in terms of categories of things and their corresponding good. He refers, not to good per se, but to the good of the human being. Thomas Aquinas, the thirteenth-century philosopher and theologian, is able to mediate between Plato (that is, *the* singular and universal good) and Aristotle (that is, good as the form of a kind of material thing) because his thinking is shaped by the biblical account of creation by a loving God. The goods of specific things are unified by their relationships to God—who is one, changeless, ever-present-in-relation to the world, and of course, the Good (Luke 18:19).

6. Aristotle, *Nicomachean Ethics*, 1094a.

7. Aristotle holds that politics is the most comprehensive science because it aims at the human good. It is worth thinking about how modern politics has strayed from this task, which by and large has been privatized. The inquiry about the pursuit of happiness is considered a private matter (and hardly a "science" or disciplined inquiry).

8. *The Republic*, trans. Robin Waterfield (New York: Oxford University Press, 1993), 508b (p. 235).

9. Aristotle, *Nicomachean Ethics*, 1096a.

Fulfillment in the Good Life

Our concern, at this point, is to understand the significance of notions such as a "good for its own sake," "the human good," and the good as our "end." (Issues between Plato, Aristotle, and Aquinas do not need to be sorted out here.) Questions like "What is our end?" and "What is good?" are not going to have answers that we can settle and walk away from. However, terms like "good," "end," and "fulfillment" do point us in a promising direction of inquiry. Questions like "What is good in itself?" set us on a journey of discovery. When we think about our own good as "the human good," we begin to seek out and see the good that is beyond us. We begin to see our lives and who we are now in terms of where we are going, who we are becoming, and the meaning (the "end") of life. My life is assumed to have a relationship to the meaning of life in an inclusive sense.

The question of our "end" sets the moral life in terms of our capacities and their fulfillment. Thomas Aquinas holds that, when some created thing is fully itself, it is good.[10] The statement is based on a distinction between potentiality and actuality. When a seed has the potential to be a flower, it is most fully itself when it actually becomes a flower. When the seed fails to grow, its potential is not actualized. When a flower fails to grow, we do not say that the seed is meant to remain a seed. We have planted it, and something has gone wrong. Likewise, the "true" self is not uncovered or discovered, but grown and developed.

Someone might have the potential to be a great musician, but a lifetime of training, discipline, love, and wisdom are required for the potential to become actual in the person. The violin player will be aware of both her talents and her shortcomings. She will have to see an end of mastery—of perfection in the craft. To get there, she will desire to play the violin and learn to love it. Given her relationship to the violin as her end, she will also be given a pathway for progress. She will have to be obedient to the course before her, to the end—to the violin and to music. Along the way, she will begin to see herself as a violinist. She will start to become a visible embodiment of the end to which she strives. Likewise, when she ceases to strive, the end will become more obscure. We will not see it in her.[11]

10. Thomas Aquinas, *Summa theologica* I, question 5.

11. MacIntyre, *After Virtue*, 53. MacIntyre outlines three elements required of a workable moral scheme: "the conception of untutored human nature, the conception of the precepts of rational ethics and the conception of human-nature-as-it-could-be-if-it-realized-its-*telos* [end]."

One way of outlining human capacities for goodness (potential that can become actual) is through a list of the virtues. The virtues point us to good and draw us outside of ourselves. Within the Western tradition (for example, Plato, Aristotle, and Cicero), four virtues come to provide focal points for how we think about the good of the human being. They are called cardinal (or "hinge") virtues: prudence, justice, fortitude, and temperance.

- Prudence is seeing the good, deliberating how to achieve the good end, and putting the plan into action. It presupposes virtues like wisdom and understanding (and what we have been calling "attention" and moral vision).
- Justice highlights our capacity to order our lives well in relationship to others and to give them what they deserve. "Justice is simply the habit of acting in a manner that nourishes right relations with others, and these relations are essential to our identities and thus essential to living a good life."[12] To be just, we must also be brave.
- The virtue of fortitude is facing fears, enduring trials, and accepting suffering for the sake of a good greater than ourselves.
- Temperance pertains to things that are to be enjoyed. It is often defined as moderation, but such a definition misses the point. Temperance is ordering ourselves to the reality of things (for instance, sex, money, and food) so that we are fulfilled in relationship to them.

These cardinal virtues imply an understanding of what is our good end. We are creatures who are most fully ourselves when we deliberate and set a course to the good, sustain the goodness of our relationships, willingly face up to obstacles to living well, and intentionally order ourselves to the goodness of creation.

In the medieval era, the cardinal virtues are integrated with the theological virtues of faith, hope, and love. These theological virtues are directed explicitly to God as our good. God is not known and loved as objects or facts in the world are known. For this reason, God is not only the "object" of the theological virtues but also the source. God's self-giving to us is the origin of faith, hope, and love in us.

12. William C. Mattison III, *Introducing Moral Theology* (Grand Rapids: Brazos, 2008), 139.

- God's ever-present self-giving is love. God is love–a love that gathers us in and sends us out to live "into" and "out from" divine life.
- God is received through faith, through our disposition of openness and trust in God's self-revelation as Father, Son, and Spirit.
- Hope is very near to faith. It is continuing to love and to strive through the trials of life, sometimes amid terrible suffering, with the firm conviction that God is all we need, because God is our one true good.

In effect, the theological virtues show God to be our good end, not only in the future, but today. God is the fulfillment of human life in a special way that only God's self-giving can activate.

Another approach to a vision of human good is through an outline of rights and responsibilities. The outline is necessarily general, for in reality each of us is formed and called within a particular set of relationships, such as sister, daughter, student, friend, neighbor, coworker, citizen, and so on. None of these roles are experienced in a general way. We are friends, neighbors, and citizens of persons and peoples with specific wants, needs, gifts, and struggles. However, human beings have a common nature and end. This claim is especially important to how philosophers and theologians, through the ages, have approached questions about the meaning of life. It is necessary to develop an understanding of human nature and goods common to human beings. Both rights and responsibilities are based in convictions about human capacities and fulfillment, our potential, and how the potential becomes actual–like the seed becoming the flower. For example, if we say that human beings have the right to be free, we are assuming that freedom accords with their nature. We don't say the same thing about goldfish in a bowl. If we say that freedom accords with human nature, we are claiming that it is essential to the human good and end.

Here, we will consider a section from Pope St. John XXIII's *Pacem in terris* (Peace on Earth)(1963), where he outlines "that order which should prevail among men."[13] At the beginning and the end of the section (nos. 8–38), St. John frames the discussion by noting that human beings are rational, social, and free, have their source and end in God, and are bound together in truth, justice, love, and freedom. The placement of justice and love with reason and freedom is significant. Neither rationality nor freedom is "centered" in the individual; we are not isolated territories. Justice nourishes good relationships, and through

13. John XXIII, *Pacem in terris* (1963), http://www.vatican.va/holy_father/john_xxiii/encyclicals/documents/hf_j-xxiii_enc_11041963_pacem_en.html.

love, we are energized to seek good for others (even our enemies).[14] Together with justice and love, our intelligence and free will actually de-self-center us in relation to common life and common goods that are rightly ordered to higher goods (wrongly centered on "lower" goods like wealth, fame, and glory of a person or one's family and nation).[15] In short, mature people take responsibility for others and for how we live together. This responsibility—properly responding to others—is how we human beings are fulfilled.

When John XXIII gives a summary of rights and duties, he highlights the theme of reciprocity. "In human society to one man's right there corresponds a duty to other persons . . . for every fundamental right . . . a corresponding obligation" (no. 30). The list of rights begins with the right to life, "to bodily integrity and to the means necessary for the proper development of life, particularly food, clothing, shelter, medical care, rest, and, finally, the necessary social services" (no. 11). From this level, Pope John goes on to opportunities for education and for moral, social, and cultural development, for the interchange of ideas, and for taking on "positions of responsibility in society" (nos. 12-13). He cites fundamental rights of conscience, religion, religious communities, family and civic associations, as well as basic economic and political participation. The list of duties follows the same pattern. It begins with the duty to preserve one's life, to follow one's conscience, to develop one's talents and abilities, to join with others to better our communities, to take responsibility in society, to help the needy, and to live responsively (not only responsibly) to who we are as created by God.

Conclusion

Like the virtues, these rights and duties point to our fulfillment (our end) and to the various goods of human life. Consider the person that we introduced at the beginning of the chapter. Her coworkers agree that she is a "great person." But some of them focus on her goodness as self-expression, while others make reference to her selflessness. These opinions seem to contradict. Do we focus on her "self," or on her lack of "self-regard"? With just our

---

14. See Vatican II, *Gaudium et spes: Pastoral Constitution of the Church in the Modern World*, no. 28.

15. Because they are not "centered" in the individual, persons with mental/intellectual disabilities, for example, inhabit relational-purposeful ordering, but do so to a different degree than others—not a difference in kind. For all of us—to different degrees—the relational and rational are given and carried also by others within common life.

brief reference to rights, duties, and virtues, it is clear that both of these views are partly correct but not entirely right. Our "great person" is—from within and outwardly—directed to the human good which is outside of her but in which she can participate and find fulfillment. Her life is ordered to a good end. Her fulfillment is ordered by responding to her good and the good of others (rights and responsibilities) and by a desire to become good (the virtues). She looks to go through her days, step by step, on a journey to becoming a better person.

For Reflection and Further Study

1. Can being good make us happy?

In his *Nicomachean Ethics*, Aristotle claims that becoming a good person and having the means to express goodness is the only thing that will bring fulfillment in life. Like today, people in Aristotle's time tried to be fulfilled through wealth, fame, honors, and pleasures. Most agree that these pursuits will not bring true happiness. We often think being good will bring us happiness in life after death. But Aristotle holds that being good brings the best possibility of happiness in earthly life.

If this is true, what does he mean by "happiness"? We often think of happiness in terms of going on vacation or spending leisure time with our friends. Aristotle thinks of happiness, not simply in terms of goodness or virtue, but virtuous activity. When is a carpenter most happy? We are quick to give answers that point to what we do when the work is done: taking pride or honor in the well-made desk; enjoying the income from the sale of the well-made desk; taking pleasure in the use of a well-made desk. Aristotle, however, seems to suggest that the carpenter is "happy" while performing well the tasks of carpentry. The honor we might take in a well-made desk—in a job well done and finished—really just sends us back to the workshop where the real happiness is found.

Read chapters 4 and 5 of book 1 of Aristotle's *Nicomachean Ethics*.[16] Consider his treatment of pleasure, wealth, and honor as means to attain happiness.

16. The *Nicomachean Ethics* can be found at the Internet Classics Archive, http://classics.mit.edu/Aristotle/nicomachaen.html.

2. The function argument

Read book 1, chapter 7, of Aristotle's *Nicomachean Ethics*. It is about five pages long and gives what is called the "function" argument. The idea of function relates to what something is—how its capacities imply a form of fulfillment. In this chapter, we used the analogy of a seed and flower to illustrate this framework: the seed has potential to become something, and the flower is the potential become actual.

Consider this framework of potential and fulfillment in terms of analogies that Aristotle uses, for example, the performance of a flute player or a sculptor. You will notice that Aristotle uses examples of crafts like carpentry and horsemanship. How do his examples help us understand what he calls an "end"? How do his analogies and his concept of an end help us to understand human happiness as "human flourishing"? What does human flourishing mean?

3. Rights and responsibilities

Consider St. John XXIII's *Pacem in terris* (Peace on Earth), nos. 8–38.[17] In the encyclical, Pope John provides an outline of responsibilities and rights. The whole section is framed by an appeal to human nature and human fulfillment in God and the goodness of creation. According to John XXIII, what are key elements of human flourishing? What is the human end?

4. Grace as our good

Take a look at Thomas Aquinas's examination of "Things in Which Man's Happiness Consists." Aquinas's work is readily available online.[18] Search using "Aquinas, Things in Which Man's Happiness Consists" or "*Summa theologica*, First Part of the Second Part, Question 2." You will find that Aquinas organizes the work by questions. When you look at the questions, focus on the section where Aquinas states, "I answer that . . ." You will notice that

17. John XXIII's *Pacem in terris* can be found on the Vatican website, http://w2.vatican.va/content/vatican/en.html. Or go directly to it at http://w2.vatican.va/content/john-xxiii/en/encyclicals/documents/hf_j-xxiii_enc_11041963_pacem.html.

18. An online version of the *Summa theologica* is maintained by the Dominican House of Studies, Priory of the Immaculate Conception in Washington, DC, http://dhspriory.org/thomas/summa/. Also at the New Advent website, http://www.newadvent.org/summa/. Online versions of the *Summa theologica* are usually a translation by the Fathers of the English Dominican Province (New York: Benziger Brothers, 1948).

Aquinas follows Aristotle closely. However, take a look at article 7, "Whether some good of the soul constitutes man's happiness?" Note that Aquinas states that happiness is not a good found in the soul. His point is that full happiness is discovered in what we receive from God. Aquinas is thinking of God's grace. Consider how our fulfillment in God affects the way we think about happiness. It is a big question, which we consider more carefully in Part 2 of this book.

However, we think it will be helpful in understanding the concept of an "end" if we review the logic of emphasizing the good of the soul and also going beyond it. If happiness is an activity then it must be more than simply the good of the body. Our bodies—in their capacities—hit a peak, level off, and then start a downward trajectory. Both of us, Jim and David, have been active all of our lives.

CHAPTER 5

Passions

W e worry a bit whenever we introduce moral theories. Often they are not helpful guides for living. By analogy, knowing how the inside of a piano works will not help a person play the piano. Imagine a piano teacher with his students. He would not make them first study the relations of soundboard, wires, jacks, levers, and hammers. Instead, students learn the relationships of the keys and notes, but the learning comes through practice—through the training of the hands as the media of knowing. Likewise, many of our ethics students, young and old, find the study of the moral *life* fascinating, but they do not find the study of moral *theory* interesting. Learning theory is like learning about the inside of a piano. With this analogy of the piano, our concern—in reference to moral vision—is to direct your attention to the music and to the possibilities of your life with the piano. Likewise, the concepts of the good and moral vision point toward our participation in the good, loving what is good, living well, and becoming good.

Thinking about Feelings

Our task in this chapter is, ultimately, to focus on the kind of seeing and knowing that inspires a desire to live well. The desire to play the piano well and the discipline of practicing do require an understanding of mechanics, not of hammer and soundboard, but of notes, meter, posture, technical movements of hands, and so on. Likewise, moral theories can be helpful if they direct our attention to what is good and to a kind of performance of the good (or simply living well). Although developing moral theories is not necessary for the moral life, they are helpful to learn at least to the extent that they can widen and deepen our understanding of the good and the possibilities of goodness in our lives. Good moral theories—unlike learning about wires and hammers in a piano and more like principles of hand position and posture—set out a landscape of inquiry about the meaning of life and living lovingly, truthfully, and justly.

The case that we have been making for moral vision assumes that goodness is something toward which the moral life aims. We are made for it; we have capacities for it, and are fulfilled in it.[1] When the moral life has an aim (an end), the passions—our emotions and desires—are essential to how we are attracted to and impelled to move toward what is good. The passions also can lead us astray (for example, greed or lust). To this degree, feelings and desires are natural human capacities that are shaped within our personal, socio-psychological, bodily, and spiritual makeup. Like our love of piano (or not), we all have the potential to enjoy music, but the particular direction of this potential is formed by our environment, our choices, and our efforts. We can shape how we emotionally respond to people and events. Take anger as an example. Rather than doing nothing at all because we are apathetic (we lack anger at injustice) or doing something rash and unjust in the heat of rage, we can learn to be angry in the right way so that it moves us to do the right thing at the right time.

The passions—how we feel and what we desire—are fundamental to the moral life. We have feelings that we do not choose to have (like anger and joy), but we can make choices that shape our emotional responses. We can learn to control our anger. We can learn to stop becoming angry at insignificant things. In short, feeling and desiring, like thinking and willing, can be directed toward the good. We are drawn to the good, and yet we (through our thinking, feeling, and acting) provide the direction. This claim is not a circular argument: we are complex beings who move forward in life in the company of others and in a multifaceted world—a world where we can see and become good. Amid the journey, we are able to feel that our feelings are right or wrong, or think in a way that shapes our desires, or choose to change the way we think and feel.

In the main portion of the chapter, we will compare this classic view of the passions with some typically modern moral theories. There is a set of modern moral theories that highlights the role of the passions, but surrenders too much control to what we feel (passively) and too much to how the

---

1. This sentence is a summary of Aristotle's function argument in *Nicomachean Ethics*, book 1, chapter 7.

world makes its impression on us. This set of theories sees the passions as a set of mechanisms or laws of human nature (something like a moral gravity). Our main concern is that such theories give us a truncated (abbreviated and reduced) view of the passions, and in the end, they do not adequately illuminate for us the possibilities of participation in the good that is outside of us in the world. In the pages that follow, our topic will be a set of modern theories that locate the core of morality in the emotions, sensations, and desires. But our main concern is moral vision—in this case, how we "see" what we feel.

Passions as Impressions Alone

First, we will consider the work of Scottish philosopher David Hume (1711–1776). In our copy of his *A Treatise of Human Nature* (1739–1740), the editor calls him "the greatest of British philosophers."[2] In any case, he is a moral philosopher to be reckoned with. He proposes that the inductive and empirical methods of the natural sciences (developed by scientists such as Francis Bacon and Isaac Newton) should be applied to the "science of man."[3] Hume holds that, as Newton "determined the laws and forces, by which the revolutions of the planets are governed and directed," his philosophy could "discover, at least in some degree, the secret springs and principles, by which the human mind is actuated in its operations."[4] The passions will be to morality what gravity is to physical objects.[5]

Second, we will consider the belief that morality is the self-expression of an individual's preferences, that in our moral views we are *merely* expressing personal likes and dislikes, feelings and inclinations. We italicized the "merely" because we certainly do not want to deny that we ought to be passionate about the good. The "merely" takes a common, shared good out of the picture. This "merely" implies that the individual "self" is the center of morality. To this degree, it is often called expressive individualism

2. Ernest C. Mossner, "Introduction," in David Hume, *A Treatise of Human Nature*, ed. Ernest C. Mossner (New York: Penguin, 1969), 7.

3. Hume, *A Treatise of Human Nature*, 45.

4. David Hume, *An Enquiry Concerning Human Understanding*, ed. Tom L. Beauchamp (New York: Oxford University Press, 1999), 93.

5. Hume does not make this direct correlation to gravity. The analogy is ours, and we think it is useful. Newton's conception of physical laws replaces the received Aristotelian framework for understanding the movement of physical objects.

(which has a connection to utilitarian individualism).[6] Expressivism holds that morality is merely an expression of a person's attitudes. That is the theory. In operation, this perspective on morality carries a moral imperative. The imperative is to do what feels right. For some, what is right might be what is easiest or least painful. If I feel like I can't keep my promise to you, I can't deny my feelings. For another, it will be what is hard but noble. I feel bound to be faithful to my word. It is undeniable that feelings and actions go together. The problem with expressivism is that it sees (and articulates) no good beyond the feeling. This problem is the reason we are dealing with David Hume and his view of the passions. Hume and expressivism reject what we have been developing as "moral vision," through which we are drawn to a good outside of ourselves.

Although historically far from Hume's view, expressivist individualism is connected to Hume's theory. Hume is not an individualist in the contemporary sense of the term. He is looking for commonality; he puts great emphasis on social relations, and he sees an inherent connection between personal well-being and the well-being of society as a whole. He has a profound sense of human sociality and fellow-feeling. However different from contemporary expressivism, his view of morality does have a connection: if feelings are like gravity, then there is no changing them, and resistance is inauthentic. The difference is that Hume's passions tend to be more sociable. Contemporary expressivism, in contrast, assumes that the individual is arbiter of true feeling: betraying my promise to you can be authentic or inauthentic. It just depends upon how I feel and what I desire.

In contrast, the traditional view of the passions (the view we are putting forward) sees the passions as capacities that can be formed or ill-formed in relationship to the good (for instance, adultery is wrong regardless of how we might feel about someone else's husband or wife). Hume challenges this traditional view insofar as it looks to him that this "relationship to the good" floats in some Platonic ether—in no place real. The problem with Hume's theory (and with expressivism) is that there is no account of a good to which we are directed and can be formed. If we treat passions like gravity, but if, in fact, they are formed one way or another by effort and environment, then

6. Utilitarian individualism and expressive individualism are two dominant moral languages in American culture. They are identified and described by sociologist Robert Bellah and a team of researchers (Richard Madsen, William Sullivan, Ann Swidler, and Steven Tipton) in their *Habits of the Heart: Individualism and Commitment in American Life* (Berkeley: University of California Press, 1985/1996). Utility (usefulness) is connected to expression of feeling as use and pleasure are connected in David Hume and classic utilitarian theory.

the passions will not provide a common source of morality (that is, they will not be like gravity at all). They will not unite us, but we will nevertheless treat them as the standard of what we must do. Morality will be a matter merely of personal desires and preferences.

We have to be fair to Hume. He develops sophisticated insights into how people think and feel about themselves, others, and the world, and about the trials and joys of life. He is at his best when he unflinchingly investigates our common motives and desires. He is honest about the difference between the reasons that we give for an action (like giving to charity) and our actual motives and intentions (like increasing our reputation). Central to his inquiry is the insight that factual or logical statements, like "malnutrition is harmful," do not move people to act. When you see a commercial or billboard about the harm of malnutrition, you will not see a list of facts. You will see images that stir the passions; you will see malnourished children, hungry and despondent. You might see images that help you recall your own experiences of hunger. You will see images that move you to sympathy and compassion, and if you feel compassion, you are likely to act. You are far more likely to act than if we were to tell you a fact: "Malnutrition is harmful."

Hume does not stop at showing the importance of the passions. He also hopes to dismantle what may be called the normative or regulating function of reason. In fact, if you were to study Hume in a philosophy course, you would—it is likely—study his work as a prime example of an empiricist arguing against eighteenth-century rationalism. This debate is not our concern.[7] In our consideration of moral vision, our concern is Hume's relationship to Aristotle. Insofar as Aristotle thinks about the good in terms of ends (that is, the fulfillment of what something is), Aristotelian thinking will be metaphysical. In moral matters, we will be thinking beyond what is now to what will be when things reach their completion/fulfillment. For Hume, this looking beyond provides an insufficient foundation for ethics. In this regard, the passions—for Hume—provide an experiential foundation in things as they are, here and now. When studying the physical world as well, Aristotle considers the tendencies and fulfillment of things. Isaac Newton, in contrast, shows that the movement and relationships of things are governed by physical laws. Likewise, Hume, in contrast to an Aristotelian framework, looks for an entirely experiential foundation of human behavior. He finds this foundation in the passions.

7. The best thing to say, in this short space, is that we certainly do not wish to defend Hume's rationalist opponents.

Hume looks to the passions as a common, fixed foundation. Looking for a natural mechanism of morality, he holds that we arrive at ideas like good and bad from the affective impressions that experiences make upon us.[8] These passions are sentiments like esteem, aversion, satisfaction, uneasiness, pride, shame, and various other feelings that can be categorized as either pleasurable or painful. Hume develops a complex ordering of passions and their relationship to ideas. The key point, in our brief treatment here, is that he claims that the passions are the basis for all moral actions and ideas.[9] An affective reaction to images of hunger reproduces our own feelings of hunger (although obviously more vague than real hunger) and develops into sympathy for the suffering, which produces an idea of suffering, so that we don't actually have to see the particular person suffer to be "impressed" by it. The impressions produce in us such feelings as compassion and sympathy. What we think— ideas like good and bad—is always reducible to these facts of sense impressions.

The important point, for us, is that Hume excludes key elements of "moral vision." His claim is certainly correct: people are moved by sympathy and compassion, and when we suffer we tend to have more sensitivity to the suffering of others. The problem is that Hume narrows our field of vision. The problem is Hume's either/or—either reason or passions. He sets up an opposition between thinking and feeling, but the opposition is not necessary. Hume simplifies our internal process of "knowing" and "experiencing" too much. He does not allow that thinking can be a primary mode of engagement. He does not allow that contemplating, pondering, and forming deductions are fundamental intellectual "experiences" in themselves. Granted, they are not "sense experiences," but they are inner movements in themselves in response to life in the world. Contrary to Hume, who always puts the passions first, it seems more sensible to allow that thinking and feeling have a reciprocal relationship. In the case of the passions, when we learn to direct our feelings to the human good, we call these well-ordered feelings "reasonable." We form and develop our passions by reflection, self-criticism, and effort—with a view to the good.

Our proposal for moral vision assumes that we can set our sights on who we should become. In the case of passions, we can say to ourselves, "I

8. Hume, *A Treatise of Human Nature*, book 3, part 1, chapters 1–2.

9. Passions are the basis for moral reasoning and the reasons that we give. We might think that giving to the poor is good; we might think that we ought to do it. But, according to Hume, it is not the "thought" of giving that moves us to action. We are moved to act because of the way we are "impressed" by suffering. And because the suffering of others makes us feel sympathy and act, we arrive at thoughts about it.

should become less envious and more joyful when my friends experience good fortune." David Hume, in his attempt to be scientific about the passions, is famous for rejecting the idea that we can reason about what should be.[10] The form of observation recommended by Hume—an eighteenth-century thinker—assumes that there are neutral facts about how human beings function, analogous to Newton's discovery of gravity. Gravity just is, and it has always been in operation—long before Newton discovered its principles. Likewise, Hume is looking for a kind of moral gravity—the laws of moral responsiveness, which are "just there" and have always been there regardless of what people think or have thought. From Hume's point of view, how we think human beings *should behave*, who we think we *should become*, and what we hope life *will be* are equivalent to arguing whether gravity is good or bad. Imposing "should" upon gravity is silly.[11]

When all is said, Hume's approach is not as much empirical as it is a rejection of the kind of ends-directed approach that we have been proposing. From Hume's point of view, our approach encourages us to look at our own ideas of what we want the world to be rather than what it really is. That said, Hume's own approach is not any more inductive or empirical.[12] Hume, himself, cannot observe other people's feelings (what is going on inside of them). In fact, if he were to observe in you an expression of humility or self-effacement over some honor received, he would believe that you were either lying to yourself or to him, and in both cases, your so-called humility, in his view, just amounts to a useful social strategy. In other words, he might observe humility, but he would not trust that observation. (He often does not believe what he sees.) He assumes that expressions of humility in response

10. In arguing about reason and passions, there really is no way to settle the argument with Hume. If we say, "We think we should control our anger," Hume would say, "It is not thinking, but some other passion—a sense of disapproval of others—that motivates us to change." Then we say, "Actually, we get wrapped up in the anger of other fans. They approve, but we don't." Hume would then come back with some other passion, and we would reply with a reason, and it would go on and on.

11. However, although Hume claims that the basis for thinking is in feeling, he is inclined to call people unreasonable if they are too quick to believe what they feel about their experience. If passions are like gravity, then a proper account of them will require critical examination. In short, we have to be clearheaded and detached from what we feel.

12. Hume's whole project is not entirely empirical or based in observation. It is dependent on his powers of reflection, in large part on his abilities of inner, self-reflection. He assumes that the human mind has a common "structure and composition" that allows him to look within to determine common modes of thinking and feeling. See his "Of Pride and Humility," book 2, part 1, section 2 in *A Treatise of Human Nature*.

to personal achievements are false. The only true response to achievement is pride—given that Hume correlates achievement with pleasure and pleasure with pride. In contrast, humility—as a theological virtue—recognizes our own gifts and achievements but puts them in reference to higher goods—to what we are called by God and with God to be. Hume just assumes—with an eighteenth-century view of science as his leverage—that there is no transcendent goodness outside of ourselves to which we are drawn.

Utilitarian and Expressive Individualism

For Hume, we experience things in the world that impress sensations upon us; it is not goodness that draws us, but passions that are already within. If, for Hume, all moral reason is reducible to sense impressions—pleasure and pain, attraction and aversion—then what we reason to be good will be what is pleasurable and therefore useful to us. You might be loyal to a friend at great cost to yourself. Hume would hold that, although costly in some way, you must have gained some benefit, some satisfaction and good feeling from it. Certainly, it is true that when we are loyal, we do experience a sense of goodness and satisfaction. The difference with Hume is that he holds that this sense of satisfaction and good feeling is the reason for the action. He would object if you claimed: I was loyal because I believe it was right and good; I did feel good in the end, but this feeling was not the reason for my action. Your claim would be that there is a real difference between taking pleasure in being faithful to a friend and holding that you were faithful only because it was pleasurable.

On this point, we will shift to our contemporaries—to utilitarian and expressive individualism. Utilitarian individualism holds that one's life is properly directed to pursuing one's own material interests. In Robert Bellah's *Habits of the Heart*, the view is represented by Benjamin Franklin. Franklin emphasizes virtues of self-improvement and socio-economic advancement. Bellah shows how Franklin's focus on self-advancement, over time, becomes thought of as one's contribution to society.[13] The view is that we contribute to socio-economic life by pursuing self-interest. Likewise (but quite different in its development from Franklin), standard economic theory defines the rational individual as one who is motivated primarily by self-interest. The rational will is equivalent to the choice that will maximize an individ-

13. Bellah, *Habits of the Heart*, 33.

ual's material self-interest. What is rational is useful to the individual. This economics-based view is certainly a narrow conception of the human being and of the human good. In game theory—a mathematical model of economic decision-making—such things as loyalty and promise-keeping are considered irrational if they do not serve self-interest, that is, if we keep promises because it is the right thing to do.

The expressivist view or an ethics of authenticity is focused less on success and more on personal, emotional satisfaction. It is more suited to what we often call the private sphere—marriage, family, friendships, and involvement in community organizations.[14] Expressivism is evident in the promise, "Let's stay married as long as it feels right." We would like to note that the alternative to "as long as it feels right" is not "Let's stay married even if one of us is miserable." Rather, some couples share a commitment not only to each other, but also to the institution of marriage. When they marry, they say, in effect, "Sometimes it will feel right; sometimes it will be very difficult. But we will try to become the kind of people who can work through good times and bad and have a happy marriage." This view sees marriage as a journey to an end—to learning to love and to be more loving. It is risky. The expressivist view sees marriage as an expression of a love that already exists. Likewise, contributing to community—organizing a neighborhood association, for example—will be pursued *because* it gives us personal satisfaction. On this point, it is close to utilitarian individualism.

These individualist perspectives are not directly attributable to Hume. Hume is an influential philosopher of the eighteenth century, but he is part of a wider tradition that focuses on sentiment and utility. He held a belief in the fundamental importance of social utility. Through the centuries, this tradition has developed beyond Hume's own views. It has developed in a variety of directions. Hume advances a tradition of thought that becomes influential in the development of utilitarian political and economic philosophies in the eighteenth and nineteenth centuries. This same tradition also has a connection to scientific materialism and sociobiology in the nineteenth and twentieth centuries. One way to divide the various directions is to note that some undertake the questions of pleasure and utility with greater scientific detachment, while others do so with greater personal commitment to self-expression and self-interest. Neither direction represents Hume. He takes for granted a connection between self-expression and fellow-feeling that subsequent generations often did not (that is, "sympathy" is a funda-

14. Bellah, *Habits of the Heart*, 41.

mental passion for Hume). In effect, Hume assumes that passions like social benevolence are stable human traits. But his proposals develop in a variety of different directions because the passions change through formation and culture, effort and environment.[15] Assuming his unproblematic connection between self and sympathy, Hume could claim that *feeling* is a more stable basis for action than the various conflicting opinions about what people *think* is the meaning of life. Today we can no longer make that assumption.

In contrast to Hume, it is part of a long tradition that we have a natural capacity to know what is good through intuition and insight, analysis and contemplation. We know the good, not only with the goal of doing something good, but also with the goal of understanding and wisdom. It is good to know the good for its own sake. Aristotle, toward the end of his *Nicomachean Ethics*, suggests that the life of contemplation is the most distinctively human and highest form of life.[16] Reflection and contemplation are kinds of experiences; they are experiences of thought. They are experiences deeply connected to our desires and passions. We contemplate when we desire to know, and for contemplatives, knowing is loving. Within this ancient philosophical framework, our senses (sight, touch, etc.) certainly prompt a desire to know, but it is also our intuitive understanding and intellectual virtues that give us the ability to see and love deeper and higher. Through effort, attention, and love for what is good, we can become wise. With wisdom, we can see things in light of the good and thus as they really are.

Conclusion

After our review of Hume, it is time to return to our piano analogy and our worries about moral theories. We worry that our discussion of Hume may not have been helpful in the way that learning about hammers and levers would not inspire a person to play and to love the piano. Levers, wires, and soundboard might be interesting for those already interested in the engineering and mechanics, but not necessarily for those who want to learn the skills and virtues of putting their fingers to the keys. Unavoidably, our discussion of Hume has focused on the moral equivalent of the piano hammers and levers because these are his concerns. In effect, our claim is that Hume

---

15. Alasdair MacIntyre, *A Short History of Ethics* (Notre Dame: University of Notre Dame Press, 1988), 175.

16. Aristotle, *Nicomachean Ethics*, book 10, chapters 7-8.

is not asking the most important question. His inquiries are important and insightful. He attends to the passions as mechanisms of the moral life. In contrast to Hume, we want to encourage you to think about the passions as pointers to what is good, to our desires, cares and worries, and loves as directing our vision beyond ourselves.

We ask different kinds of moral questions when we set our eyes to the good, to a journey of becoming better people and to participating more deeply in the good of music, carpentry, friendship, and life itself. What fulfills the human being? What is the human being for? What role do I play? What is the good of my work? What is the end of family life? What is the purpose of citizenship in community? As we ask these questions more consistently, we are likely to see more clearly. And as we see beyond the surface of things, we are likely to love more deeply. Sometimes, we first love more deeply, and then we work to see better what we love. In short, the passions (emotions and desires) are fundamental to a just and loving vision of the world. They are essential because they can be shaped by our thinking, efforts, choices, and convictions. Part of moral vision is learning to feel in the right way.

For Reflection and Further Study

1. Feeling and thinking

We have found that feeling and thinking about what to do tends to vary from person to person. By temperament and personality, some people feel first and then think things through. Others think about what they feel. Reflect on what leads you to action. Think about bold actions; these tend to stand out. If you had to have a difficult and painful discussion with a coworker or friend, what moved you to do it? Did you primarily reason it through? Or did you feel impelled to act? Both?

2. Reason—the slave of the passions?

"Reason is, and ought only to be the slave of the passions, and can never pretend to any other office than to serve and obey them."[17] David Hume makes

---

17. For these quotations, we are using the edition of *A Treatise of Human Nature* edited by L. A. Selby-Bigge (1888), published by Oxford University Press in 1965. This edition is widely available. But in the event that the reader is consulting a different edition, we will cite passages

this famous (or infamous) claim in *A Treatise of Human Nature*. The section, titled "Of the Influencing Motives of the Will," is ten paragraphs long and can be found online—either separately or as part of the full text of *A Treatise of Human Nature*. Hume's text is difficult to read. We will ask you, when all is said, to focus on the eighth paragraph, which begins, "'Tis natural for one, that does not examine objects with a strict philosophic eye, to imagine, that those actions of the mind are entirely the same, which produce not a different sensation, and are not immediately distinguishable to the feeling and perception."[18] In this line, notice that Hume is making a contrast between how most people see things and the philosopher's point of view. Hume is asking us to distrust our ordinary observations. In the end, we will ask you to make your own observations and reflect on the intimate relationship between our thinking and feeling in the moral life.

At the very beginning of the section, "Of the influencing motives of the will," Hume states the view of his opposition. He argues against the history of philosophy (since the Greeks) and everyday people who claim that reason ought to "regulate" our actions—that our passions might contradict reason (at first) and can be made to conform to what is reasonable (in terms of anger for example). In contrast to this view, Hume seeks "to prove *first*, that reason alone can never be a motive to any action of the will; and *secondly*, that it can never oppose passion in the direction of the will."[19] Before we move forward, we want to note that Hume's first claim might not be controversial at all, depending upon what he means by "reason alone."

Hume's "reason alone" seems to be naming what is traditionally called speculative or theoretical reason (such as principles of logic). On this point, Aristotle and Thomas Aquinas, for example, agree with Hume. Speculative reason does not produce action. However, Aristotle and Aquinas also see at work in us a practical form of reason. In trying to understand this kind of reason, Aristotle makes analogies with crafts and craftsmanship. How a carpenter makes decisions about the practical matters in making a good desk has an analogy to how we aim toward and craft the good in our various practical endeavors. Like the carpenter, we gain knowledge, wisdom, skill, and a feel for what we are doing. Through doing (rather than feeling), we learn to reason. In this sense, practical reason is not "reason alone" (however

---

by book, part, and section. In this case, the quotation is from book 2, part 2, section 3, "Of the influencing motives of the will," p. 415 in the Selby-Bigge (1965) edition.

18. Hume, *A Treatise of Human Nature*, book 2, part 2, section 3, "Of the influencing motives of the will," p. 417 in the Selby-Bigge (1965) edition.

19. Hume, *A Treatise of Human Nature*, 413.

Hume imagines it). It is reasoning through our doing and living. This kind of practical reason orders and guides what we do.

In any case, Hume seems to give examples of speculative (rather than practical) reason when he refers to "reason alone." Likewise, in his second claim (that reason can never oppose the passions), he seems to hold to a view of "passions alone"—that is, of passions as prior to our knowledge or judgment of them. With his conjecture about "passions alone," prior to our naming of them, he is able to put passions in a pure realm beyond our reach. As soon as we name passions, we have thought about them. As soon as we identify a passion with a label or concept, we have mixed reason with the passion. So, argues Hume, when a passion seems to contradict reason, it is not the passion per se but our faulty reasoning or action that accompanies the passion. When reason seems to contradict a passion, reason actually contradicts reason (not the passion). We have misnamed or wrongly understood what we feel. See the end of the sixth paragraph: "In short, a passion must be accompany'd with some false judgment, in order to its being unreasonable; and even then 'tis not the passion, properly speaking, which is unreasonable, but the judgment."[20]

This point leads us to the eighth paragraph. Hume is setting up an argument that he is guaranteed to win. "'Tis natural for one, that does not examine objects with a strict philosophic eye, to imagine, that those actions of the mind are entirely the same, which produce not a different sensation, and are not immediately distinguishable to the feeling and perception." In short, what we think are thoughts are really feelings. We experience thoughts (promptings of reason) such as "do good," but at bottom—according to Hume—they are not thoughts but passions. Hume explains:

> Reason, for instance, exerts itself without producing any sensible emotion; and except in the more sublime disquisitions of philosophy, or in the frivolous subtilties of the schools, scarce ever conveys any pleasure or uneasiness. Hence it proceeds, that every action of the mind, which operates with the same calmness and tranquillity, is confounded with reason by all those, who judge of things from the first view and appearance. Now 'tis certain, there are certain calm desires and tendencies, which, tho' they be real passions, produce little emotion in the mind, and are more known by their effects than by the immediate feeling or sensation. These desires are of two kinds;

20. Hume, *A Treatise of Human Nature*, 417.

either certain instincts originally implanted in our natures, such as benevolence and resentment, the love of life, and kindness to children; or the general appetite to good, and aversion to evil, consider'd merely as such. When any of these passions are calm, and cause no disorder in the soul, they are very readily taken for the determinations of reason, and are suppos'd to proceed from the same faculty, with that, which judges of truth and falshood. Their nature and principles have been suppos'd the same, because their sensations are not evidently different.[21]

We experience thoughts and judgments (like "do good and avoid evil"), but they are, according to Hume, really passions. In effect, any evidence that we can give of basic moral reason, Hume will reject for the sake of his theory that we are first of all moved by passions.

Where does this set of arguments leave us? At least we can say that passions (emotions and desires) and practical reasoning are intimately connected. What Hume calls a "calm passion," such as "the general appetite to good, and aversion to evil," Thomas Aquinas will call a first principle of practical reason. On this point, Hume asserts that thoughts are really passions. In contrast, Aquinas makes a commonsense claim (which Hume rejects). While Hume tries to convince us that our "reasons for acting" are really driven by passions, Aquinas trusts that we know what we are about. What we think of as reasons for acting do, in fact, come from our capacity to act according to reason (the intellect).

Regardless of the debate with Hume, it is worth discussing the basic reasons that we give for acting and how our emotions move us to act. Anger or distress about injustice can move us to make the world a better place. They can also move us to hurt others and make things worse. How do we begin to understand that it is better to feel one way rather than another? What is the connection between the passions and the moral life?

3. Utilitarianism

John Stuart Mill develops the moral philosophy of utilitarianism. He follows in David Hume's path in some important ways. He thinks of passions

---

21. Hume, *A Treatise of Human Nature*, 417. In addition, the text can be found online at either of these websites: www.gutenberg.org/files/4705/4705-h/4705-h.htm#link2H_4_0075; and http://people.rit.edu/wlrgsh/HumeTreatise.pdf.

as the cause and, in this sense, the "end" (goal/purpose) of human action. However, there are key differences. For example, Hume thinks of pleasure and pain (fundamental passions) as a result—in a moral sense—that comes from *doing* good and bad actions. He distinguishes these moral feelings from the pleasure and pain that comes from fortune or misfortune, that is, from experiencing the *consequences* of someone else's actions and things out of our control. Mill, in contrast, thinks about pleasure and pain—morally speaking—entirely in terms of the *consequences*. In short, Hume thinks of moral pleasure and pain in terms of the person doing the action (it gives pleasure to do it). Mill thinks of moral pleasure and pain in terms of the aggregate results of the action (the amount of pleasure distributed in the doing of the action).

Although there are important differences, Mill is working within the same tradition as Hume and appeals to a similar understanding of pleasure and utility. We suggest that you look at the beginning of chapter 2 in Mill's *Utilitarianism*. Notice his appeal to pleasure and utility as a single mechanism of morality. At the beginning of the chapter, Mill explains that "the 'greatest happiness principle' holds that actions are right in proportion as they tend to promote happiness, wrong as they tend to produce the reverse of happiness. By happiness is intended pleasure, and the absence of pain; by unhappiness, pain, and the privation of pleasure."[22] In the next paragraph, Mill will introduce an Aristotelian objection: if life has "no higher end than pleasure," Mill supposes his critics will say, then his "doctrine is worthy only of swine." Mill's critics will argue that there are higher goals of human life than mere pleasure. After stating the objections, Mill will defend his view and show that pleasure is the proper end of human life.

Consider how Mill answers his critics through the first ten paragraphs of chapter 2 in *Utilitarianism*.[23] How does Mill justify his claim that pleasure is our ultimate end? How does he argue that all morality is about pleasure/utility? Is he successful? What do his arguments imply about what makes us human?

In his arguments in defense of pleasure as our ultimate end, Mill assumes that pleasures can be judged by what could be called "objective" standards. In other words, pleasures do not amount to mere preferences

22. John Stuart Mill, *Utilitarianism*, 2nd edition, ed. George Sher (Indianapolis: Hackett, 2002), 7.

23. The full text of Mill's *Utilitarianism* can be found online, for example, at www.util itarianism.com/mill2.htm.

of individuals. He is a bit elitist in this regard. Some pleasures are more basic, like a desire for meat and bread. Other pleasures appeal to the higher—intellectual and noble—character of the human being. These higher pleasures are distinctively human. In comparing lower and higher pleasures, Mill claims that a preference for higher pleasures is obvious to those who are able to judge between the two. Those who have experienced high and low pleasures—studying philosophy and watching mindless YouTube clips—can give us a clear judgment. "The test of quality and the rule for measuring it against quantity [is] the preference felt by those who, in their opportunities of experience, to which must be added their habits of self-consciousness and self-observation, are best furnished with the means of comparison."[24] The implication of this statement is that a class of people who have experienced higher-quality pleasures (education? culture?) is better situated than commoners are to judge the value of pleasures.

If we accept Mill's claim that pleasure is our ultimate end and if, at the same time, we reject Mill's arguments about those who are best situated to judge—if we put Lady GaGa at the level of Beethoven or getting drunk on the level of cleaning up the neighborhood—then we are headed toward expressive and utilitarian individualism. The ultimate end of the human being becomes a matter of individual preference. Is there any harm in this point of view?

24. Mill, *Utilitarianism*, ed. George Sher, 12.

CHAPTER 6

Moral Reason

C onsider the difficult decisions that we make in life. Our students are faced with a common set of questions: where to go to school, what to choose as a major, whom to have as a roommate, whom to date and whether it should become "serious," and even simple day-to-day questions like, should I study for an extra few hours or mess around with my friends? The factors involved in making these decisions are numerous—what do I think are the pros and cons, the cost and benefit, what do I think that I *should* do and why, what do parents and friends say, how do I feel about doing one thing rather than another? Do I want the right thing? How do I know what the right thing is? When faced with a difficult decision, we often wonder why it has to be so hard. Sometimes a person will say in exasperation, "Somebody just tell me what to do!" But then we don't listen. After we are told what to do, we have to struggle with the decision anyway. The reason, perhaps, is because difficult and important decisions require all of who we are: our thoughts, convictions, feelings, relationships, hopes, desires, courage, and more. Likewise, all of who we are—our character—is the matrix for moral decisions.

Living and Seeing

The simple point for this chapter is that moral reason does not stand alone but is part of a whole setting of life and the whole makeup of persons (for example, desires, relationships, and habits of life). From this simple point, thinking about moral reasoning becomes very complicated. You might have had the experience of trying to teach someone (or to learn for yourself) a complicated dance step or a musical instrument or the proper way to strike a soccer ball. Try to teach a seven-year-old how to shoot a slapshot. You will find that far more is involved in the shot than you had originally thought (least of which is being able to skate well enough). Because of the complications, you are likely to emphasize one thing for the child to learn. You might even be tempted to say that everything follows from this one thing, say, how a hockey player squares up his feet. But the reality is far more complicated.[1]

In this book, our focus on moral vision will help keep manageable the very complicated topic of moral decisions. Moral vision begins long before we confront a particular moral issue. It is not narrowly "moral"—if moral means some specific issue, problem, or decision. It is how we see the world, the people in our lives, our relationships, ourselves, and on and on. Moral vision is intentional. We have to be critical and root out misconceptions and misunderstandings. It is loving; it develops with the conviction that what is true is good, that when we learn to see the world and others rightly we learn to see and desire their good. It is possible, of course, for someone to have a proper intellectual grasp of something and then use the knowledge for some bad purpose (for instance, knowledge of chemistry used for making illegal drugs). This is why morality cannot be reduced to our focus on "vision." Nonetheless, we want to attend to the importance of how we see the world apart from specific moral questions.

Thomas Aquinas (drawing from the works of Aristotle) outlines what he calls intellectual virtues—mainly the speculative virtues of understanding, science, and wisdom.[2] The terms "understanding" and "wisdom," for Aquinas, have meanings that are close to how we use the words today. We have the ability to understand things as they are. Wisdom goes deeper than understanding. Wisdom pertains to the meaning of life; we can attain wisdom about the common source and goal of all things. Science, for Aquinas, is a bit different than its modern meaning. For Aquinas, science means the intellectual capacity to attain knowledge by moving from principles of understanding to subsequent levels of knowledge. Science, for Aquinas, applies to the fields we call the natural sciences, like physics, but also mathematics, theology, and philosophy.

1. Charles Pinches calls this reduction of morality to a single principle, "principle monism." See his *Theology and Action: After Theory in Christian Ethics* (Grand Rapids: Eerdmans, 2002), 39-58.

2. Thomas Aquinas, *Summa theologica* I-II, question 57.

Along with the speculative virtues, Aquinas outlines virtues of reasoning required for making things (the virtue of "art") and for acting well, which is prudence. Art, for instance, is an intellectual grasp of the knowledge required for carpentry and plumbing. Art involves a way of seeing and thinking through a task. No doubt, visual and performing artists have a definite "know-how." They are able to see much more than the average person. To give an example that some people think is far from art, good automobile mechanics have gained knowledge and insight through years of working on engines, and for this reason, are able to see problems and solutions more readily than those with little experience. Similarly, prudence is the virtue of moral action; it shapes our capacity to find the right means to a good end. It converts the vision of the speculative virtues to a course of action, to see how to move step by step to achieve a goal.

The practices of accounting provide a good example of how these intellectual virtues come together. To be a good accountant, one will need to understand the basic principles of accounting, which include general principles of mathematics and more specific knowledge of how the general principles apply to accounting. In Aquinas's use of the term, accounting is a science. In addition, a student will have to study and perform the practical operations and tasks. Aquinas might call the virtues of these operations the "art" of accounting. All of these intellectual virtues are required to have the ability to even see a moral problem in accounting. Accounting scandals are reduced to simple terms by news reporters. But the actual accounting issues are usually quite sophisticated. To see the problem, one needs to understand the science of accounting, that is, to know how good accounting is done. Even more important, one needs to have the skills of accounting in order to deal with difficulties. Prudence is the virtue that sees a pathway and is able to take the steps to do things right, especially in a situation where they threaten to go wrong.[3]

Moral reasoning, like moral vision, cannot be reduced to a narrow view of what counts as moral or practical. In the last chapter, we considered a theory proposed by David Hume (1711–1776) and its reduction of morality to feelings and emotions. Hume argued that the passions were the sole source of morality. To do so, he committed himself to an indiscriminating view of how we arrive at some feelings rather than others. He did not consider that someone could *reason* that she had gone overboard with anger and use her

3. See Ronald F. Duska and Brenda Shay Duska, *Accounting Ethics* (Oxford: Blackwell, 2003).

reasoning to form her emotions, little by little, during subsequent fits of rage. Over time, keeping in mind the importance of being reasonable, she would no longer overreact. Her passions would change. In this case, reason would be the source that formed the passions. This common experience is overlooked if we take Hume's view.

Reason Alone

At this point in this chapter, we will turn to Immanuel Kant (1724-1804). Kant answered Hume's criticisms of reason. Hume argued against the view that morality is based in what the intellectual virtues can grasp—against the idea that the moral good is understood through reason first of all. Hume held that we are moved only by feelings and desires, by sentiments about what seems good and bad. Kant defended reason, but not the structure of reasoning that we have been discussing under the heading "moral vision." Kant accepted Hume's critique of speculative reasoning as it is understood by the likes of Aristotle and Aquinas. He accepted that we cannot have a rational grasp of what is good as an object of understanding—as truly good and really existing outside of ourselves. But, he argued, human reason itself is a reality and structure that we can know as we study our own powers of knowing. Using a camera as analogy, we cannot know the object in view for itself (this would be the goal of the speculative virtues). But we can understand the operation of the lens. We cannot know goodness and truth in the world as existents in themselves. We cannot know what goodness requires of us. But we can know what our powers of reason are and what our reasonableness requires of us. If thinkers of ages past thought that what was morally right corresponded to some real goodness, Kant held that what is morally right corresponds to consistent and autonomous ("pure") reasoning. In effect, what is purely rational is good.

Our concern with Kant is shaped by our focus on moral vision: How does Kant help us understand our relationships to others and life as a whole? How do we view the human being and human morality? To Kant's credit, he managed to defend a view of practical reason, and he was a champion of freedom and human dignity. However, he created a set of problems in the process. We will focus on a few. In looking for a pure principle of morality, Kant extracts and separates his concepts of the "rational will" and "duty" from a person's purposes/ends for acting and the concrete duties of her life (for example, duties as friend, daughter, coworker, etc.). In doing so, he confines "morality" to a narrow area of our lives. We can reason well about what not to do ("do not lie"), but we have much more difficulty connecting purposes and ends of our personal lives (for instance, being an accountant) with moral duty. The two, in Kant's system, are quite separate, and occasionally, when some moral problem arises, the two might come together. The question "What are my moral duties?" is considered entirely separate from the question "How do I become a good accountant?"[4]

Kant proposes that the only appropriate area of moral judgment is the will. The will is the facility in us to act on our own or, as the apt phrase puts it, by our own free will. As the intellect has thoughts, desires have goals and intentions, and the passions have feelings, the will has action. The will is our capacity to act freely. As will, it is free, and as a good will, it is rational. For Kant, this point about the good will includes an important distinction. If free and rational, the will is autonomous. It is self-ruled. The rational will is guided only by the intellect and its reasoning—by nothing personal, not by feelings, inclinations, goals, or intentions. In the preface to his Foundations of the Metaphysics of Morals, Kant notes that he is looking to establish "the supreme principle of morality" (p. 8 [392]) that is purified of any view of what fulfills human life and any conception of what it is good to be, to want, or to have. Kant names this supreme principle as the good will.

In the first section of his Foundations, Kant is like a scientist trying to identify a fundamental cause. Imagine a researcher going through a process of excluding variables. In trying to identify the cause of a kind of cancer, the scientist will test environmental conditions, one by one, genetic traits, one by one, diet and lifestyle habits, and so on. Likewise, to find the source of morality, Kant tests and excludes various elements of life: pleasures, goals, and happiness. He holds that all adulterate the reasonable good (p. 11 [395]). He tests and excludes human desires and needs because they are best served by mere instinct (p. 12 [396]). He rejects feelings—even sympathy: if I feed the poor because I feel the pain of compassion, then my actions lack moral

---

4. Immanuel Kant, *Foundations of the Metaphysics of Morals*, trans. Lewis White Beck (New York: Macmillan, 1959), 13 [397]. (In this section we will give the references to Kant's work in the text, citing the page number first and then the standard numbering in brackets, so that the reader will not have to rely on the translation that we are using.) Here, Kant gives the example of a merchant or shopkeeper. If the person in business sees that acting morally is good for business, then his or her actions lack moral worth. The businessperson's actions would be selfish rather than moral. In this example, Kant makes it appear that being moral has to undermine good business sense for an act to have moral worth.

worth (p. 14 [398]). Kant excludes intentions insofar as he thinks of intentions as encouraging of personal desires rather than objective, moral goods (p. 16 [400]). He excludes judgments based on the consequences or results of one's actions. These are not in a person's control. (Too often we act poorly for a good end, such as lying to spare someone's feelings.) Kant tests the idea that a morally good action can be judged by the good that is done, and he finds the idea lacking (p. 10 [394]).

For Kant, the only possibility of a good in itself is the good will. On this point, he is unlike the scientist. Kant rejects all material causes. In fact, he excludes consequences, intentions, and desires because each introduces some material element that will make reason impure and will adulterate the moral good. He excludes our friendships, worldly concerns, and personal commitments. Here, we can see the basic assumptions that Kant makes. He is writing at a time when modern science is emerging and an Aristotelian science has been replaced. While Aristotelian science considered matter in terms of forms and purposes, modern physics developed causes in terms of invariant laws of matter. Likewise, Kant's older contemporary David Hume rejects the rational basis of morality in terms of the material operations of passions (how experiences make an impression on us). Hume criticizes moral "reasoning" because it is not its own source. He looks for a material source and finds "passions" based in experience. In order to defend moral reason, Kant goes the other direction, but stays within the same basic framework. He seeks to identify a pure reason, unadulterated by experience. In a sense, he shifts from natural science to mathematics, from physics to geometry. He is looking for a moral theorem or maxim (like the law of the angles of a right triangle) that can be seen in experience but can also exist in a pure idea in reason alone.

In his *Foundations*, Kant sets forth the maxim of the rational will with two basic formulations. Because they are imperatives of reason only, Kant calls these versions of the categorical imperative. They are categorical because they are commands that have no qualifications and are applicable for all always. The first formulation is "I should never act in such a way that I could not also will that my maxim should be universal law" (p. 18 [402]). Kant's best example for this formulation is "Do not lie." If everyone were to lie as a universal law, then words could not be trusted. In this case, neither telling the truth nor lying would have any credibility. Lying, to be effective, depends upon the assumption that one tells the truth as a universal law, that telling the truth is the general rule. It is only in this context where lying "makes sense." Therefore, one cannot lie and at the same time will that lying be universal law. "Do not lie" is a categorical imperative. There is no "if" clause . . . "if you want to be a good friend, then don't lie." It is categorical because it is universal: "Do not lie" needs no qualification.

The second basic formulation of the categorical imperative is: "Act so that you treat humanity, whether in your own person or in that of another, always as an end and never as a means only" (p. 47 [429]). Following this formulation, Kant turns to the example of suicide. "If, in order to escape burdensome circumstances, he destroys himself, he uses a person [here himself] merely as a means to maintain a tolerable condition up to the end of life." In other words, he uses himself (by ending his own life) as a means to end suffering. This example and others that follow are not as tightly constructed as the examples following the first formulation. But this second formulation is necessary inasmuch as Kant claims that the rational will is a good in itself so that the rational person is an end in herself.

Given our concern for moral vision, two problems emerge in Kant's defense of moral reasoning. These problems have been noted by prominent moral philosophers. The first problem is that acts that Kant wants to disallow, such as lying, can be included in the categorical imperative.[5] The second problem is related to the first: Kant's own use of his formula can arrive at conclusions that look to be irrational and blind to a real good.[6]

Concerning the first problem, we can use the categorical imperative to include what Kant wants to reject. The following fits the requirements of the categorical imperative: "Do not cheat on a test, unless one needs the class to graduate; one will fail otherwise, and one wouldn't cheat for a lesser reason." A person might make this claim a positive, universal claim: the rational person ought to cheat under the conditions outlined above; otherwise, the person would be irresponsible. To cheat would be the responsible thing to do because so much is at stake. Kant would not like the self-interest involved in our formulation of the command, but it is consistent with his requirement of universalizability. It does fit his first formulation of the categorical imperative. And he claims that the formula is all that we need. We do *will* that our cheating in this narrow framework should be a universal law. Hopefully, dear readers, you see our universal law of cheating to be a mere rationalization of bad behavior. Maybe not. In any case, Kant's formula is not decisive. It can be used to show both that cheating is rational and that it is not. This

5. Alasdair MacIntyre, *A Short History of Ethics* (Notre Dame: University of Notre Dame Press, 1988), 193-94.

6. Hannah Arendt, *Eichmann in Jerusalem* (New York: Penguin Classics, 2006), 135-37.

problem is evidence that some other factors, not Kant's formula, are at work to make the moral determination.[7]

Second, we have the problem of irrationality that is produced by the categorical imperative. Our example, again, is telling the truth, but this time to Nazis. Following the second formulation, we ought not to use Nazis as a means to an end; we ought to tell them the truth. So when SS officers ask us if we know the location of some Jews, we tell them where they can find them. In this case, the categorical imperative leads to an act that appears to be blind to obvious moral concerns. We might protest that the Nazis are using the Jews as a means to an end. But Kant tells us that what Nazis do is not our concern. Our concern is the autonomy of our will in reference to the universal law. In reality, our commitment to universal law ends up being a commitment to Nazis. If a Jewish person asks us to lie for her, we would have to say, "No, sorry, I cannot violate the universal law." We hope you agree that this commitment to the Nazis is irrational and immoral. (We are not in favor of lying, and the Catholic tradition has developed ways of understanding what does and does not constitute a lie in this kind of situation.) In effect, Kant's categorical imperative, used consistently, can arrive at irrational conclusions.

Conclusion

What is the point of our critique of Kant? What is the lesson learned? The main point is that moral vision is directed to reality. Kant, in contrast, accepts the view that "values" are simply the meanings that we ascribe to things, that we humans and the world are not objectively good. He turns from the "good" of reality to the good of our rational will—to abstract rational consistency as the final test. In contrast, moral vision starts with the conviction that what is true about the world and our lives is good. Following this point, moral vision draws us outside of ourselves to what is real—what is good and true. Because we are drawn to the good, our moral reasoning need not be separated from the whole of ourselves, our circumstances of life and our relationships. Certainly, moral reasoning has a distinctive role in the moral life. But it is joined by our desires, passions, intentions, goals, and community with others. Moral reasoning requires

---

7. MacIntyre, *A Short History of Ethics*, 197. MacIntyre argues that "Kantian doctrine is parasitic upon some already existing morality."

all of who we are, and those who become wise attain a high degree of unity and consistency of self.

A second and related point is that the moral reasoning does not proceed in the abstract. Kant wants to protect the clarity and certainty of moral decisions by keeping them separate from everything else. He cordons off the realm of the will from desire and intentions. But moral reason does not exist in a distinct realm of pure thought, and all of who we are (for example, our desires and hopes) and all of our lives (for example, friendships and work) are important to moral decisions and issues. Duties and moral imperatives (for example, being truthful to others) are experienced as part of everyday life within our day-to-day relationships and commitments. When we struggle to live well with our brothers, sisters, friends, and neighbors, we start the processes of conforming our desires to what is good. We fight against all the things that worry Kant—our self-centeredness, tendencies to let our emotions get the best of us, and a narrow view of what is good. But the goal in day-to-day life is to conform ourselves to what is good, so that we no longer fight with our desires and emotions. Rather, we start to want what is good for another. Our duties toward others become a profound and rich part of who we are.

For Reflection and Further Study

1. Reason and emotion

Consider Kant's examples in the first section of his *Foundations of the Metaphysics of Morals*. They are found on pages 13-15 of the translation we are using and 398-99 in the standard numbering system. Kant is trying to determine the moral worth of actions. In the third example, he argues that if we help the needy through a sense of sympathy, our actions will not have moral worth. But if we are cold and indifferent but act on behalf of the needy, our actions will have moral worth. Discuss this example and the role of emotions like sympathy and empathy in the moral life.

2. Categorical imperative

Consider Kant's categorical imperative. The first formulation is: "I should never act in such a way that I could not also will that my maxim should be universal law." The second formulation is: "Act so that you treat humanity, whether in your own person or in that of another, always as an end and never as a means only." We noted in the chapter that the second formulation of the categorical imperative seems to lack the precision of the first formulation. One reason, we think, is that Kant rejects the idea of ends (intention, goal, and purpose) as determinative in moral judgments, but then he uses the concept in the second formulation. Take a look at Kant's discussion of suicide and meritorious duty in the second section of the *Foundations* (429-30 in the standard numbering).

It seems to us that Kant's categorical imperative can be used to countenance suicide and to help others commit suicide. Keeping people alive who are suffering great psychological pain can seem like using them rather than seeing them as ends in themselves. Discuss this point.

If the categorical imperative can be used consistently to argue both for and against suicide, then some other moral concept is at work. Discuss the other concepts that come into play.

3. Moral purpose
A common criticism of Kant's approach is that it tells us what not to do, but fails to set out a vision for being a good person. In his *Landscapes of the Soul*, sociologist Douglas Porpora finds that this criticism is supported by social research. In his research he finds that "the problem with a morality that is largely procedural is that it does not identify any moral purpose we ought to fulfill with our lives. The procedural constraints tell us what we should refrain from doing but offer little moral vision as to what we actually should be about doing."[8] Discuss the concepts, people, things, and/or convictions that inspire us to live well and to strive to be better people.

---

8. Douglas Porpora, *Landscapes of the Soul: The Loss of Moral Meaning in American Life* (New York: Oxford University Press, 2001), 72.

CHAPTER 7

Art, Virtue, and Law

E arly on in chapter 6, we made reference to Thomas Aquinas's distinction between speculative virtues, art as a virtue, and the moral virtues. Our concern, here, will be to connect what Aquinas means by the virtue of "art" to moral vision. The connection will be by way of analogy: We want to think about the work of moral vision as a craft—like carpentry or medical care—where a way of doing also cultivates a way of knowing and seeing.[1] This focus on practicing an art and the art of moral vision will bring us back to themes at the beginning of this book (chapter 2) where we put vision in terms of the connoisseur—a person who loves something (wine, tomatoes) and sees it as good and shapes her life accordingly—seeks the good out, wants to be near to it, spends time and money to foster a relation to it, and takes joy in it for its own sake (for the sake of the good that it is).

This framework of the connoisseur's life is different than performing a craft, but it has a connection to what we (following Aquinas) will develop as the virtue of art. Art pertains to how things are made. Consider, for example, the winemaker. She needs to understand fermentation and the properties and chemical behavior of grapes (the theoretical or speculative knowledge), but she also needs to apply the knowledge to making excellent wine. This application is an art. Art in this sense is not, strictly speaking, a moral activity: good wine could be made in a morally corrupt way, by a vicious person. The winemaker's end/purpose of making good wine does not lead necessarily or by definition to a moral action. Nonetheless, we believe that attention to the vision required of practicing an "art" will help

---

1. See Aristotle, *Nicomachean Ethics*, trans. Martin Ostwald (New York: Macmillan, 1962), book 6.

us understand moral vision. In this chapter, artistic vision will provide a window into seeing moral virtue as a craft. From the craft analogy, we will attend to the happiness that comes through doing something well—a joy that comes through the labors and struggles of a craft—the excellences of doing good things. From this point, we offer a re-visioning of moral law. Here, the reader will see that we are emphasizing our account of the passions and moral rules as developed in chapters 5 and 6.

Vision Is an Art

We will start with visual art. To understand the vision required for drawing, I (David) went to visit Professor Nick Hutchings at an art studio at Mount St. Mary's University. He showed me the object for the first assignment in his Drawing I course. It was three pieces of different-colored and patterned cloth, about three feet long and two wide, twisted together and mounted on the wall. I looked, stared, concentrated, and told Professor Hutchings that I was baffled. If I were a student in the class I would not know where to begin. I have no artistic talent at all. Hutchings passionately disagreed. He argued that, although I might never have the talent to be a great artist, I certainly could, with perhaps some but probably great effort, become a good one. He told me that my problem was not, first of all, how I put pencil to paper, but how I viewed the object.

Professor Hutchings went to the wall hanging and showed me. He blocked my vision for the most part. His body was in the way, and I could see only a bottom corner of the twisted cloth. In front of that portion he made a triangle with his hands. I could see an orderly shape with manageable shading and detail. Then Hutchings stepped back and asked me to divide the whole into manageable parts. In about thirty seconds, he transformed what looked to me like a chaotic image of twisted cloth into an ordered arrangement of shapes. Upon a bit of reflection and discussion, I came to realize that my basic problem with drawing was not primarily in my pencil strokes but my seeing. Previously, if I were to look at an apple in order to draw it, I would not see in the way that Professor Hutchings had just shown me. I would see an apple, and then construct a picture of the apple in my mind. From the image in my mind, I would then put something on paper. What I would get on paper was exactly that: the idea of an apple—the equivalent of a stick figure that signifies the idea of a person, but not a real person. I would make a "stick-figure" apple. Think about how often we do this with people. Something that a person says prompts something in our minds, and we react to what is already in our minds rather than what the person actually is saying or feeling or thinking. In terms of drawing, I give attention, not to the particular apple before my eyes, but to an apple in the abstract.

Seeing the object (the hanging cloth) differently is not the same as actually drawing it well, but there is an indispensable relationship between the two. Seeing the twisted cloth as an ordering of triangles gives me a place to begin—to see a manageable part in relationship to the whole. My drawing would not immediately improve, but at least I would have the possibility of improving. In contrast, with my previous process of drawing—"looking" at a mental picture and not really at the actual object—I was not free to draw an apple (for example) because I really was not attending to the apple before my eyes. When attending to the actual apple, my drawing will improve only as I practice, as I draw and draw and draw, through which I will gradually learn to see better—to see particularities and nuances that I was blind to before. As I learn to see as an artist, I will become attentive to shapes, contours, shades, previously noticed but not appreciated.

The Art of Moral Vision

This analogy of drawing can be used to understand the art of understanding people—both ourselves and others—and the contours and shades of moral intentions and actions. Remember that the example of seeing in drawing is just an analogy—that the view of "art" that we are seeking to understand is not about visual art per se. To use an analogy unrelated to visual art (from chapter 6), the art of automobile making and repair requires that we start to see car engines in the way that an engineer or mechanic would see it. Likewise, the moral art—the art of "producing" goodness and becoming a better person through our actions—is connected to how we see (that is, the virtue of prudence). Consider my problem with drawing an apple: I don't attend to the apple that I see; instead, I tend to draw an image of an apple that I have in my mind (prior to seeing a particular apple). In the same way, we often don't attend to the people, relationships, and situations in our lives day-to-day. We see, instead, the idea of something that is already in our heads. The most blatant form of this problem is stereotyping a person according to how he or she appears to us at first glance, when we don't look carefully or attentively enough. Like learning to see in visual art, learning "moral vision" requires attentiveness, effort, and practice.

We want to elaborate on these points about the art of moral vision—to show the "hows" rather than merely to define terms. To do so, we will turn to one of G. K. Chesterton's detective stories, "The Man in the Passage," featuring Father Brown.[2] In this story, Father Brown is an unassuming and comparatively diminutive figure, among extraordinary and important people. The first is Sir Wilson Seymour, an aristocrat who—in manner and appearance—could be described as the Edwardian version of a metrosexual. The second person of note is Captain Cutler, a soldier of some renown—large-headed (apparently not in a bad way), broad-shouldered, and handsome. The two are introduced in the story at the same time, but not together, arriving backstage at the Apollo Theatre at the dressing room of the attractive and charming Miss Aurora Rome. The aristocrat and soldier are obviously rivals for the actress's attention. Sir Wilson and Captain Cutler are admitted into the suite of rooms by Miss Rome's shabby and tottering servant (her "dresser"). The dresser, Parkinson, also appears to be a rival for Aurora's affections, but is clearly outmatched by the visitors. He quietly follows her every move.

The actress's dressing room contains the usual accoutrements, along with what seems to be an inordinate number of mirrors—"at every angle of refraction . . . [as if] inside a diamond" (50). We, the readers, do not know the significance of the mirrors at this juncture. But by the end, we will find that the mirror (Chesterton's "looking glass") is an apt image at multiple levels. Miss Rome will be murdered, and key to solving the crime is the looking glass and its relation to habits of vanity, distorted or refracted appearances, and our ability (or inability) to properly look at ourselves. At this juncture, however, the mirrors simply add to the glitter of the setting. Aurora greets the two distinguished gentlemen, and shortly after, her theatrical partner bursts in. Isidore Bruno is also a renowned actor, and at this moment he appears larger than life. He is "six-foot-six . . . of more than theatrical thews and muscles . . . like a barbaric god . . . [leaning on a prop from his recent performance] on a sort of hunting-spear." Finally, Father Brown appears at the door, noting to the others that Miss Rome had sent for him. In contrast to Aurora and the others, he looks "rather like the wooden Noah out of an ark" (51).

Aurora Rome is murdered, and, as noted, the looking glass is a key feature of the crime. We are not attempting to reproduce Chesterton's subtle

---

2. G. K. Chesterton, *Favorite Father Brown Stories* (New York: Dover, 1993), 48–61. In the next few paragraphs we will give the page numbers in parentheses in the text.

and clever way of introducing essential details. Allow us a prosaic summary of events. When Father Brown arrives, the actress wants to talk to him alone. She sizes the other men up and finds a way to get rid of them—each in relation to his fragile self-possession. The valiant Captain is sent off to a flower shop. Bruno stomps off to his own adjoining dressing room in jealous indignation. Sir Wilson is brought into Aurora's confidence about getting rid of the Captain just before she steps out with the Captain to show him where he will need to go. Shortly after, Sir Wilson steps out into the hall, now concerned that Aurora might have gone through the hallway entrance to Bruno's room. Father Brown is left with Parkinson, who fiddles about with sliding full-length mirrors—panels—in and out of the walls and then shuffles off to Bruno's room, ostensibly to stow away the actor's theatrical spear.

Moments later, Aurora Rome will lie dead in the hall. An art of seeing oneself and others (and the world) plainly and candidly is at the heart of Father Brown's ability to solve the crime. When Aurora is discovered dead, we see the actor, aristocrat, and soldier as rivals—as the principal suspects. Almost immediately, the doddering Parkinson reenters the scene and dies of shock. After some wrestling about and wild accusations among the remaining suitors, Bruno is finally accused by Sir Wilson and Captain Cutler. They can account for their whereabouts. Bruno, purportedly alone in his dressing room, cannot. He is arrested and put on trial.

Sir Wilson and Captain Cutler are the principal witnesses. At different moments during and just after the murder, each had seen a figure in the dark hall, as did Father Brown. The three witnesses see very different "murderers"; nonetheless, the evidence points toward Bruno. When questioned at the trial, Sir Wilson explains that he saw the outline of a tall, effeminate person, "not exactly a woman and yet . . . not quite a man," suggesting (but not naming explicitly) none other than Isidore Bruno (58). The Captain indicates that he saw a beast, with "huge humped shoulders like a chimpanzee, and bristles sticking out of its head like a pig," also suggesting (but not naming explicitly) none other than Bruno (59). Father Brown tells the prosecutor that he saw the silhouette of a figure that was "short and thick" with horns like the devil. Father Brown, however, does not point a tacit accusation at Bruno. In the demonic figure, he recognizes himself—his own reflection in a mirror panel like the ones Parkinson had been moving back and forth in the dressing room.

Immediately after the crime is committed, Father Brown realized that it was Parkinson who killed Miss Rome. Parkinson murdered her with the stage-prop spear, thrust at her in the hall from Bruno's room through a gap in a sliding mirror panel. Seeing his own reflection in the hall (while others couldn't recognize themselves), Father Brown deduced that the killer had slid out a mirror panel, lunged with the spear, and quickly slid the panel back into the wall. Parkinson's own death was induced by horror at what he had done—he simply "died of being penitent," says Father Brown (60). At the end of the story, we learn that Parkinson and Aurora Rome were married and having marital troubles. These troubles were the reason Aurora had summoned Father Brown.

Father Brown's understanding of the people involved in the crime and trial displays "seeing" as an art—analogous to a craft. The murder is solved, but the real punchline of the whole story is set up when the judge finally asks Father Brown why he was able to recognize his own reflection in the mirror (as the outline of Satan no less) when "two such distinguished men" could not recognize themselves. Father Brown stammers a reply, "I don't know . . . unless it's because I don't look at it so often" (61). The implication here (we think) is that, for Sir Wilson and Captain Cutler, vanity inhibited their ability to know what they were seeing. These distinguished men knew the basic principle of the matter: do not falsely accuse an innocent man. If you read the story, you will see that they are careful in their testimony before the court. Each dispassionately describes what he saw. Neither says, "I saw Bruno kill Miss Rome." In this sense, their misjudgment is an error, not in moral rule, code, or principle. Likewise, they do not commit an error in action—not in their practical reasoning. They do not act precipitously. Both Sir Wilson and Captain Cutler had learned to see the world with himself at the center—as the main character, the hero, of events in his own life. Which one of us does not do the same? Chesterton's answer to that question is: Father Brown. Throughout the Father Brown stories, his way of seeing is the key to his talent in solving crimes and other riddles of human behavior. He is able to see the world of human folly and wisdom (of himself and others) truthfully—because he sees it as God's story and not his own.

From Chesterton's story of Father Brown, we can see the significance of "art" as an analogy to moral vision. In Thomas Aquinas's distinctions, art is an intellectual virtue that is between the speculative and moral virtues.[3] The speculative virtues are like the knowledge of gravity. We have an immediate understanding of what things do when we drop them, and we also can learn the physics—the scientific accounting—of it. Both instances (intuitive and

---

3. Thomas Aquinas, *Summa theologica* I-II, question 57. See also Aristotle, *Nicomachean Ethics*, book 6.

scientific) are concerns of the speculative virtues, because gravity cannot be other than it is. Gravity just is. As noted above, the principle against murdering innocent people has the same status. It can't be other than it is.[4] For their part, the moral virtues are about things that could be different. Moral virtues move the will to action; moral reasoning is about seeing an action (or set of actions) to achieve a good end—like helping someone who is falling (where we intuitively put our knowledge of gravity to work) or in protecting an innocent person who is under threat.

The virtue of art is between speculative and moral virtues. It is *like* the moral virtues because we attain the virtue of an art through engagement in practical endeavors: as the carpenter learns to see how wood will behave. Art is *unlike* the moral virtues because it does not necessarily lead to a moral action: Father Brown could have seen the shadowy figure correctly but lied on the witness stand (because he worried that Bruno had killed Aurora even if he had not been seen in the hall). For this reason, the virtue of art is *like* a speculative virtue. But it is *unlike* a speculative virtue because art, as a way of seeing and knowing, is attained through practical endeavors. In Father Brown's case, the implication is that he learns to see people and situations truthfully because he has consciously undertaken the practical work of living with God (not himself) at the center.

The Just and Loving Gaze (Back to Murdoch)

Aquinas defines the virtue of art as "the right reason about certain works to be made."[5] He calls it an "operative habit," which means that it requires goodness in the doing. One learns to see as an artist by getting better at it. As in a craft, the "knowing" of the art is judged by the consistency of the product. We will call a person an artist and trust that she has the eyes of an artist, not after a single good drawing, but after a consistent demonstration of the craft. She has attained the art when she embodies an approach to what she sees, when she starts to see what she did not expect, when she sees the ordinary with an extra-ordinary depth. Professor Hutchings says that one problem with teaching art students to see objects properly is that they have success at one thing and simply continue to replicate the creation of that object. In

4. "Murder is wrong" is what logicians call a tautology. Murder by definition is the killing of a person without justification; therefore, "murder is wrong" is—like gravity—always true.
5. Aquinas, *Summa theologica* I-II, question 57, article 3.

other words, they fail to develop art as a virtue; that is, they do not persist in developing a habit that becomes a quality of who they are becoming. By analogy, we are calling moral vision an art because it is attained, not simply by knowing principles and rules, but through the difficult craft of seeing and understanding what is going on around us. This seeing may or may not lead to a particular action; the seeing itself is something to be done well. Principles and rules are important, of course, and will be treated in the discussion questions at the end of the chapter. At this juncture, we want to emphasize the importance of vision—seeing and understanding as an architect sees and understands the art and construction of a building.

To illuminate the difficult art of moral vision, we return to Professor Hutchings's course in drawing. The most difficult challenge of a drawing class, he explains, is not the drawing itself and not developing the artist's way of viewing an object. The most challenging element of learning to draw is receiving criticism and learning self-criticism. "Criticism," here, does not mean disapproval or condemnation. It means what is sometimes called "constructive criticism"—an analysis that is directed toward improvement, an evaluation that serves the one who is evaluated by helping that person become better. This kind of criticism is also analogous to an art. Through experience, the teacher learns how to help the student see and hear his or her shortcomings. Criticism is effective in a context of trust and fidelity, where the one criticized experiences and understands the teacher's attentiveness and charity.

This evaluation—in relationship to art as a virtue—is always put in terms of the product. Professor Hutchings does not say to a student, "You are a bad person or a horrendous artist." Rather, he evaluates the craft—the drawing itself: "You need to do a better job isolating manageable segments of the twisted cloth." Likewise, moral vision is attained through opening ourselves to evaluations by others and self-criticism of our actions. We start to see the world more truthfully when we are open to others to tell us when we have treated them or others uncharitably, impatiently, unfairly, etc. Likewise, we have to open ourselves to the recognition of goodness, to the gratitude of others, to the way that others make a claim on and become a part of the good that we do. We open ourselves to become better and to see others and the world in a more graceful way when we work to see what we do and various events in the world from another person's point of view, when we make distinctions between what is advantageous for us and what might be better for others, when we resist inserting ourselves as the hero of every rivalry and challenge. The list can go on here with what we can do to cultivate the art of moral vision. Suffice it to say that we have to commit ourselves to the craft of doing good and being good, that we become a connoisseur of goodness as it grows and is crafted around us in the world.

The "crafting" of the good leads us back to the moral virtues (prudence, justice, fortitude, and temperance), which were introduced in chapter 4 as a means to provide a picture of the moral journey of human beings. We have basic capacities (potentialities), and when we act in such a way that these capacities become actual in us, we are fulfilled. Along the line of our analogy to art, if a person were to have gifts and talents for painting, and if she were to dedicate herself to developing those talents, then it is very likely that she would paint beautifully, create wonderful paintings, become an artist in the process, and—as an artist—find that she is never happier than when she is at the sketchpad or easel with pencil or brush in hand. As she is developing a painting, she is also shaping who she is and her capacity to see and to love the good that she is doing. Likewise, a virtue-based vision of the person holds that by seeing and doing what is good, we begin to become good and to be fulfilled in seeing, being, and doing what is loving and just. We are fulfilled in what is good.

The moral life is about the happiness that comes from doing things well (beautifully and truly) and becoming good—as the skills, qualities, and gifts needed for doing become the mainstay of who we are—as the pleasure of painting becomes the joy of being an artist. The cardinal moral virtues provide a basic outline for the art of the moral life. The virtues are "habitual"—they are in us as the formation of our dispositions to act in ways that achieve what is good. Prudence is the "habit" of seeing and setting out a course for doing what is right and good. Because of its deep connection to moral vision, prudence is treated in greater detail in chapter 8. At this juncture, we will say that prudence follows from what Iris Murdoch calls a "just and loving gaze" (chapter 2). Justice is the virtue of giving others what is their due, of balancing give-and-take, of responsibilities and rights. In this sense, justice requires us to size up who we are and our relationships to others. It is a virtue of both friendship and citizenship, where our responsibilities and our rights come together—where we take joy in our responsibilities as gifts—where we feel abiding gratitude for the good we are given the opportunity to do.

This gratitude and happiness are not without struggle and failure. It is not the kind of happiness that comes from a problem-free life or "living on easy street." It is the joy of excellence. For this reason, fortitude and temperance are required. Fortitude—moral resilience and strength—is the habit of enduring, resisting, and when need be, challenging obstacles to standing with, standing firm on, or doing the good. Temperance (not abstinence) is the habit of desiring and feeling what is in balance with having and doing what is good. Temperance, in the usual sense, is desire for the healthy and pleasurable amount of food and drink. It is not limiting our pleasure, but taking the greater pleasure in what is good for us. It also is a hunger for justice, as we become angry at injustice but not in a way that spills over toward revenge, as our thirst for what is good also is our desire in avoiding doing harm (as we might be tempted to do harm as a means to achieve good). Fortitude and temperance put our passions and appetites in harmony with our vision of the good.

Vision and Law

As a final inquiry into art, we want to take a look at moral rules and law. The first step is to resist the contrast implied in the phrase, "it is more an art than a science." The phrase appears to mean that we make stuff up (creatively) rather than appeal to rules and procedures (methodically). In relationship to a craft as well as moral law, the contrast is false. In carpentry, the methods (rule and law) are determined by the reality of the wood; one cannot develop the artistry without conforming to the rules. An analogy of a sport will help us go deeper. Rules are not merely limits to behavior, but outline the world in which one sees and acts. For example, to grasp a puck in your hand and throw it into a goal is not simply a violation. It is not hockey. If someone were to ask, "Why can't a player carry the puck like a football?" the proper answer is: because that is not how hockey is played.

The rule establishes the environment for membership and the excellences found through dedication to that membership.[6] The person who asks the question "Why not grab the puck and skate away?" might be wondering why hockey players are limited in their behavior. A hockey stick is a poor tool for keeping possession of something. Wouldn't it be easier to hold on to the puck? The answer is that the rule is not a limitation on otherwise effective behavior. Rather, the rule provides the structure—the very possibility of—not only the game itself but also the excellences that make the game

6. See David Matzko McCarthy and Charles R. Pinches, "Natural Law and Our Contemporary Institutions," *Political Theology* 16, no. 5 (September 2015): 442–62; McCarthy and Pinches, "Craft as a Place of Knowing in Natural Law," *Studies in Christian Ethics* 29, no. 4 (November 2016): 387–408.

wonderful.[7] Consider other sports, dance, or musical performance in the same sense. To play the piano, one must submit to the reality of the instrument, and the rules applicable to playing the piano draw from and name that inescapable reality. Those who submit and strive for excellence claim membership; they are pianists. Likewise, rules of justice and the moral law set out membership in the same way. They set out a structure of human community and the excellences that come from living into this membership, such excellences as prudence, justice, fortitude, and temperance.

This claim about moral law, that it sets a structure for human community and excellences, has a direct relationship to moral vision. For example, consider the command "do not lie" as a membership rule like "don't grasp the puck in your hand and throw it in the goal." Lying undermines all human relationships—from friendship to economic exchange. Every life-giving activity depends upon presumptions that we are truthful with each other. We have used "all human relationships" and "every life-giving activity" intentionally. You are likely to object. (1) There are activities, like card games and sports, where deception, bluffing, and faking are part of the game. Along these lines, we should add the deceptions required in humor and joking and the untruths involved in embellishing an interesting story. (2) Everyone lies to get out of a difficulty or an awkward situation at some point in their lives, if not at some point every day. Answering these objections will help us connect the fundamental moral law "do not lie" with moral vision.

The basic point concerning objection #1 is that the application of the rule against lying requires an incredibly complex set of judgments and ways of seeing and sizing up situations that we learn over a lifetime. The point concerning objection #2 is that every issue, temptation, and opportunity for lying requires us to see situations differently—to learn ways of seeing the truth. Because it is so complex, an answer to objection #1 could go on for pages and pages. Suffice it to say that deception in card games, for example, is an accepted and agreed-upon part of the game. What is not agreed upon—and what would undermine the game—is called cheating. An analogy can be made with jokes and exaggeration: when they exceed or undermine the communication games of humor and storytelling, they are understood as lying.

---

7. It is an interesting matter when secondary (not foundational) rules are introduced, like not allowing players to check other players (to use physical contact) until they are "old enough." The rule is not simply to avoid injury. Its primary function is to develop other more fundamental excellences of the game, such as skating and puck handling.

These lines between acceptable and unacceptable deception are what makes the classic case of lying to Nazis (to protect Jews and others) so complex. The Nazis have already undermined truthful communication. Where do we go from there? Would you lie to the Nazis? One thing that we do know: exemplary people and communities who worked to protect Jews during World War II worried a great deal about having to lie, if it came to that, because they cared about the truth and because their care for the oppressed was a rejection of the lies of the Nazis. Lying was to be avoided, and part of the effectiveness of their operations was setting up a process where few, if any, would have to lie. In other words, if one fights for truth, one will not think readily of lying as a good means to a truthful end.[8]

With this point, objection #2 comes into play. Our everyday lies, big and small, usually have something to do with self-promotion or self-preservation—making ourselves look good and avoiding conflict. In terms of moral vision, we have a narrow view of what we are about and the relationships we are sustaining (through a lie). Often, the reason we lie is because we see the truth poorly. Consider a simple example. A friend has just given a speech, and it was not well done. He asks us how it was. We waffle and say in vague and encouraging terms that it was good. We don't want to hurt his feelings. We are worried for his good, but this "good" is narrow and momentary. To broaden our vision, we would have to think about how our friend can become better. But to think about him becoming better, we need a keen eye to what he does that is good. We would have had to focus on his speech far more carefully than we did, noticing and analyzing the subtle positives that were overshadowed by the blatant negatives. In short, when our friend asks us, "How did I do?," a common reaction is to spare our friend's feelings and to shut out and ignore the errors, problems, and failures that we did see. In contrast, honesty will require, first, that we see our friend's good in much broader terms, and second, that we open our vision more (rather than less) to what he did and said during his speech.

---

8. A good example is André Trocmé who, with the people of Le Chambon, hid and rescued Jews in Nazi-occupied France. The community set up a system that alerted refugees to scatter into the woods when Nazis appeared in the town. No one had to lie: they just invited the Nazis to go ahead and take any Jews that they could find (and they never were successful). See Philip Hallie, *Lest Innocent Blood Be Shed* (New York: HarperCollins, 1994). Another is Corrie Ten Boom and her family. They set up a system in Haarlem, Holland, for helping Jews escape the city and go into hiding. See Corrie Ten Boom (with John and Elizabeth Sherrill), *The Hiding Place* (Grand Rapids: Chosen Books, 1971).

Conclusion

In effect, the need to be honest (the command, "Do not lie") will widen our vision to a greater good and focus our vision to nuance and subtlety that we might otherwise overlook. In a craft as well as moral vision, virtues, skills, rules, principles, and law come together in a common purpose. Speaking a difficult truth to another—in a life-giving way—is certainly an art. It certainly requires virtues of wisdom and understanding as well as prudential considerations like when and where to have the best kind of conversation. No doubt, by committing ourselves to say a hard truth we submit ourselves to a moral law, "Do not lie." However, we are likely, also, to be motivated by love and care for a friend, or perhaps by respect and fairness to an enemy. In both cases, law and virtue broaden our horizons. Speaking honestly to an enemy is difficult, but it is usually even harder to do so to a friend, when we are likely to risk our peaceful and affable friendship. The moral vision (law as well as virtue) broadens us in this way; however, the art of moral vision also focuses our attention on particulars. To speak the truth well, we often need to see with a shrewd and discerning eye (like Father Brown's). In cultivating a "just and loving gaze," we are called to see an expansive good in the particulars of everyday life.

For Reflection and Further Study

1. Seeing people with a detective's eye

Along the lines of Father Brown in "The Man in the Passage," consider how one's character affects one's moral vision. In this context, "character" identifies virtues and vices that become set in us through habits of behavior and point of view. In "The Man in the Passage," Chesterton develops characters in this way. For example, in his descriptions of Sir Wilson Seymour, he notes, "He was so unique that nobody could quite decide whether he was a great aristocrat who had taken up Art, or a great artist whom the aristocrats had taken up. But you could not meet him for five minutes without realizing that you had really been ruled by him all your life."[9] Sir Wilson's studied appearance and actions suggest the kind of self-possession that makes him unable to see himself accurately. You can take up the question

9. Chesterton, "The Man in the Passage," 49.

of moral vision and character through another Father Brown story, which is readily available online, full-text. We suggest G. K. Chesterton's "The Secret Garden."

2. Art and prudence

Please remember we are using Thomas Aquinas's virtue of art as an analogy to focus on a way of seeing—or, rather, doing—that is connected nonetheless to practical endeavors (to arts). To this degree, some treatment of prudence is required (see chapter 8). Consider the section from the *Summa theologica* II-II, below, on prudence. Aquinas notes that prudence is an intellectual virtue related to action. It is the seeing and deciding what to do in order to act well and "produce" good. In making this distinction, he begins with what we have identified in the chapter as "speculative" virtues.

> "Wisdom," "knowledge" and "understanding" [speculative virtues] are about necessary things, whereas "art" and "prudence" are about contingent things, art being concerned with "things made," that is, with things produced in external matter, such as a house, a knife and so forth; and prudence, being concerned with "things done," that is, with things that have their being in the doer himself.[10]

The distinction between art and prudence, therefore, is that prudence is judged and attained through moral action. The phrase "things that have their being in the doer himself" is important. It means that the good is something we are: a single good painting does not make a person into an artist, but if a person possesses qualities that lead to good paintings, we call that person an artist.

We have appealed, at this juncture, to the virtue of art because we want to attend to a level of seeing and understanding that is, on one hand, not about first principles (that is, moral gravity) and, on the other hand, not about moral action strictly speaking. However, by speaking of morality at all, we are moving from Aquinas's definition of art (for instance, carpentry)

10. Aquinas, *Summa theologica* II-II, question 47, article 5. For an online version of the *Summa theologica* go to the Dominican House of Studies, Priory of the Immaculate Conception, http://dhspriory.org/thomas/summa/. Also New Advent: http://www.newadvent.org/summa/.

to prudence. For the moment, we want to forestall that talking about prudence and specific moral judgments. Consider, first, the various crafts that you and others undertake, such as soccer and learning to see the field of play or playing clarinet and playing as part of an ensemble. How does excellence in these activities teach us to see?

Now, consider the "activity" of understanding and appreciating people, of seeing the world from another's point of view. We are getting, here, to what Iris Murdoch calls a "just and loving gaze" (see chapters 2 and 3). In any given situation, developing this "gaze" might not lead to or require an action. But overall, seeing others with love and compassion is the groundwork of prudence, which we will consider in the next chapter.

3. Law

The function of law in the moral life is an area of study in itself. The text to consider is Thomas Aquinas's treatise on law, *Summa theologica* I-II, questions 90–108, which includes topics such as the structure of law in general, divine providence, the law that is constitutive of human nature, and laws made by human beings (for example, governments). In terms of moral vision, our purpose in treating law is to see law as reasonable and directed toward virtue and human happiness. Remember (as noted in this chapter) that happiness is the gratification and fulfillment that comes from living well (also see chapter 4). Consider the following reference points in Aquinas's treatise on law.

In the *Summa theologica* I-II, question 90, Aquinas explains that law is reasonable and purposeful. (Recall the discussion of reason in chapter 6.) The purpose of law is human fulfillment—a good end that we share as human beings. As shared, law is disseminated to members of a community (human or local) in some fashion. Consider the definition of law offered in the *Summa* I-II, question 90, articles 1 and 2.

> Law is a rule and measure of acts, whereby man is induced to act or is restrained from acting: for "lex" [law] is derived from "ligare" [to bind], because it binds one to act. Now the rule and measure of human acts is the reason, which is the first principle of human acts . . . since it belongs to the reason to direct to the end, which is the first principle in all matters of action. . . .
>
> Consequently the law must needs regard principally the relationship to happiness. Moreover, since every part is ordained to the

whole, as imperfect to perfect; and since one man is a part of the perfect community, the law must needs regard properly the relationship to universal happiness.[11]

All levels of law (eternal, natural, human-made) are connected by the end of happiness. Eternal law is God's creative ordering of everything to its purpose and fulfillment. It "is nothing else than the type of Divine Wisdom" (I-II, q. 93, a. 1). Human beings are a particular kind of creature, with intellect and will, knowledge and freedom. Given human nature (rational and free), it is essential to God's ordering of human beings to their purpose and fulfillment that we participate in eternal law by making and disseminating laws that organize human life. According to our natures, we participate in the fulfillment (perfection) of our natures. Our capacity to participate through law-making does not mean we always hit the mark. The measure of justice, in this regard, is the natural law, which—to repeat the point—is how our natural makeup is directed to our fulfillment in human community and in relationship to God. This natural law may or may not be evident to any particular person. It is part of our natures that we do not know what to do by mere instinct, but we have to deliberate, share ideas, and think things through. Consider Aquinas's discussion on natural law in the *Summa*, I-II, question 94, article 2.[12]

[S]o "good" is the first thing that falls under the apprehension of the practical reason, which is directed to action: since every agent acts for an end under the aspect of good. Consequently the first principle of practical reason is one founded on the notion of good, viz. that "good is that which all things seek after." Hence this is the first precept of law, that "good is to be done and pursued, and evil is to be avoided." All other precepts of the natural law are based upon this. . . .

Since, however, good has the nature of an end, and evil, the nature of a contrary, hence it is that all those things to which man has a natural inclination, are naturally apprehended by reason as being good, and consequently as objects of pursuit, and their contraries as evil, and objects of avoidance.

[I]nasmuch as every substance seeks the preservation of its own being, according to its nature: and by reason of this inclination,

11. Find this translation and the full text of question 90 on the New Advent site: http://www.newadvent.org/summa/2090.htm.
12. For the entirety of question 94, see http://www.newadvent.org/summa/2094.htm.

whatever is a means of preserving human life, and of warding off its obstacles, belongs to the natural law.

Secondly, there is in man an inclination to things that pertain to him more specially, according to that nature which he has in common with other animals: and in virtue of this inclination, those things are said to belong to the natural law, "which nature has taught to all animals," such as sexual intercourse, education of offspring and so forth.

Thirdly, there is in man an inclination to good, according to the nature of his reason, which nature is proper to him: thus man has a natural inclination to know the truth about God, and to live in society.

Our overall point in pointing you to matters of natural law is to develop our vision of the human good: we are made to see, know, and participate in what brings us to our fulfillment. Here, under the matter of natural law, we are dealing with human beings in general. In the next part of the book, we attend to a view of the world that is discovered in relationship to God in Jesus Christ, who calls us to live out God's love and justice for the sake of the world.

4. Justice

In this chapter, we noted that justice is based on giving others what is their due, of balancing give-and-take, of seeing and fulfilling responsibilities in terms of what is good and right, including a person's rights. At the end of chapter 4, we asked you to consider St. John XXIII's *Pacem in terris* (Peace on Earth), nos. 8–38, so far as this section of the document outlines what is "due" to human beings and how we are responsible to and for others.[13] Also notice that the whole section is introduced by claims based on natural law:

> Any well-regulated and productive association of men in society demands the acceptance of one fundamental principle: that each individual man is truly a person. His is a nature, that is, endowed with intelligence and free will. As such he has rights and duties, which

13. John XXIII's *Pacem in terris* can be found on the Vatican website: http://w2.vatican.va /content/john-xxiii/en/encyclicals/documents/hf_j-xxiii_enc_11041963_pacem.html.

together flow as a direct consequence from his nature. These rights and duties are universal and inviolable, and therefore altogether inalienable. (no. 9)

Pacem in terris gives a broad and general picture of the human being and the requirements of justice. In a sense, reading the document is an academic or intellectual exercise. Our hope for this chapter has been to make clear that seeing human beings with love and justice in the concrete in our lives and in the world is an art and virtue, a craft of moral vision.

PART 2

Reenvisioning

CHAPTER 8

Prudence

Growing up at an age when we did not have propane barbeques with automatic starters, I (Jim) remember well that my father would light the barbeque by touching a match to the right amount of lighter fluid applied to the coals. This usual procedure was not failsafe, and at times—actually, many times—it did not serve to ignite the coals properly. My dad had several other tricks up his sleeve, and the most common one involved squeezing more lighter fluid onto the almost-hot coals. If my mother happened to be watching out the window, she would usually shout out, "Gene, are you crazy? What happened to prudence?" He would usually mutter something like, "You're right, Betty," and then continue squirting the lighter fluid when she had turned away. This would usually end in a bonfire of sorts, perhaps some singed arm hairs, and a word from my father to me and my brothers that my mother was right after all. My mother, of course, was correct in that she saw rightly that squeezing more lighter fluid onto almost-hot coals was dangerous. Indeed, you could say that my father shared her right view in this venture, acknowledging that this was not a good thing to do. Even though he also saw rightly, he did not act accordingly. In other words, he did not follow through in what he was seeing correctly. This little story serves the purpose of introducing the virtue of prudence, which has two aspects to it. As a virtue, prudence is defined as seeing *and* acting correctly or truthfully.

A King's Wisdom and Folly

There is a biblical person who serves as an example of one who did not see or act rightly—his name is Solomon. Solomon was the successor to his father,

King David, and we learn from chapter 3 of 1 Kings that God appeared in a dream to Solomon, asking him to request anything at all from God. Solomon does not ask for a long life, or great wealth, or the life of his enemies, but for an understanding heart, so that he can discern good from evil as he rules God's people. God is very pleased that Solomon has asked for this gift and grants it to him, as well as all the things that he does not ask for.

The very next story in chapter 3 of 1 Kings—a familiar one to many readers of the Bible—is evidence that God had indeed granted the gift of wisdom to Solomon. There were two women, each with a small baby, who had gone to sleep at night. One of the women rolled over and smothered her baby. Realizing what she had done, she switched her dead baby with the second woman's live baby. When the second woman awoke and saw that the baby in her arms was dead, she looked more carefully and knew that it was the other woman's child. But the first woman insisted that this was not true. So the dispute was taken to King Solomon—the one with the gift of wisdom. Once Solomon heard the stories of the two women, he ordered a sword to be brought out in order to cut the living child in two, giving one half to each mother. So much for wisdom! But before this deed could be carried out, the second woman shouted for the king to stop and to give the baby to the other woman; for her part, the other woman seemed content to let things run their course. Because of the different reactions of the two women, Solomon, with his gift of wisdom, was able to identify the true mother, for he knew that no true mother would ever be able to stand by and watch her child be killed. God had, indeed, given this gift of wisdom to King Solomon!

With this gift of wisdom, God expected much from Solomon. In chapter 9 of 1 Kings, we are told that God appeared in a second dream to Solomon. God promises that if Solomon follows his father David in integrity of heart, in uprightness, and keeps God's statutes and commandments, then God will establish Solomon's throne upon Israel forever, just as God had promised his father David. But there is also a warning from God. God warns Solomon that if he does not keep the commandments and statutes, and if Solomon worships and serves other gods, then God will cut off Israel from the land that had been given them, and that the house of David and Solomon will be cast away. Indeed, God indicates that bystanders to this disaster will look at the destruction of Israel and ask how this happened. When they do, others will answer: "Because they forsook the Lord their God, who brought forth their fathers out of the land of Egypt, and have taken hold upon other gods, and have worshiped them and served them; therefore has the Lord brought upon them all this evil" (1 Kings 9:9).

In the end, things don't turn out well for Solomon at all—despite the fact that he was given the gift of wisdom to judge between good and evil. For while he had the gift of wisdom, one could say that he still did not have prudence, the virtue of seeing and acting rightly or truthfully. He certainly did not see rightly, which means that he really could not act rightly. Chapter 11 in 1 Kings recounts how Solomon had seven hundred wives and three hundred concubines. Astounding as this number may seem to us today, it can distract us from the real problem that Solomon encountered. These women, including the daughter of Pharaoh, and women of the Moabites, Ammonites, Edomites, Zidonians, and Hittites, had brought with them to Israel their strange gods. Over time, these women turned the heart of Solomon away from God, and he even built many altars, which allowed his wives to burn incense and sacrifice to these strange gods. These foreign women had influenced how Solomon saw things. He no longer saw rightly or truthfully that the source of all his life and blessing was God. His foreign wives turned his heart so that he saw differently, believing that these strange gods and their ways would sustain and assist him in ruling Israel. Perhaps among all these wives and concubines, Solomon needed someone like my mother, Betty, to remind him that this would not be prudent! For if Solomon could see rightly or truthfully, then he would be able to use the gift of wisdom to act rightly as he had done in the story of the two women with their babies.

We have suggested that the influence of his foreign wives prevented Solomon from seeing, and by extension, acting rightly or truthfully. Their influence clouded his vision, obscuring what was good. Here we would agree that he was not seeing rightly, that he was imprudent. But there might be some other possibilities to explore. In another scenario, we might also agree that Solomon just made a bad choice, and that he knew he should follow God, but instead chose to follow the strange gods under the influence of his foreign wives. Here we could say that he did see rightly, but chose not to act rightly. Again, we would say that Solomon was imprudent—not because he did not see rightly, but because he did not act rightly. But there still remains another possibility—even if only hypothetically, because after all, God appeared to Solomon in several dreams! What if Solomon thought that what he was doing was correct and right? What if Solomon were to utter the words that we often hear people say today: "I was just following my conscience"? In other words, what if Solomon was convinced that he was just following his conscience, carrying out what he thought he should do? Is it possible that he really did think that he was seeing rightly or truthfully, and that is why he chose to worship the strange gods of his foreign wives?

It is important to say a word about conscience because an erroneous conscience could prevent us from acting rightly. Whenever we talk about conscience, we recognize that a person's conscience could be correct or in error.[1] If the person is following what we call an erroneous conscience, then there is another distinction we could make. In the first case of an erroneous conscience, we would say that the person's conscience is in error, but she is not responsible for not knowing any better. Here, the person operating under this erroneous conscience is referred to as being invincibly ignorant. In other words, the person is following her conscience and would have no way of knowing any better that what she is doing is wrong. Because this is the case, the person is doing something wrong, but would not be culpable or responsible for this wrong. It would be hard to apply this to the case of Solomon, however, for we would have to argue that he could not have known any better and therefore, even though he was seeing wrongly and acting wrongly, he was not guilty of any sin because he had no way of seeing and doing otherwise. But since the story in 1 Kings clearly tells us that Solomon did, in fact, have several revelations from God in his dreams, he ought to have known better. Unlike the case of an erroneous conscience, where the person could not have known better (invincible ignorance), Solomon *should* have known better. We would say that his conscience was in error, but that he was responsible for being in this state; we call this state of an erroneous conscience as having vincible ignorance. God had appeared to Solomon twice in dreams and revealed to him how he should see as God sees and how he should act accordingly as the ruler of God's people. Solomon failed to do this. Since he was responsible for knowing better, we would say that Solomon was acting in vincible ignorance. He came to see, not as God expected him to see, but only dimly under the influence of the strange gods of his foreign wives. He began to see poorly, but he was responsible for not seeing rightly by discarding the vision with which God entrusted him.

Getting Order to Life

Focusing upon Solomon has helped us to understand the importance of seeing rightly if we are to exercise the virtue of prudence. But remember, prudence also involves acting rightly. We could imagine situations where we see

---

1. William C. Mattison III, *Introducing Moral Theology: True Happiness and the Virtues* (Grand Rapids: Brazos, 2008), 106–10, includes helpful distinctions concerning conscience.

rightly or truthfully, but still do not act accordingly. I (Jim) have one such personal example that clearly depicts this situation. Some years ago, I was at the point in my graduate studies where I was working on my dissertation. I was fortunate that I had an interesting topic and a good faculty director. However, I found the solitary work of the dissertation to be a challenge, especially as I spent hour after hour, day after day, translating medieval prayers from Latin to English. Almost everything else looked more interesting and inviting. So, as people asked me to help at parish, or give a talk or presentation, or conduct a retreat, or go to a conference, I would say yes. After all, I told myself, these are good things to do and people need my help. A fortunate turn of events happened when I read an advertisement from the local diocese to attend a conference on how to apply Stephen Covey's *The 7 Habits of Highly Effective People* to ministry. Looking back, I can see that this is exactly the type of thing I was saying yes to that was preventing me from acting rightly! I really should have ignored this opportunity and continued to work on my dissertation. It turned out, however, to be providential that I went on this workshop, for through the workshop I learned how imprudent I had become.

Two of Stephen Covey's habits helped me to see more clearly and to act accordingly. Habit 2, "Begin with the End in Mind," helped me to see what I was doing more particularly with my dissertation in the larger context of my life story. Through various exercises, I wrote a mission statement—which over the years, with some revisions, still guides me. Covey indicates that a personal mission statement "becomes a personal constitution, the basis for making major, life-directing decisions, the basis for making daily decisions in the midst of the circumstances and emotions that affect our lives. It empowers individuals with the same timeless strength in the midst of change."[2] Reflections leading to my own mission statement reminded me of my call to be a Resurrectionist priest exercising my ministry as a teacher in higher education. This was a "place of meeting" for me where I experienced God's call and my own gifts to make a difference in service to the world. I realized that finishing my dissertation would allow me to follow through on this call. It was not enough for me to embrace this major, life-directing decision; I also needed to make daily decisions that would bring it to realization. I began to see more rightfully and truthfully what I needed to do.

2. Stephen Covey, *The 7 Habits of Highly Effective People: Restoring the Character Ethic* (New York: Simon & Schuster, 1989), 108.

Stephen Covey's Habit 3, "Put First Things First," helped me to put into practice what I began to see more rightly. Through the various workshop exercises, I began to address two questions that Covey poses: What is the most important aspect of your personal life, and what is the most important aspect of your professional life? Clearly, for me, the most important aspect of my professional life was to finish my dissertation. Covey's Habit 3 encouraged me to organize and execute around this priority, learning not to manage my time, but to manage my life.[3]

One of the most helpful features that Covey includes in Habit 3 is the "Time Management Matrix."[4] This matrix is divided into four quadrants. Quadrant I is comprised of activities that are both urgent and important, such as crises, pressing problems, and deadline-driven projects. I found myself in Quadrant I most often when I was on the verge of meeting with my dissertation director, trying to finish neglected work quickly at the last minute. Quadrant II is comprised of activities that are important but not urgent. These activities include prevention, preserving and maintaining assets, relationship building, planning, and recreation. I realized that I spent little time in this quadrant, seemingly more satisfied with the heightened urgency that I created by committing myself to too many things, including ones that distracted me from my top priority. And because I found myself so busy with crisis-created activities of Quadrant I, I also felt guilty whenever I took time for prayer, recreation and exercise, and friendships—things that would ensure a healthy person spiritually, emotionally, and physically.

For its part, Quadrant III includes activities that are not important, but are urgent. These activities include interruptions, some phone calls, emails and meetings, and proximate pressing matters. I found that I spent more time in this quadrant than I should because I wanted to be interrupted by phone calls and emails! I realized that I was in control of these things and could make a decision to answer or respond to these interruptions after I faithfully completed my day's commitment to work on the dissertation. In this light, I made one practical decision to silence the sound on the computer that alerted me to a new email—something that tempted me to leave what I was working on in order to be distracted by what was probably not very important. Instead, I checked my email once in the morning and once at the end of the day, bringing some personal control over these distractions

3. Covey, *The 7 Habits of Highly Effective People*, 149–50.
4. Covey, *The 7 Habits of Highly Effective People*, 151. The examples that follow are taken from the illustration on the same page.

that were truly preventing me from getting done what was more important. Quadrant IV is comprised of activities that are both unimportant and not urgent. I found that the more time I spent in Quadrant I responding to various crises—and not in Quadrant II where planning and process are conducted to minimize crises—the more time I spent in Quadrant IV. Here I found a place to escape from the pressure and energy that it took to deal with Quadrant I problems, watching too much television, playing computer games, and generally wasting time. Covey's insights helped me to become aware that I needed to manage myself, not my time. In other words, I needed to clearly see rightly what I needed to do, but just as importantly, I needed a practical approach that would help me to meet my goal through certain right actions.

Conclusion

Prudence grows or diminishes within the whole framework (or "environs") of our lives. Little decisions and ways of doing things accrue to habits of seeing (or not seeing) good ways to achieve good ends. William Mattison, in *Introducing Moral Theology*, provides other insights about living the virtue of prudence when he reminds us about other virtues that will enable prudence: memory, docility, and nimble decisiveness.[5] In terms of *memory*, if I had reflected truthfully on my past of studying and working alone—which was not a very good one—I would have been better prepared to see and act rightly concerning my dissertation. Instead of not paying attention to or covering over the past, I could have acknowledged that I had difficulties working on my own over long stretches of time and, perhaps, talked this through with my dissertation director and some close friends who had completed similar work. Similarly, instead of a blind trust in my ability to plow through this work on my own, I would have benefited from having more *docility* in asking for and accepting the guidance and advice of others who had been through this process before. Finally, a dose of *nimble decisiveness* would have helped me to size up my situation more quickly and honestly in order to help me achieve the goal of completing my dissertation in a timely manner. In short, prudence develops as we are attentive day-to-day to what is going on in our lives.

5. Mattison, *Introducing Moral Theology*, 103-4.

For Reflection and Further Study

1. Seeing and acting rightly

Both aspects of seeing and acting are part of the exercise of the virtue of prudence. But it is seeing that is likely to present the greater challenge. Consider Aristotle's remarks in book 6 of his *Nicomachean Ethics*. Learning wisdom to see properly everyday matters of life is perhaps more challenging than geometry.

> While young men become geometricians and mathematicians and wise in matters like these, it is thought that a young man of practical wisdom cannot be found. The cause is that such wisdom is concerned not only with universals but with particulars, which become familiar from experience, but a young man has no experience, for it is length of time that gives experience; indeed one might ask this question too, why a boy may become a mathematician, but not a philosopher or a physicist. It is because the objects of mathematics exist by abstraction, while the first principles of these other subjects come from experience, and because young men have no conviction about the latter but merely use the proper language, while the essence of mathematical objects is plain enough to them.[6]

It would be helpful to go back to chapter 5 of the same book, where Aristotle begins, "Now it is thought to be the mark of a man of practical wisdom to be able to deliberate well about what is good and expedient for himself, not in some particular respect, e.g. about what sorts of thing conduce to health or to strength, but about what sorts of thing conduce to the good life in general."[7]

In our world today, we are much more youth oriented. Is Aristotle's dismissal of the possibility of wisdom among the young offensive? He assumes that his listeners are going to have a proper education and grow to be wise. Can we assume the same? What social pressures get in the way? What role does education have in shaping our views? How is one put in a good situation where he or she is likely to become wise?

6. Aristotle, *Nicomachean Ethics*, book 6, chapter 8, at http://classics.mit.edu/Aristotle/nicomachaen.6.vi.html.

7. Also at http://classics.mit.edu/Aristotle/nicomachaen.6.vi.html.

2. Importance of prudence among the cardinal virtues
There is a mutual dependence between prudence and the exercise of other virtues, particularly the other cardinal virtues of justice, temperance, and fortitude. In fact, the *Catechism of the Catholic Church* refers to prudence as the "charioteer of the virtues."

> It guides the other virtues by setting rule and measure. It is prudence that immediately guides the judgment of conscience. The prudent man determines and directs his conduct in accordance with this judgment. With the help of this virtue we apply moral principles to particular cases without error and overcome doubts about the good to achieve and the evil to avoid.[8]

Consider the descriptions of justice, fortitude, and temperance in the *Catechism*, nos. 1807-9. How do you think prudence and its moral vision are needed to guide these virtues?

3. Foresight
This chapter noted that memory, docility, and nimble decisiveness are virtues related to prudence. It is worth looking at other aspects of prudence like circumspection and caution. See the *Summa theologica*, II-II, question 49, on the "quasi-integral" parts of prudence.[9] Our emphasis has been on the role of prudence in setting out steps and following them to attain a good end. To this degree, consider the role of foresight in prudence.

> Prudence is properly about the means to an end, and its proper work is to set them in due order to the end. . . . Now the past has become a kind of necessity, since what has been done cannot be undone. In like manner, the present as such, has a kind of necessity. . . .
>
> Consequently, future contingents, in so far as they can be directed by man to the end of human life, are the matter of prudence: and each of these things is implied in the word foresight, for it implies

---

8. *Catechism of the Catholic Church* (Vatican City: Libreria Editrice Vaticana, 1993), no. 1806, http://www.vatican.va/archive/ccc_css/archive/catechism/p3s1c1a7.htm.
9. The full text of *Summa theologica* II-II, question 49, can be found at http://www.newadvent.org/summa/3049.htm.

the notion of something distant, to which that which occurs in the present has to be directed. Therefore foresight is part of prudence.[10]

As you imagine completing some project (writing a paper or cleaning the house), what practical steps do you need to take in order to reach your goal? Now think about how to tell a friend that a certain behavior is annoying and crude. Your goal is to help the friend change her behavior. Do you go through a similar process of thinking through steps?

---

10. Aquinas, *Summa theologica* II-II, question 48, article 6, http://www.newadvent.org /summa/3048.htm.

CHAPTER 9

Faith

W hen I (Jim) first entered the world of Catholic youth ministry, I went to a conference in the archdiocese in which I was ministering. The conference was led by some incredibly gifted and committed people who left a permanent mark upon me because of their love for and dedication to young people. One recurring plea that I heard from participants in the different breakout sessions and over the course of conversation and meals was the need for our young people to have a better "knowledge of the faith." In fact, many voiced the concern that the children of our Protestant brothers and sisters had a better "knowledge of the faith" than their own children, and that these young Protestants could even quote Scripture passages by heart! Clearly, many parents thought that youth ministry should shore up these shortcomings so that their young people would "know" the faith better.

Clearly, faith in this regard is being understood in terms of content, or what we refer to as *fides quae*, or the faith which is believed. I am the first to support the need for every Christian to grow in their understanding of what they believe. But there is something more—and I dare say, something more important—and that is that people also be committed to the human dynamic of believing, or what we refer to as *fides qua*. For the Christian, this involves the personal response to God's revelation of self-communication through the Holy Spirit in Christ Jesus. To put it simply, it is important for a Christian to know his or her faith, to know about the story of salvation that culminates in Christ, but every bit as important for a Christian to come to know God through Christ in the Holy Spirit. This is, of course, why we not only teach our young people to *know things about* Jesus, but we also teach them to come to *know* Jesus. The latter comes about through teaching our youngsters how to pray—and this involves more than "saying" prayers—so that they can learn to listen to the voice of Jesus and be able to share in their own words their cares and concerns, their hopes and their dreams, with the one who continues to be with us always as the Risen Lord. We have also discovered, over the years, the importance of retreats so that young people can meet or encounter Jesus in their personal prayer, in the celebration of the sacraments, and in service to the poor. All of these efforts are made so that we can enkindle a personal relationship with Jesus.

This chapter delves into the human dynamic of having faith in Christ, especially when we experience the pains, struggles, and difficulties of life. After some preliminary thoughts on having faith, we will examine several gospel stories that illustrate that the real challenge in this dynamic is to shift our vision so that we have faith in Christ's plan and not in our own plans. It is common to define faith as "belief" in God. This definition is certainly true. Too often, however, belief in God is understood only as a statement about the existence or about some quality that God possesses, like mercy, compassion, and love. Faith includes these beliefs and much more. Faith is trust in God as the goal and purpose of our lives—of human life and creation as a whole. There is a parallel here between faith and prudence. Faith is not only trust in God as our end; it is also trust in God as the pathway to that end. Faith in the God of Jesus Christ is trust that God is revealed in Jesus and, in Jesus, reveals a way for us (the path that we follow) to play a role in how creation fulfills its purpose and reaches its end. Faith in God is trust in how God loves the world and our willingness to follow and to claim that way as our own.

Lamentations and Hope

Coming to a personal relationship with Jesus, and learning to trust in him and his ways, can be built upon good, healthy relationships that we have with others, including family, friends, and coworkers. But having faith in someone is, of course, a difficult undertaking because many of us have had the experience of being let down and hurt by someone in whom we placed our trust and faith. In this regard, our relationships with others can present obstacles to overcome in our relationship with Jesus. It is normal to think that this relationship with Jesus will be just like all the others that include broken promises and unfilled assurances. It is the faith journey of each of us that leads us to discover that a relationship with Jesus is not like all the other ones in life, and that Jesus is one who can be trusted and is worthy of our placing our faith in him.

The ability to place our trust and faith in God is a central theme of the Bible. Israel, the disciples, and the early church had difficulty in trusting God's ways of dealing with the world. But, in the face of distrust in God's ways, God continues to reveal Godself as one who has humanity's best interests at heart. Even in the darkest times, God's steadfast love is present. Perhaps a most striking example of God's faithfulness comes through in the Book of Lamentations. It is an interesting book, as its style communicates something of its message. It is written as an acrostic poem in which the initial letters of each line of poetry follow a pattern. In this case, the first letters of each line form the Hebrew alphabet of twenty-two letters. In the case of Lamentations, the author is conveying grief, and doing it in a way that expresses the completeness of grief—covering it "from A to Z," as we might say.[1]

Clearly, at the heart of this poem is the absolute grief that the author experiences as he ponders his life and all the terrible afflictions that Israel, in general, and he, in particular, have had to bear—afflictions for which the author blames God! Thinking of Jerusalem, which has been destroyed by the Babylonians, the author believes it is God who has "brought to the ground in dishonor a kingdom and its princes," and who "in blazing wrath cut down entirely the horn of Israel, withdrawing the support of his right hand when the enemy approached" (2:2-3). And when reflecting upon his own wretched condition, the author cries out,

I am one who has known affliction under the rod of God's anger, one whom he has driven and forced to walk in darkness, not in light. . . .
He has worn away my flesh and my skin, he has broken my bones; he has besieged me all around with poverty and hardship; he has left me to dwell in dark places like those long dead. (3:1-6)

As the author remembers the terrible things that have happened "over and over," his soul is downcast. However, the poem takes a turn and the author states that in the midst of all this grief, he will call to mind something that will always bring him hope: "The Lord's acts of mercy are not exhausted, his compassion is not spent; they are renewed each morning—great is your faithfulness! The Lord is my portion, I tell myself, therefore, I will hope in him" (3:22-24).

1. *Catholic Study Bible*, New American Bible Revised Edition, ed. Donald Senior, John J. Collins, and Mary Ann Getty (New York: Oxford University Press, 2011), 1146.

Of course, it is most difficult to have faith in the midst of difficulty and struggles. The author of the Book of Lamentations gives witness to belief in God's steadfast love when there is little evidence around him to support this faith. This is actually the basic definition of faith, taken from Hebrews 11:1, that St. Thomas Aquinas provides: "the realization of what is hoped for, the evidence of things not seen."[2] This is the basis of faith: despite a lack of evidence in the moment, one continues to hope and trust in God's steadfast love. This phrase "in the moment" is key because it is the present struggle that can cloud our memory of God's faithfulness in the past, as well as our hope for a future founded upon a plan that is crafted by God for our welfare, not our woe (see Jer. 29:11).

The Good Shepherd

The Gospel of John is permeated with stories showing that Jesus is the one who is worthy of having faith placed in him. In John 5, we encounter a man who had been ill for thirty-eight years. The story takes place at the pool by the Sheep Gate, and the man, like a "large number of ill, blind, lame, and crippled," has been trying to get into the pool when the water was stirred up. Legend had it that an angel of the Lord would come down into the pool, and the first person to enter the water when it was stirred up would be healed. Jesus, realizing that the man had been there for a very long time, asks him a question: "Do you want to be well?" (John 5:6). One might think that the answer is obvious, but, upon further reflection, we have to realize that in thirty-eight years the man was never the first to enter the water! So this is a pointed question that Jesus asks the man. Perhaps our own experiences of choosing to live less than the fullness of life make this question pertinent for every reader of this gospel passage. Do you want to be well? In other words, Jesus is asking: Do you want to continue living less than the fullness of life when you can embrace the one who offers life to the full? Jesus is asking this man if he wants to continue to trust in his own path, or if he chooses to put his faith in Jesus.

Interestingly, this gospel passage appears in the weekday lectionary on Tuesday of the Fourth Week of Lent. The gospel passage is accompanied by portions of Psalm 46 as the responsorial psalm, including these verses:

---

2. *Summa theologica*, II-II, question 4, article 1, http://www.newadvent.org/summa/3004 .htm.

There is a stream whose runlets gladden the city of God,
the holy dwelling of the Most High.
God is in its midst; it shall not be disturbed.
God will help it at the break of dawn. (Ps. 46:5–6)

As I (Jim) was preparing my homily, I was baffled as to why these particular verses were selected to accompany a gospel that has as its context the story of the waters being disturbed in order to bring healing. Why choose a psalm verse that talks about the water *not being disturbed*? Then, it dawned on me. In the previous chapter of John's gospel, Jesus has revealed himself to the Samaritan woman as the Living Water: "Whoever drinks of the water I give will never thirst; the water I shall give will become in him a spring of water welling up to eternal life" (John 4:14). There is no need for the angel of the Lord to disturb this water in order to bring healing to this man. Jesus, the Living Water, is before him, offering him the fullness of life. What path will one choose: trust in one's own path of "life limping along," or faith in Jesus, the Way itself?

John's gospel includes another story about the struggle to have faith in the midst of difficulty. The crisis "in the moment" for Martha and Mary was that their brother, Lazarus, had died. Both Martha and Mary, separately, when they see Jesus, utter the same cry: "Lord, if you had been here, my brother would not have died" (John 11:21, 32). There is something here that touches upon the universal experience that we seem to have when something bad happens to us: if only God had been paying attention, if only God had cared, if only God had wanted to help us, then . . . then this terrible thing would not have happened to us. The gospel story reports that "Jesus loved Martha and her sister and Lazarus" (11:5), but the evidence of the situation for Martha and Mary indicates that Jesus really did not care about them. Or worse, perhaps, that he did care about them, but chose not to help them. After all, if Jesus really loved them, he would have come sooner or he would have done something to prevent the death of the one they loved.

In response to Martha, Jesus tells her, "I am the resurrection and the life; whoever believes in me, even if he dies, will live, and everyone who lives and believes in me will never die. Do you believe this?" (John 11:25–26). Now, evidence to support this claim is absent. In fact, the only evidence that Martha has before her is her dead brother. Yet she professes faith when she responds, "Yes, Lord. I have come to believe that you are the Messiah, the Son of God, the one who is coming into the world" (11:27). At first sight, Martha's response is praiseworthy. Many of us in similar situations would find it difficult to make such a faith-filled response in face of the death of a loved one. But, looking deeper, Martha is very much like us, and her faith, admirable as it might seem at first glance, is rooted more in her own beliefs than in belief in Jesus.

Francis J. Moloney's commentary on the Gospel of John provides some background that will help us to delve deeper into the question of what it means to have faith in Jesus and how, in the face of difficulty, we often are more comfortable in putting faith into our own plan than in God's plan. Interestingly, although both women utter the same cry—"Lord, if you had been here, my brother would not have died"—only Martha continues with the words: "But even now I know that whatever you ask of God, God will give you" (John 11:22). As Moloney points out, the reason for her belief in Jesus comes from her conviction of Jesus's ability to work miracles. Like previous characters in John's gospel, Nicodemus (3:2) and the man born blind (9:31–32), Martha expresses her belief that Jesus has special access to God and he will be able to work a miracle.[3] One can begin to see that Martha's faith lies in her plan of what Jesus should do in the face of her brother's death—for even now, Jesus should be able to do something for Lazarus.

When Jesus replies that her brother will rise, Martha interrupts him, explaining that she accepts a current Jewish view of the final resurrection of the dead.[4] As Moloney notes, "*She tells* Jesus what resurrection means: resurrection at the last day."[5] But, in response, his words transcend the limited eschatological expectation uttered by Martha and center on his person as the resurrection and the life (John 11:25). When Jesus asks Martha if she believes this, she responds that she has believed for some time (*egō pepisteuka*). In other words, in the past Martha came to an understanding of Jesus as the Christ, as the Son of God, and as the one who is coming into the world.[6] But, as Moloney points out, "All of these expressions have been

3. Francis J. Moloney, *The Gospel of John*, Sacra Pagina, vol. 4 (Collegeville, MN: Liturgical Press, 1998), 327.

4. This view of the end of time, current at the time of Jesus, is rooted in the Jewish persecutions inflicted by the Seleucid tyrant Antiochus Epiphanes IV who reigned over Syria from 175 BCE until 164 BCE. The resurrection of the dead included everyone at the end of time, providing vindication of the faithful and judgment of the unjust.

5. Moloney, *The Gospel of John*, 327–28.

6. Moloney, *The Gospel of John*, 328. Further evidence of Martha's lack of faith in Jesus comes later in the story when Martha objects to Jesus's command to "take away the stone" (11:39). Although she earlier had expressed belief in Jesus as a miracle worker, she is unable to accept that Jesus is the resurrection and the life. She declares that Jesus has no authority over a person who is dead (332).

used by others who fell short of true faith."[7] The first disciples (1:41) and the Samaritan woman (4:25, 29) called Jesus "the Christ," Nathanael (1:49) called Jesus "the Son of God," and the crowds confessed that Jesus was the one who was coming into the world (6:14). But, in each case, Jesus corrects these views, promising the disciples "greater things," asking the Samaritan woman to reach beyond her messianic hopes to see him as the "Savior of the world," and warning the crowds that they should long, not for bread that perishes, but for the food provided by the Son of Man. In other words, Martha has limited faith, matching that of the disciples, Nicodemus, the Samaritan woman, and the crowds, who used traditional Jewish messianic expressions to voice their faith in Jesus.[8]

What of Mary? Is her response of faith in Jesus different from that of her sister? While "the Jews"[9]—who are focused on the dead Lazarus rather than on Jesus—expect that Mary will join them at the tomb in their lamentations over Lazarus, Mary has heard that Jesus "is calling her" and responds immediately: "She rose quickly and went to him." Moloney notes that "every reference to the 'voice' (*phōnē*) of Jesus is a call to fullness of life with him (cf. 3:8, 29; 5:25, 28; 10:3, 4, 16, 27)."[10] When she meets Jesus, she greets him differently than Martha: she falls at his feet and repeats part of Martha's confession—but Martha's expectation of Jesus as a miracle worker is not repeated. She simply states her unconditional trust in Jesus as the resurrection and the life.[11]

To this point, Mary responds to the voice of the Good Shepherd and emerges as the character in the story who demonstrates true faith in Jesus in the face of Lazarus's death. Moloney, however, points out that this

7. Moloney, *The Gospel of John*, 328.

8. Moloney, *The Gospel of John*, 328.

9. Pheme Perkins notes that the Gospel of John often uses the expression "the Jews" as a symbol for all those who oppose Jesus. She reminds us that John is not making a statement about the Jewish people when he uses "the Jews" as the "bad guys." The Vatican has pointed out that, in the past, people did not distinguish between John's use of "the Jews" as characters of opposition and the Jewish people, leading to an anti-Semitic reading of the gospel. Perkins suggests that it might be appropriate to substitute the phrase "Jesus's enemies" for "the Jews" in order to avoid this confusion. See Pheme Perkins, "Reading Guide: John," *Catholic Study Bible*, 413.

10. Moloney, *The Gospel of John*, 329.

11. Moloney, *The Gospel of John*, 330. There are echoes here of another story of Martha and Mary in the Gospel of Luke. As in this story, Mary is at the feet of Jesus—the posture of a disciple—and comes off better than her sister Martha who is busy about many things (see Luke 10:38-42).

situation suddenly shifts in verse 33, where it states that Jesus "became perturbed and deeply troubled" when "Jesus saw [Mary] weeping and the Jews who had come with her weeping." This emotional response of Jesus is not about compassion or a lack of compassion for Lazarus. This same description of Jesus's frustration and disappointment occurred previously in the gospel as his public ministry drew to a close.[12] Up to this point, only "the Jews" have been reported as weeping. But now Mary joins "the Jews" in their tears. Moloney sees in this action an indication that Mary is turning away from her authentic belief in Jesus as the resurrection and the life, which generates anger and severe disappointment in Jesus. Mary earlier showed signs of transcending the limited expectations of "the Jews" (11:31), of the disciples (11:12, 16), and of Martha (11:21-22, 24, 27), but in making the death of Lazarus the center of attention, she has abandoned her earlier unconditional faith in Jesus.[13]

As the story of the raising of Lazarus illustrates, having unconditional faith in Jesus, rather than in our own understandings and plans, is a struggle. In the midst of Lazarus's death, Martha has faith in Jesus's ability to work miracles and in the resurrection on the last day. She is not able to have faith in what Jesus has more fully revealed to her—that he is the resurrection and the life. For her part, Mary at first responds to Jesus's revelation that he is the Good Shepherd who calls all to the fullness of life, but she turns from this and begins to weep with "the Jews." Rather than be critical of these two sisters who loved their dead brother deeply, we can see their struggles to have faith are similar to our own. In the midst of such loss, we too grasp for faith in what makes sense for us, rather than in Jesus, the resurrection and the life.

There might be no better example of this tendency to trust in our own plan than the story of Jairus, the synagogue official (Mark 5:21-43). Jairus has a twelve-year-old daughter who is so sick that he is willing to try anything to help her recover. Jairus is willing to leave his daughter alone in order to go to Jesus and ask for his help. Surely, this is a demonstration of great faith on the part of Jairus! After all, he risks not being with his daughter if she were to die while he is reaching out to Jesus. On the way to Jairus's house, the narrative is interrupted by the story of a woman who demonstrates great faith, believing that if she only touches Jesus's clothing, she will be healed.

---

12. Moloney, *The Gospel of John*, 330 and 340-41. Note that Jesus weeps again (11:35). Moloney maintains that the tears of Jesus are not shed as a demonstration of Jesus's love for Lazarus; it is Mary's total association with the mourning of "the Jews" at this point in the story that again moves Jesus to tears (331).

13. Moloney, *The Gospel of John*, 330.

After Jesus tells the woman that her faith has saved her, people from the synagogue official's house arrive and tell Jairus that he should not bother Jesus anymore because his daughter has died.

We might imagine what this experience would be like for Jairus. He really does have faith in Jesus. After all, he has risked leaving his very sick daughter to go to him. Yet, despite his faith, his worst fears have been realized—his daughter has died. We could imagine Jairus second-guessing not only his decision to leave his little girl but, even more, putting his faith in Jesus. What good did that do? It would seem that his faith only brought death, not life. Remarkably, it is precisely *at this moment* that Jesus speaks to Jairus. Disregarding the message that has been reported, Jesus says to the synagogue official, "Do not be afraid; just have faith" (Mark 5:36). In other words, Jesus is asking Jairus to lay aside faith in his own plan and to trust in Jesus's plan. Jairus had, after all, worked all this out. Much like Martha who understood Jesus as a miracle-worker, Jairus had already figured out what the outcome of his daughter's sickness would be—Jesus would come and heal her. But Jairus's plan did not work out. Jesus is now asking him to trust in him, for he is the resurrection and the life. Jesus is asking Jairus to allow him to bring about an outcome that Jairus could not possibly imagine: to bring life out of death itself.

Conclusion

For Christians, having faith in Jesus is a struggle. We have ample evidence in the gospels of how hard it is for the disciples and others to do this. We know that this is true for us as well. Often, in the midst of our own difficulties, our prayer is like a lesson plan for God to follow in order for us to experience new life. But deeper reflection on our own faith journey leads us to a different conclusion. We realize that over time and with reluctance, we must let go of our plans, and try to be open to God's plan. It is a plan for our welfare, not our woe. It is a plan that will bring new life, but most often in ways that we had not anticipated.

Christians have two wonderful examples of what faith in God and God's plan might look like. One example is Mary in the Gospel of Luke. She is greatly troubled by the angel's message, for she has been told that as a young woman who has had "no relations with a man," she will conceive and give birth to a child who "will be called holy, the Son of God" (Luke 1:34–35). Mary makes an incredible response: "Behold, I am the handmaid of the Lord. May it be done to me according to your word" (1:38). The other example is Jesus. Like Jairus, Jesus is mulling over a plan that might bring life out of the struggles of death as he contemplates his agony in the garden. But, in his prayer, he gives himself over to God's plan, not his own: "Father, if you are willing, take this cup away from me; still, not my will but yours be done" (22:42). Jesus trusts that God's promises will be fulfilled despite evidence to the contrary in the moment of his trial and suffering, and even his death.

For Reflection and Further Study

1. Faith as *fides quae* and *fides qua*

First Peter 3:15 says, "Always be ready to give an explanation to anyone who asks you for a reason for your hope." Usually, this challenge is thought to mean: How can I explain the existence of God? As a thought-experiment, consider that "reason for your hope" means the reason you think that God's justice and love will gather up creation in the end, that God's goodness will win the day, not because the bad people are somehow vaporized so that only the good remain, but because God—through a way of peace—has transformed (that is, "resurrected") the world. How might someone respond to this challenge, understanding faith both as *fides quae* (the content of belief) and *fides qua* (the dynamic of believing)?

It is not an easy question. In an address on "The Year of Faith," Pope Benedict XVI says this about faith:

> The encounter with Christ renews our human relationships, directing them, from day to day, to greater solidarity and brotherhood in the logic of love. Having faith in the Lord is not something that solely involves our intelligence, the area of intellectual knowledge; rather, it is a change that involves our life, our whole self: feelings, heart, intelligence, will, corporeity, emotions and human relationships. With faith everything truly changes, in us and for us, and our future destiny is clearly revealed, the truth of our vocation in history, the meaning of life, the pleasure of being pilgrims bound for the heavenly Homeland. . . . Faith in a God who is love . . . clearly indicates that man's fullness consists solely in love.[14]

14. Pope Benedict XVI, "General Audience: Year of Faith, Introduction" (October 17,

In Pope Benedict's statement, *fides qua* flows together with *fides quae*; the manner of believing (the whole self) flows with the content of believing in the God who is love. He worries that Christians have unwittingly accepted a content of belief that is individualist and relativist (everyone has their own gods) and therefore our manner of belief has become private, as a way to make our own life secure and better. We are not likely to share God's love for the world.

Consider the challenges of faith: too often we settle in to belief by keeping it in a safe place, what Pope Benedict refers to as the "intellectual knowledge" of faith. Consider what it would look like to believe and to live in such a way that we need a continual renewal of trust in God's way to keep carrying on. How might the way we live look different?

2. Tradition

The Christian faith is apostolic in the sense that what happened in a long-ago past is the measure of how we think about the future. In a sense, this comment is a restatement of the relationship between the content of belief (*fides quae*) and the manner of believing (*fides qua*). The content of faith is carried forward through how we believe. Aquinas's definition of faith is "the realization of what is hoped for, the evidence of things not seen" (Heb. 11:1). In the *Summa theologica* II-II, he explains:

> "We hope for that which we see not" because to see the truth is to possess it. Now one hopes not for what one has already, but for what one has not. . . . Accordingly the relation of the act of faith to its end which is the object of the will, is indicated by the words: "Faith is the substance of things to be hoped for . . ." [I]n us the first beginning of things to be hoped for is brought about by the assent of faith.[15]

Certainly, we do not see God and cannot grasp or possess God. This is why the unseen is deeply connected to hope. Through faith, we have trust now in God's future. But, as noted, the future is set out in the past—in a biblical and apostolic era. Christians in the present live between a biblical past and a

---

2012), https://w2.vatican.va/content/benedict-xvi/en/audiences/2012/documents/hf_ben-xvi_aud_20121017.html.

15. Aquinas, *Summa theologica* II-II, question 4, article 1, http://www.newadvent.org/summa/3004.htm.

future completion of that history as it continues to unfold—"Christ has died, Christ has risen, Christ will come again."

The word/concept most often used to link this past and future is *tradition*, that is, how a people (not simply individuals) become the link between what has been done and what will be. It is helpful to think about tradition in a variety of senses, for example, how we organize our year around holidays, what we do during holidays to keep continuity with the past, and headier matters like how academic disciplines carry forward research and key ideas (in biology or philosophy) as well as how churches pass on the faith. Consider these various ways of tradition, how they change, and how we come to try to get back on track. For example, many complain about the commercialization of Christmas. How do we know or realize that it has been "commercialized"? After considering these matters of how we "hand on" (that is, how we can be a link from past to future), consider how our memory of God's past actions will assist us in having hope for a future crafted by God—in seeing the ways of God in the present.

CHAPTER 10

Seeing the Way of God

This chapter will focus on the challenging, surprising, and joyful way of God. We will follow the disciples through the Gospel of Mark and see challenges and joys that they experience as they follow Jesus. Recall that Part 1 of this book framed moral vision as the course of a journey where we learn to see the good more clearly and in the process learn to live better and participate more fully in the goodness of creation. Life is a moral journey. Indeed, the life of faith is a journey, and we have seen, in the previous chapter, that the journey of faith requires trust in God's self-giving love. The good news proclaimed in the Gospel of Mark is that in Jesus Christ the world is given a pathway to its fulfillment. In his gospel, Mark is focused on helping the hearer (us) to understand who Jesus is and what it might mean to be his disciple.

Seeing Anew

To know Jesus as he is revealed in Mark's gospel is to see and to trust in the way of God, which is not only challenging, but also frightening. After all, Jesus suffers and dies on a cross as a criminal, deserted by his disciples, crying out in anguish, "My God, my God, why have you deserted me?" Despite the cost, to follow Jesus is to place one's trust in him like a "little child." This demands a conversion on the part of anyone who follows Jesus, for he reminds us that God's ways are not our ways. Disciples need to be open to allowing God to transform them to see as God sees, so that they may act as God acts. Indeed, to follow Jesus is to embrace certain patterns of living, such as losing oneself, being the least, and being the servant of all.

Paradoxically, these practices are the way, not to a diminished life, but to a life fulfilled. Mark's gospel provides various characters to illustrate what it looks like to follow Jesus. The religious authorities have hard hearts and never seem to be able to place their trust in Jesus. In direct contrast, we have people who are like "little children," putting all their faith and trust in Jesus in their great need. And then we have the disciples. They are trying to be open to Jesus's teaching and God's transformation of them, but they find it difficult to follow and they are afraid of the consequences of "the way." This chapter will explore each of these groups to help contemporary disciples to see more clearly the way of God in the person and actions of Jesus.

Thinking about the religious authorities of Jesus's day usually brings to mind charges of hypocrisy and how they laid unnecessary burdens upon people. In truth, there were many good and holy men among the religious authorities of Jesus's day. The gospel depiction of them might be understood as a prophetic critique of Judaism from within Judaism, and later still in Matthew's gospel, a rejection of Pharisaic Judaism that developed during the time of the early church. In any case, the religious authorities as depicted in the gospels are not open to Jesus and therefore are not open to any conversion to seeing and acting differently. Rather than being open to Jesus, they are critical of him and his ways.

Early in the gospel, Jesus begins his ministry of calling the first disciples and healing the sick. He cures a demoniac in a synagogue in Capernaum (Mark 1:21-28), Simon's mother-in-law in the house of Simon (1:29-31), and then before the day is over "many who were sick with various diseases" (1:32-34). Chapter 1 ends with the cleansing of a leper, whom Jesus touches and heals (1:40-44). In the midst of this evidence that the "kingdom of God is at hand," chapter 2 of Mark's gospel illustrates the inclination of the religious authorities to question and complain about Jesus's inauguration of "the time of fulfillment." This chapter has four stories, each of which is punctuated by a question that the religious authorities pose in response to Jesus's actions. When he heals the paralytic, they ask, "Who but God alone can forgive sins?" When he eats with tax collectors and sinners in the house of Levi, they ask, "Why does he eat with tax collectors and sinners?" In light of the accepted custom of fasting, they object, "Why do the disciples of John and disciples of the Pharisees fast, but your disciples do not fast?" Finally, in response to the disciples picking the heads of grain as they walked through a field, they say, "Look, why are they doing what is unlawful on the Sabbath?"

Rather than understanding that they are witnessing the in-breaking of God's kingdom, the religious authorities resort to criticism. Jesus tries to respond to each complaint. In response to the claim that he does not have the power to forgive sins, Jesus asks what is more convincing: to say to the paralytic that his sins are forgiven or to tell him to rise and walk? Clearly, a greater show of "power" would be the latter, for the former is not discernible to the eye. Jesus is indicating through his healing of the paralytic—something astounding and visible—that he does indeed have the power to forgive sins. In response to the complaint that he is eating with the wrong sort of people—those who would render him ritually "unclean" in his association with them—Jesus responds that, like a physician who is called to heal the sick, he is called, not for the righteous, but for the sinner. To the third critique, Jesus tries to help the religious authorities to see that something new and wonderful is happening. This is the joyful time of the messianic fulfillment, and the wedding image that Jesus introduces suggests a new relationship of love between God and the world that is manifested in Jesus's healing and table fellowship. The images of sewing a piece of unshrunken cloth onto an old cloak or of pouring new wine into old wineskins illustrate the futility of holding on to the "old ways." Finally, in answer to the fourth criticism, Jesus manifests a clear understanding of the purpose of the law: it is for the benefit of humanity to bring them life.

The next story, in the beginning of chapter 3, serves not only as an illustration of Jesus's understanding of the law, but also of the religious authorities' reaction to Jesus and his ways. As Jesus enters the synagogue on the Sabbath, the religious authorities watch closely to see if Jesus will cure a man with a withered hand. As the man stands before him, Jesus asks, "Is it lawful to do good on the Sabbath rather than to do evil, to save life rather than to destroy it?" (Mark 3:1). The religious authorities say nothing, and Jesus is "grieved at their hardness of heart." They have not understood that the Sabbath, the day of re-creation from Genesis, would be the perfect day to bring restoration and new life to this man in his affliction. The last verse in this story is a haunting one: "The Pharisees went out and immediately took counsel with the Herodians against him to put him to death" (3:6). Mark's irony is not lost on the reader, who realizes that the religious authorities have gone further than misunderstanding the purpose of the Sabbath—they are now actually plotting the death of Jesus on the Sabbath. Their hearts are hard, and they are not open to the good news of God that Jesus preaches in his words and deeds.

The disciples, in contrast to the religious authorities, are open to Jesus, but they find his teaching hard to understand and difficult to follow. Mark provides lessons for the disciples in chapters 8-10 of his gospel. In three particular places, he follows a pattern wherein: (1) Jesus announces his upcoming suffering and death; (2) the disciples indicate that they do not understand what this message entails; and (3) Jesus uses this misunderstanding to teach the disciples what it means to follow him on the way. This expression—on the way—can be taken literally as Jesus and the disciples wander through Galilee, but it is also an image for what it entails to follow Jesus in discipleship. Indeed, the first disciples were called followers of "the Way" (Acts 9:2).

The Way of God

Mark 8 includes the first of these encounters between Jesus and his chosen followers about discipleship. Jesus shares with his disciples that he must go to Jerusalem to suffer and die. Peter, hearing this, rebukes Jesus, urging him not to go. In turn, Jesus—in the strongest rebuke of the gospel—says in response, "Get behind me, Satan. You are thinking not as God thinks, but as human beings do" (Mark 8:33). Jesus then begins to teach his followers that in order to follow him, they must take up their cross and follow him. He goes further, using a paradox, telling them that "Whoever wishes to save his life will lose it, but whoever loses his life for my sake and that of the gospel will save it" (8:35).

We see the second of these encounters between Jesus and the disciples in chapter 9. Again, Jesus indicates that he must go to Jerusalem to suffer and die. This news seems to have fallen on deaf ears, as the disciples discuss among themselves "on the way" who is the greatest! Indeed, Jesus asks them, "What were you arguing about on the way?" This provides another opportunity for Jesus to teach about discipleship, again in the form of a paradox: "If anyone wishes to be first, he shall be the last of all and the servant of all" (Mark 9:35).

The third of these lessons in discipleship occurs in chapter 10. Here, Jesus announces his upcoming passion and death and, in response, James and John ask for seats at his right and left when he comes in glory! Jesus responds with a similar message to the one we have already heard: "Whoever wishes to be great among you will be your servant; whoever wishes to be first among you will be the slave of all" (Mark 10:43–44).

There are two things worth noting in this third lesson in discipleship. First, Jesus points out that they will drink from the cup that he will drink from. Indeed, they do. In Mark's gospel, we are told that "they all drank from it [the cup]" (14:23) at the Last Supper. But, rather than being a mark of pride, it becomes one of shame. This gesture, which is underlined by Peter's insistence that he will never desert Jesus, is symbolic of their solidarity and commitment to stay with Jesus throughout his ordeal. But the gesture stands in stark contrast to what really happens; they do, in fact, abandon him when he is arrested. Mark's gospel makes this clear in the verse: "And they all left him and fled" (14:50). Even Peter, who has boldly claimed, "Even though all should have their faith shaken, mine will not be" (14:29), deserts Jesus in his hour of need and denies that he ever knew the man. Despite Jesus's efforts, the disciples have remained "blind" to seeing what it means and costs to be a disciple.

Second, the story that follows the lesson in chapter 10 is about the blind man, Bartimaeus. Like James and John, Jesus asks the blind man what he wants Jesus to do for him. While James and John ask for prestige and power and glory, the blind man asks to see. Throughout Mark's gospel, this image of seeing is about having faith, about understanding God's ways and trusting that these ways are the path to a life fulfilled. The gospel, in fact, presents us with those who can "see," who are really "blind," and those who are "blind," who can really "see." Unlike the disciples who can see, this poor, seemingly insignificant character who is blind asks Jesus for what is important in the life of discipleship—not wealth or prestige or power, but sight into God and God's ways. It is significant that Mark ends this encounter with the cryptic phrase that this man now began "to follow him on the way"—a metaphor for what a true disciple does.

The story of the healing of the blind man, Bartimaeus, forms an end to this collection of stories on discipleship. Interestingly, the beginning of the block of stories about discipleship also contains a story about a blind man, the blind man of Bethsaida (Mark 8:22-26). The fact that this story about a blind man begins an arrangement of stories should immediately clue us in to the fact that Mark does not think that becoming a disciple is something that is easily "seen." In fact, disciples might be "blind" to the requirements of discipleship. Indeed, the story itself is instructive, for the man is healed in stages. After touching him, Jesus asks him if he can see, but the man responds, "I see people looking like trees and walking." The gospel then reports that Jesus "laid hands on his eyes a second time and he saw clearly; his sight was restored and he could see everything distinctly" (8:24-25). Mark's subsequent stories that are related to Jesus's pronouncements of his suffering and death illustrate that the disciples clearly are "thinking not as God does, but as human beings do." Mark's aim is to use the examples of the disciples to help the members of his community to see as God does, but he realizes that people will need to embark on a process of transformation in order to do this.

While the religious authorities are hard-hearted and plot to have Jesus killed, the disciples, despite their openness to being with Jesus on the way, are portrayed as failures. Judas betrays Jesus, Peter denies him, and all the others run away when he is arrested. In fact, Mark includes this detail: when Jesus is arrested, those with swords and clubs try to seize a young man dressed only in a linen cloth. As they go to grab him, he slips their grasp and runs away naked (Mark 14:51-52). This story stands in sharp contrast to the beginning of the gospel, when the disciples are willing to leave everything to follow him. Now they are leaving everything to get away from him!

In contrast to the hard-heartedness of the religious authorities and the failure of the disciples, Mark presents us with still another group of people who seem to put their trust in Jesus unreservedly. We have already mentioned some of these "little" people briefly in a few stories—the healings of the leper, the paralytic, the blind man of Bethsaida, and the blind Bartimaeus. Each of these stories presents people who are seemingly insignificant—only Bartimaeus is named—yet all put their complete trust in Jesus.

The first of these "little" people is the leper in chapter 1. As a leper, he is required to keep his distance from healthy people, warning them of his close proximity. Yet he approaches Jesus and begs him, "If you wish, you can make me clean" (Mark 1:41). Many translations indicate that Jesus is moved with pity, but a better translation of the Greek word *splanchnizomai* is "being filled with compassion."[1] This attribute of Jesus, as well as his intention to include all people, portrays the heart of Jesus's ministry. In fact, Jesus reaches out and touches the leper, an unthinkable action for those concerned with ritual purity. His compassion for this man is what motivates Jesus's action. Further, he tells the man to show himself to the priest so that he can be reunited with the community. Here we see, in concrete, the chief concerns of Jesus: compassion and the inclusion of all, especially those on the margins. For his part, the man suffering from leprosy is like a "little child" who places all his trust in Jesus. His disease and exclusion from others have left him with little to depend upon. He is open to what Jesus can do for him, and he takes a bold step to trust that Jesus will respond and make him whole.

A similar Marcan account that depicts a "little" person who is in great need arises in the story of the woman who has been hemorrhaging for twelve

---

1. Bruce M. Metzger, *A Textual Commentary on the Greek New Testament*, 3rd ed. (Stuttgart: United Bible Societies, 1971), 76.

years. Like the leper, she has no resources to depend upon, and her trust in Jesus is strong. She also shares the boldness of the leper, being convinced that she will be healed if she can just touch the fringe of his garment. After being identified, she approaches Jesus "in fear and trembling," but she hears only words of good news: "Daughter, your faith has saved you. Go in peace and be cured of your affliction" (Mark 5:34). Like in the story of the leper, we see another example of what happens when a person is open to Jesus, trusting in him.

The blind man, Bartimaeus, provides us with another example of one who, like a little child, places his trust in Jesus. He has many obstacles to overcome, but he is determined to encounter Jesus so that he may be healed. In addition to his physical blindness, the crowds are pressing upon him and urging him to be quiet as he calls out to Jesus. Once Jesus does hear his voice and calls him forward, "he threw aside his cloak, sprang up, and came to Jesus." The text does not indicate clearly, however, that as he comes to Jesus, he is still blind! He responds to the call of Jesus, trusting in him. In many ways, he models the true way of discipleship, walking by faith and not by sight. Indeed, Jesus acknowledges this when he says, "Go your way; your faith has saved you" (Mark 10:52). And in a final note—an indictment of both the religious authorities and the failed disciples—Bartimaeus begins to "follow him on the way." He is, through his trust in Jesus, a true disciple.

Conclusion

These teachings on discipleship remind us that "the way" of Jesus is about trusting Jesus like a little child (Mark 10:15). This trust will be tested as disciples are called to imitate Jesus in service and sacrifice for the sake of others—learning to give themselves away in love for others. The fact that these stories are framed in Mark's gospel by stories of the healing of blind men indicates that we might struggle to "see" this clearly. However, lest we become afraid and fear that discipleship is beyond our reach, we might reflect further on the disciples. Their hearts were not hardened like the religious authorities, but they lacked the trust of the many "little" people in the gospel. What hope is there for them, and for those who try to follow Jesus today? For those of us with "more to lose" than the little people, chapter 10 provides some hope that God can still work good within us despite our shortcomings. In this chapter, Mark includes the story of a rich young man, who goes away sad because he has many possessions (10:17-22). It is difficult for him to trust like a little child because he has much. This situation leads Jesus to comment: "How hard it is for those who have wealth to enter the kingdom of God!" (10:23). The disciples, in turn, are "amazed at his words." This prompts Jesus to repeat his teaching, announcing that "it is easier for a camel to pass through the eye of a needle than for one who is rich to enter the kingdom of God" (10:25). Now, the gospel tells us, the disciples are "exceedingly astonished and [say] among themselves, 'Then who can be saved?'" And now come the words of hope from the mouth of Jesus! He looks at the disciples and says, "For human beings it is impossible, but not for God. All things are possible for God" (10:27).

This is why all disciples, well aware of their frailties and sinfulness, can place their trust in God, who, through the Spirit of the Risen Lord, continues to work within us as long as we are not hard-hearted. If we are open, this Spirit has the power to transform us just as the Spirit of the Risen Lord transformed Peter and the other disciples from utter failures to those who took up their cross and died as followers of the Way. Perhaps Paul—another disciple who underwent a transformation by the Spirit of the Risen Lord—says it best in Ephesians: "Now to him who is able to accomplish far more than all we ask or imagine, by the power at work within us, to him be glory in the church and in Christ Jesus to all generations, forever and ever" (Eph. 3:20).

For Reflection and Further Study

1. Clouded vision

Consider the failures of disciples to see and to understand in the Gospel of Mark: Peter (8:31-38), the whole group of twelve (9:33-37), and James and John (10:35-45).[2] What inhibits their vision? Think about analogies between their misunderstandings and our own lives. For example, Peter, like most of his fellow Jews, seems to believe that the Messiah will liberate the people of God, by force, from the bonds of Roman oppression. His presumptions about what the Messiah is all about cloud his ability to see and understand Jesus's vocation. Likewise, we often expect God to "fight our battles" in the sense that we unintentionally decide what God's concerns should be and what "victory" will look like. What are our presumptions about what God is going to do (or should do) in the world? How might these pre-set views cloud our vision?

2. If you are without a Bible, the Gospel of Mark can be found at USCCB.org: http://www.usccb.org/bible/books-of-the-bible/index.cfm.

2. Human fulfillment

The chapter notes that Jesus's life, death, and resurrection bring God's promises to fulfillment. It also highlights an apparent paradox of the gospels: the way of "losing" oneself is the way to find happiness. By setting our vision in terms of fulfillment in God, the chapter parallels the philosophical framework of "journey" and "end" that was introduced in chapter 4. Goodness is the route to a good life, and in making this point, we made sure (in chapter 4) to explain how the cardinal virtues of prudence, justice, fortitude, and temperance "point us to good and draw us outside of ourselves." Throughout the book, we have already shown the importance of faith, hope, and love.

At this juncture, it is important to put these theological virtues together in terms of fulfillment in God and God's love for the world. A theological virtue has its source and raison d'être in God. The love of God (charity) unites us with God and through God with our neighbors (whether enemies or friends). Faith is the gift of trust and certainty in God, which on an intellectual level, gives us the capacity to see God as our fulfillment and end. Hope gives us the ability to carry on along the journey of life, to draw on God's goodness and to continually see God's goodness as our end. Consider this concise description from Thomas Aquinas's *Summa theologica* II-II:

> A virtue is said to be theological from having God for the object to which it adheres. . . . Accordingly charity makes us adhere to God for His own sake, uniting our minds to God by the emotion of love. . . . [H]ope and faith make man adhere to God as to a principle wherefrom certain things accrue to us. Now we derive from God both knowledge of truth and the attainment of perfect goodness. Accordingly faith makes us adhere to God, as the source whence we derive the knowledge of truth, since we believe that what God tells us is true: while hope makes us adhere to God, as the source whence we derive perfect goodness, i.e. in so far as, by hope, we trust to the Divine assistance for obtaining happiness.[3]

Given that God is the source of the theological virtues, it is important to ask how they elevate our lives to higher goods. How does the love of God connect us to people in such a way that justice becomes more complete?

3. Aquinas, *Summa theologica* II-II, question 17, article 6, http://www.newadvent.org /summa/3017.htm#article6.

How does faith see and understand others more clearly and more truthfully? On this point, recall the story of Father Brown in chapter 7. How does hope give us the capacity to persist in doing what is good beyond our narrow self-interests?

2. Eyes to see

Given the functions of faith, hope, and love, consider why the "little" people are able to recognize Jesus for who he really is. Reflect upon the story of the woman with the hemorrhage (Mark 5:25–34) and blind Bartimaeus (10:46–52). What allows them to see differently than the disciples and good upstanding people?

3. Love in truth–authentic human development

Pope Benedict XVI, in his encyclical *Caritas in veritate*, treats a variety of social and economic questions in terms of justice, the common good, and authentic human development. In the conclusion, he repeats a point made several times in the document. Justice and openness to the common good depend upon personal and social transformation.

> [E]ven in the most difficult and complex times, besides recognizing what is happening, we must above all else turn to God's love. Development requires attention to the spiritual life, a serious consideration of the experiences of trust in God, spiritual fellowship in Christ, reliance upon God's providence and mercy, love and forgiveness, self-denial, acceptance of others, justice and peace. All this is essential if "hearts of stone" are to be transformed into "hearts of flesh" (Ezek 36:26), rendering life on earth "divine" and thus more worthy of humanity.[4]

On the topic of transformation, you might find it helpful to review chapter 3 on seeing the good. The important point to retrieve from that chapter is that seeing the good requires that we make "the way" of love and justice an ordinary part of our lives.

---

4. *Caritas in veritate* (Vatican City: Libreria Editrice Vaticana, 2009), no. 79, http://w2 .vatican.va/content/benedict-xvi/en/encyclicals/documents/hf_ben-xvi_enc_20090629_cari tas-in-veritate.html.

Chapter 2 of *Caritas in veritate* is titled "Human Development in Our Time" (nos. 21-33). Read this section and consider how our lives—on a personal, social, and economic level—will need to change in order to sustain a proper vision of the human good and authentic human development.

CHAPTER 11

Providence

W henever I (Jim) set out to accomplish something, I have always found that it is helpful to have the final end or goal in sight. Studying for a small quiz may seem pointless if the goal of passing the course or graduating from school is lost. Likewise, practicing a shot over and over may seem pointless unless I realize that the goal is to be a better player and to contribute to a winning game or season. Even everyday tasks such as reading the newspaper or going for a walk or setting aside time to pray make more sense if they are put into the larger perspective of wanting to be a happy, healthy, well-rounded person. If I can see what I am aiming for, the smaller choices and actions begin to make more sense to me. But what about taking this approach to an even greater level? What effect would it have on us if we kept in sight the ultimate question about creation and God's providence—God's plan for creation?

Creation

Jumping ahead to the answer, I would say that God's plan for us is a lofty one. In fact, it may be almost too much for us to comprehend, for the plan is to be one with God who has created us. In his second letter, Peter suggests that the goal is nothing less than "to share in the divine nature" (2 Pet. 1:4). Certainly, humanity has done its part to thwart this plan, but throughout history God has taken different initiatives and patiently waited for humanity to respond freely to the invitation that has been given. God has called a people, Israel, and made a covenant with them, providing them with the Torah, with judges and kings, and with the prophets to guide them. At different points in time, God has saved God's chosen people, Israel, from captivity in Egypt, from death in face of Pharaoh and the desert, from the consequences of their rebellion and rejection of God's ways, and from exile in Babylon.

God's greatest deed in revealing God's plan, of course, is the incarnation, where the invisible God is made visible. This is what the author of the Letter to the Hebrews writes when he says, "In times past, God spoke in partial and various ways to our ancestors through the prophets; in these last days, he spoke to us through a son, whom he made heir of all things and through whom he created the universe" (Heb. 1:1-2). In other words, the God who was veiled is now made manifest in Jesus so that all can come to know most fully who God is—that God is love (1 John 4:8). But Jesus also reveals to us what it is to be a human being—what is at the core of being human, what brings us happiness and fulfillment, and what is our destiny. It is the incarnation that not only makes this destiny clear but also makes it possible; it is through the incarnation that humanity achieves its deification, or as 2 Peter states it, becomes partakers of the divine nature. This might startle and amaze us! Yet it is something that is repeated at every Eucharist when the priest adds a few drops of water into the wine as he prepares the gifts, saying, "By the mystery of this water and wine, may we come to share in the divinity of Christ, who humbled himself to share in our humanity." In other words, God humbled himself to share in our humanity so that we might become partakers of the divine nature. What a plan! What a destiny! What a perspective for us to have as we live our lives each day!

But we have jumped ahead, and it would be helpful to provide some of the details of God's plan and humanity's response to this plan throughout history. We might start at the beginning. The Book of Genesis starts with those very words: "In the beginning. . . ." Here we hear the story of creation and of how God lovingly creates a world out of nothing. There is a pattern and order to God's creation; after each day, the author tells us that "God saw that it was good." The day and the night, the sky and the earth, the two great lights to govern the day and the night, the water and the earth and all its creatures, and finally humans created in God's image—all created by God who "looked at everything he had made, and found it very good" (Gen. 1:31). We can take the goodness and the beauty of this creation story for granted, not realizing that this story stands as a particular understanding of how we might think about God and how we might think about creation in general, and of human beings in particular.

The creation story emerges from the people of Israel as a story that stands in contradistinction to what other people—their Babylonian captors—

thought about their deity and creation. After Jerusalem fell to the Babylonian King Nebuchadnezzar in 586, the leading citizens of status, skill, and wealth were deported to Babylon where they lived in exile from their homeland for about seventy years. In their exile, the people of Israel came into contact with the Babylonian people and their gods and were exposed to the Babylonian creation story—the *Enuma Elish*—which promoted a very different view of their gods and creation. It turns out that the Babylonians believed in many gods, and at the heart of their creation story is a great battle between Tiamat, the great mother goddess, who decides to kill her offspring gods, and Marduk, who leads the revolt against her. Marduk kills Tiamat—crushing her skull with his mace—and makes the heaven and the earth out of her carcass. From the blood and guts of her consort, Kingu, Marduk makes "savage man." This is, as we can see, a very different creation story than the one we find in Genesis 1. In contrast to the story of Genesis 1, this story suggests that creation is the afterthought of a violent struggle between gods, and that human beings are made, not in the image and likeness of God, but out of the severed blood vessels of Kingu. One might ask what might be expected of such a world that comes about through war and violence, and one might ask what might be expected of a human being who is created as the result of more violence and is called "savage man." The answer, of course, is "not too much"—at least in comparison to Genesis 1, where God creates each step in an ordered and loving manner, assuring us that the result of each step is "good."

So, when we begin "in the beginning," we need to remember that creation is something that is good and that human beings are created in God's image. God has revealed something important here, for this is not what people previously thought of the world and of humans—and of God. This unique perspective on God's creation, and humanity's role within it, is furthered if we look at the story of "the fall" in Genesis 2–3. This story introduces a new perspective about God, for it reveals that God's plan will not be thwarted by humanity's lack of trust.

In Genesis 2, we see that the Lord God has created a garden and "out of the ground the Lord God made grow every tree that was delightful to look at and good for food, with the tree of life in the middle of the garden and the tree of knowledge of good and evil" (Gen. 2:9). The Lord God is careful that man has a suitable partner, so he cast the man into a deep sleep, removed his rib, and then "built the rib that he had taken from the man into a woman" (2:22). The man and woman are naked, but they feel no shame, for they are living in harmony with each other, with all of creation, and with the Lord God.

There is one command that humans must obey: "You are free to eat from any of the trees in the garden except the tree of the knowledge of good and evil. From that tree you shall not eat; when you eat from it you shall die" (Gen. 2:16-17). Neither God nor the author of Genesis justifies the prohibition; it is the commandment of God, pure and simple.[1] Humans are creatures, and not God, and there are some things that remain a mystery to them. The question is about their willingness to trust in God's plan for them. Can they trust that God will provide for them in God's time and in God's way, or do they need to grasp on their own what ultimately would be freely given to them? The "original sin" that this story reveals is that humans have a deep desire within them to be masters of their destiny; they cannot trust that God will in fact provide for them. Humans are not content to be creatures that must trust, but rather prefer to be "like gods." When God created humanity, God gave humanity a great gift—freedom—because God wants a willing partner, one who chooses God in freedom. But, unlike God, humans are creatures, not knowing all things. As creatures they are called to use the gift of freedom to trust that God's plan for humanity will be brought to fruition in God's time and in God's way.

Like the rest of the bad choices that Israel will make in the future, the decision made by the man and the woman in the garden had consequences. In addition to the etiological elements of the story,[2] the consequence for not trusting in God is really the future reality of Israel in its relationship and trust in foreign gods, instead of the Lord God. The enmity "between you and the woman, and between your offspring and hers" (Gen. 3:15) is the enmity between the strange gods that the serpent represents and the people of Israel, who will continue to distrust and reject God while trusting and embracing the strange gods they will encounter in their history as a people.[3] The story of salvation history is, however, the story of God's steadfast love in the midst

---

1. See Mary Katherine Birge, SSJ, "Genesis," in *Genesis: Evolution and the Search for a Reasoned Faith* (Winona, MN: Anselm Academic, 2011), 18, and Gerhard Lohfink, *Does God Need the Church? Toward a Theology of the People of God*, trans. Linda Maloney (Collegeville, MN: Liturgical Press, 1999), 16. Lohfink says, "Everything depends on this will of God standing in the midst of the world and being obeyed."

2. Etiology is a folkloric explanation for an event or phenomenon. When we were children and we heard thunder, our mothers might have told us that it was "the angels bowling." This story provides etiological explanations for why the snake lives on its belly, why women bear children in pain, and why people must work by "the sweat of their brow."

3. From a Christian perspective, this enmity will be overcome through Jesus, who is born of the woman, the mother of all Israel, for he comes from the House of David.

of Israel's reluctance to trust in God's plan. God's love for all of creation and humanity does not evaporate in the face of humanity's infidelity. The stories of the exodus from Egypt and the exile into Babylon are stories that illustrate this steadfast love.

Redemptive Love

In the case of the exodus, God uses Moses to deliver Israel from their captivity in Egypt and from their near destruction as they became trapped by the Red Sea. Israel saw in these events the hand of God: "Who is like you among the gods, O Lord? Who is like you, magnificent among the holy ones? Awe-inspiring in deeds of renown, worker of wonders" (Exod. 15:11). Yet it does not take Israel long to forget the mighty deeds of God and to begin to murmur and grumble that they have no water, no bread, and no meat in the desert (Exodus 16–17).

Perhaps the single word that describes the Israelites after God's mighty deeds have freed them from slavery in Egypt and from death at the Red Sea is "grumblers." Granted, they are in the desert, but they seem to have quickly forgotten all that God has done for them. Also, they do not seem able to grasp that the God who has saved them and freed them is a faithful God who will never abandon them, for they are God's people. They first complain about a lack of water, and later they complain about a lack of food. In both cases God provides for the people with water from the rock at Meribah and manna in the desert. Still, however, the continuation of these mighty deeds does not quench the grumbling of the Israelites. Eventually their grumbling turns into rebelliousness. While Moses communes with God at Mount Sinai, they fashion a calf out of precious metal. Psalm 106 depicts this act most starkly when it summarizes the grumbling and rebelliousness of Israel in these words: "They exchanged their glorious God for an image of a bull, which eats grass" (Ps. 106:20).

Gerhard Lohfink cites incidents such as these as an indication of Israel's particular relationship with God vis-à-vis other people and their gods. He maintains that while other people served gods of power—something people seem to cherish, for these gods were largely of the world itself and projections of the world—Israel was called to serve a God whose will is different. Israel realized that it was more beneficial to serve this God, and the Torah is the attempt to unite the people of God to the will of God. But Israel constantly resisted that will because it is often counter to human plans, ideas, and intentions. Israel preferred to live like other nations and, hence, its story became one of rebellion against God's will.[4] This stubbornness vis-à-vis God's will becomes for Lohfink a reflection upon the difference between religion and faith. For Lohfink, religion does not require faith. Religion seeks to satisfy human interests; it seeks to live out *our own plan for our lives* under the blessing of the gods. But faith asks about *God's interests* because it has found that God desires nothing other than the salvation of the world.[5] In other words, faith sets aside our personal plans and asks how it may serve God's plan for the world. Faith is about being anxious about God's concerns. It is about seeing the world as God does.

The story of Israel is really the story of how well they remember (or forget) what God has done for them. As they respond to Joshua, for instance, the people of Israel recommit themselves to God, who has carried out marvelous deeds on their behalf:

> Far be it from us to forsake the Lord to serve other gods. For it was the Lord, our God, who brought us and our ancestors out of the land of Egypt, out of the house of slavery. He performed those great signs before our very eyes and protected us along our entire journey and among all the peoples through whom we passed. . . . Therefore we also will serve the Lord, for he is our God. (Josh. 24:16-19)

But, despite their words of promise, Israel would forget what God had done and would be tempted to worship the strange gods of others whom they encountered in their journey and settlement in the land.

This rebellion against God's will is best exemplified in the story of Israel's desire to have a king. As Israel encounters other people, they are tempted to adopt their customs and their ways. In their cry to the prophet Samuel for a king to rule over them, God sees clearly that this is not only a rejection of the prophet: "The Lord said, 'Listen to what the people say. You are not the one they are rejecting. They are rejecting me as their king. They are acting toward you just as they have acted from the day I brought them up from Egypt to this very day, deserting me to serve other gods'" (1 Sam. 8:7-8). Respecting their freedom, God allows them to be governed by kings, despite the bad consequences that will befall them. Even Solomon, to whom God had granted the gift of wisdom to distinguish between good and evil (1 Kings 3:9-12), "turned his heart to follow other gods" (1 Kings 11:4).

4. Lohfink, *Does God Need the Church?*, 93-94.
5. Lohfink, *Does God Need the Church?*, 93-94.

When Solomon died, his son Rehoboam assumed the throne. He turned out to be more oppressive than his father. When asked for a reprieve by his people, Rehoboam responded: "My father put a heavy yoke on you, but I will make it heavier. My father beat you with whips, but I will beat you with scorpions" (1 Kings 12:11). Because of this oppressive behavior, the northern kingdom separated from the southern kingdom (1 Kings 12:1–20), leaving both more vulnerable to foreign powers. The northern kingdom fell to the Assyrians in 722 BCE, and the southern kingdom fell to the Babylonians in 586, with its leading citizens taken into exile to Babylon. Like all moments of crisis, the exile became an opportunity for Israel to reflect upon its circumstances and to ask significant questions about the covenant that God had made with Abraham, with Moses, and with David. Was God not worthy of trust? Were the promises God made not kept?

Over time and with self-reflection, the people realized that God had remained faithful to God's promises, but Israel had not lived up to its end of the relationship. Instead of trusting wholeheartedly in God, Israel continued to put its trust in other gods and was now reaping the consequences of its poor choices. As the people reached into their collective memories, they realized that their exile was much like being in captivity in Egypt and that this time of desolation was like when Israel wandered in the desert. They saw this time as an opportunity to repent, and they hoped that God would bring about a new exodus from Babylon.

Throughout, God demonstrated great patience with Israel and its wayward behavior. This does not mean that God was pleased with Israel. Indeed, a word here might help us to understand better the wrath or anger that is ascribed to God in the Old Testament. God's initial response to Israel's stubbornness was *patience*. Only after God had given them water, manna, quails, and the Torah—and the grumbling continued—did God respond with wrath. Hosea 4:1–3 stands as a prime example of God's *wrath*:

> Hear the word of the Lord, Israelites,
> for the Lord has a dispute with the inhabitants of the land.
> There is no fidelity, no loyalty, no knowledge of God in the land.
> Swearing, lying, murder, stealing and adultery break out;
> bloodshed follows bloodshed.
> Therefore the land dries up, and everything that dwells in it
> languishes:
> the beasts of the field, the birds of the air, and even the fish of the sea
> perish.

Lohfink notes that these words are a judgment on all of reality, for there will even be an end to the animals, birds, and fish. All the positive attributes of fidelity, love, and knowledge of God have disappeared and have been replaced with behaviors that mark the Israelites as blasphemers, betrayers, murderers, thieves, and adulterers. The wrath of God will lead to the very end of the universe.[6] Yet God's *wrath* quickly turns into a *lament*:

> When Israel was a child, I loved him, and out of Egypt I called my
> 	son.
> The more I called them, the farther they went from me,
> sacrificing to the Baals, and burning incense to idols.
> Yet it was I who taught Ephraim to walk, who took them in my arms;
> but they did not know that I cared for them. (Hos. 11:1–3)

Finally, we see the movement from *lament* to a rekindling of the *deep-felt love* for Israel:

> How could I give you up, Ephraim, or deliver you up, Israel?
> How could I treat you as Admah, or make you like Zeboiim?
> My heart is overwhelmed, my pity is stirred.
> I will not give vent to my blazing anger, I will not destroy Ephraim
> 	again.
> For I am God and not a man, the Holy One present among you;
> I will not come in wrath. (Hos. 11:8–9)

An analogy might help us to understand this movement from wrath to lament to love. Imagine that you have violated the freedom your parents gave you when you did something wrong. They have loved you and trusted you, but you made a bad choice. They are upset—they may be very angry at you, and they may long for the day when you were younger and more innocent—but because they love you, they will help you to move forward. Note, however, that their love is not a magic wand; it cannot undo the mistake that you have made. Their love can, however, be there to help you get through the mistake. In this process, your appreciation for your parents' love can grow, as can your understanding of freedom, responsibility, and consequences.[7]

---

6. Lohfink, *Does God Need the Church?*, 97–98.
7. Lohfink, *Does God Need the Church?*, 99–100.

Despite disappointment, God does not give up on Israel. Indeed, God will meet Israel at the place of its consequences, not abandoning them in exile in Babylon, and providing them with a message of a hope-filled future.

> For thus says the Lord: Only after seventy years have elapsed for Babylon will I deal with you and fulfill for you my promise to bring you back to this place. For I know well the plans I have in mind for you—oracle of the Lord—plans for your welfare and not for woe, so as to give you a future of hope. When you call me, and come and pray to me, I will listen to you. When you look for me, you will find me. Yes, when you seek me with all your heart, I will let you find me—oracle of the Lord—and I will change your lot; I will gather you together from all the nations and all the places to which I banished you—oracle of the Lord—and bring you back to the place from which I exiled you. (Jer. 29:10-14)

Looking forward, despite Israel's infidelity and the punishment that they brought upon themselves, God will take the initiative to establish a new covenant that will purify Israel and prepare it to follow God freely and faithfully: "I will sprinkle clean water over you and make you clean; from all your impurities and from all your idols I will cleanse you. I will give you a new heart, and a new spirit I will put within you. I will remove the heart of stone from your flesh and give you a heart of flesh" (Ezek. 36:25-26). Gathered from among the nations once again, Israel is ready to resume its task: "I will make you a light to the nations, that my salvation may reach to the ends of the earth" (Isa. 49:6).

Conclusion

The story of Israel is the story of a people that God has loved steadfastly and gathered to be a sign in the world of the gracious partnership that God offers to humanity. However, in the midst of Israel's acceptance of this partnership, there still remained infidelity and rebellion against God and God's ways. The Christian story takes up the story of Israel and sees in Jesus the one who lives in total trust of God, with no rebellion. It is through his life, death, and resurrection that Christians learn how to live in a most human and fulfilled way, trusting that God will be faithful to them in their needs, just as God was faithful to Jesus on the cross, raising him to new life in the resurrection.

Indeed, it is the resurrection of Jesus that provides hope that we will become partakers of the divine life. Through the incarnation, God has entered freely into creation and history, becoming fully human. The raising of Jesus from the dead—a bodily resurrection—means that the very "stuff" of creation is raised into the life of the Trinity. In this sense, Jesus is the "firstfruit" (1 Cor. 15:23), the "firstborn from the dead" (Col. 1:18; Rev. 1:5), and "the firstborn of many brothers and sisters" (Rom. 8:29), anticipating our destiny, which is nothing less than to be united in love with the God who created us.

For Reflection and Further Study

1. Original sin

The original sin is often recommitted or reenacted in the very way we explain it. Often, in response to the question "What is original sin?," people point to our first parents' disobedience. We get to blame someone else. We have been given this sinful baggage by the foolishness of Adam and Eve. In blaming them, however, we are like Adam in blaming Eve (Gen. 3:12), Eve in blaming the serpent (3:13), and the serpent who calls God a liar (3:4-5). We commit the original sin insofar as we think about it as something like a genetic inheritance in which we have played no role (just as a person has bad eyesight through no fault of her own).

According to the account of "the fall" in this chapter, original sin is fundamental to how we, as humans and as not God, invariably cast God as our competition. This competitive posture is the angle the serpent uses to tempt Eve to eat the forbidden fruit. "You certainly will not die! God knows well that when you eat of it your eyes will be opened and you will be like gods" (Gen. 3:4-5). The implication is that God wants the power and the fruit for himself. The fall in Genesis reveals that we humans have a deep desire to be like God without God's partnership. We want to take the prerogatives of God—"the knowledge of good and evil"—for ourselves, but separate from God (behind his back, so to say). The irony of this disposition toward God is that the divine plan, from the beginning, has been to share life with humanity and to bring creation to its fulfillment in nearness to God. Creation is good; the original sin casts a shadow (however small or large) over it.

Original sin as competition with God fits with a framework of Part 1, of the human good as moving toward fulfillment. As we struggle to become better (and struggle successfully with sin), we have to learn to see God differently. The nearer we are to God, the freer we are for happiness. This view seems to make little sense. In the world, the nearer we are to something else, the less free we are likely to be. Cooperation means we have to give up freedom and some portion of our lives that we might want for our own. However, because God is not another thing in the world, but its source, our nearness to God brings us greater freedom to become both ourselves and God's partners, simultaneously. "God looked at everything he had made, and found it very good" (Gen. 1:31). Creation is good. Our human capacity to become better with God requires the possibility that we become worse by trying to do without God. As "better" is movement toward fulfillment and as God is fullness of being, our becoming worse is a deprivation of the possibilities of our fulfillment. This is the vision of our gracious God: God is on our side, even when we are not.

This account of sin also gives us a more life-giving view of those we consider morally evil. Insofar as a human being exists, God is on the side of his existence. Life is good, pure and simple, and insofar as someone lives, she shares in the goodness of life—regardless of the things she does. The Christian tradition (following St. Augustine) sees evil as "privation." Consider a portion of Augustine's handbook of *Faith, Hope, and Love*.[8]

> What, after all, is anything we call evil except the privation of good? In animal bodies, for instance, sickness and wounds are nothing but the privation of health. When a cure is effected, the evils which were present (i.e., the sickness and the wounds) do not retreat and go elsewhere. Rather, they simply do not exist anymore. For such evil is not a substance; the wound or the disease is a defect of the bodily substance which, as a substance, is good. Evil, then, is an accident, i.e., a privation of that good which is called health. Thus, whatever defects there are in a soul are privations of a natural good. When a cure takes place, they are not transferred elsewhere but, since they are no longer present in the state of health, they no longer exist at all.[9]

As noted, this account of sin has interesting implications for how we see those we find irredeemably evil (such as a terrorist or murderer). "For good to be diminished is evil; still, however much it is diminished, something

---

8. Augustine, *Enchiridion: On Faith, Hope, and Love*, no. 4, trans. Albert Outler (1955), www.tertullian.org/fathers/augustine_enchiridion_02_trans.htm#C4.
9. Augustine, *Enchiridion*, no. 11.

must remain of its original nature as long as it exists at all."[10] That nature is God's creation, and it is good. On this point, we can say that one consequence of sin is that not only are we quick to see ourselves in competition with God but we are also quick to see God in competition with our enemies and evil ones. Evil is a challenge to us, but because God is fullness of being, evil is no threat to divine goodness. God makes goodness out of nothing.

Finally we come to a question for discussion: Genesis 1 is a story that proclaims the goodness of God's creation, especially the goodness of the creation of humanity. How do we hold onto the inherent goodness of all creation and the inherent goodness of humanity when we continue to see how poorly and carelessly we can treat the world and each other?

2. Providence, freedom, and the problem of evil

We have only scratched the surface with theological and practical quandaries pertaining to God's providence, human freedom, and the problem of evil. One resource that we have found both deep and readable, concise yet thorough, is the first section, headed "God," in Herbert McCabe's *God Matters*.[11] The *Catechism of the Catholic Church* offers a condensed discussion that can be helpful. (But as a condensed discussion it also opens up ancillary questions.)

Consider a section from the first part of the *Catechism* on creation.[12] A subsection on Divine Providence begins:

> Creation has its own goodness and proper perfection, but it did not spring forth complete from the hands of the Creator. The universe was created "in a state of journeying" (*in statu viae*) toward an ultimate perfection yet to be attained, to which God has destined it. We call "divine providence" the dispositions by which God guides his creation toward this perfection. (no. 302)

From this statement, the *Catechism* treats "primary and secondary causes," that is, a philosophical explanation of how God carries out the divine plan through human freedom. "Why would God do so?" is a theological question.

---

10. Augustine, *Enchiridion*, no. 12.

11. Herbert McCabe, *God Matters* (New York: Continuum, 1987).

12. *Catechism of the Catholic Church* (Vatican City: Libreria Editrice Vaticana, 1993), nos. 302-14, http://www.vatican.va/archive/ccc_css/archive/catechism/p1s2c1p4.htm.

Because the section is condensed (as is the nature of a catechism), this question can be easily missed. The answer has something to do with covenant and love: the divine plan is worked out through human freedom, so that human beings might "then fully become 'God's fellow workers' and co-workers for his kingdom" (no. 307).

The last part of this section is on "Providence and the scandal of evil" (nos. 309-14). It goes straight to the question, "Why did God not create a world so perfect that no evil could exist in it?" As the question is considered, notice the distinction made between physical and moral evils. Moral evil pertains to willful human acts, while physical evil includes suffering in the world such as the "destructive forces of nature." The section concludes:

> We firmly believe that God is master of the world and of its history.
> But the ways of his providence are often unknown to us. Only at
> the end, when our partial knowledge ceases, when we see God "face
> to face," will we fully know the ways by which—even through the
> dramas of evil and sin—God has guided his creation to that definitive
> sabbath rest for which he created heaven and earth. (no. 314)

This is an important conclusion. The "scandal of evil" is indeed a scandal because we have faith in a loving God and the goodness of God's creation. Amid the scandal—the mark against God's providence—Christians have reason to have faith because God's ultimate response to the evil of the world is not benign indifference, but the incarnation, to suffer the evil of the world as a way to overcome it.

CHAPTER 12

Incarnation

The sixth question in the section devoted to "The End of Man" in the *Baltimore Catechism* asks: "Why did God make you?" The succinct answer given is: "God made me to know Him, to love Him, and to serve Him in this world, and to be happy with Him forever in heaven."[1] We see in this answer the wonderful plan that God has for us—that we will ultimately be united with God. The previous chapter dealt with God's plan for humanity, a plan that demands trust on our part so that it will be brought to completion. We saw how Israel, a people chosen from among all peoples, and who were called to be light for the entire world, often responded to God's plan with distrust and even rebellion. We also saw how God's steadfast love continued in the face of this response. The first part of this chapter will focus upon how God's commitment to bring about God's plan was embodied in a partnership with Abraham, a person who was able to put such trust in God that he is named "Father of Faith." The second part of this chapter will focus upon how God ultimately brought about God's plan through the incarnation, whereby God became flesh in Jesus Christ.

Called to Be a Light

The story of the fall in the Garden of Eden is about humanity's inability to trust in God, but it is also the story about how God never compels, but continues to invite humanity into a relationship that depends upon God's

1. *Baltimore Catechism* (1891), reproduced in *The Catholic Primer* 2005, http://www
.boston-catholic-journal.com/baltimore_catechism.pdf.

graciousness. While the first man and woman could not trust in the Creator and his ways, Abraham stands as one who responds to God's invitation and is justifiably called the "Father of Faith." There are, indeed, many events in the life of Abraham that earn him this title. First, he is called by God to "go forth from your land, your relatives, and from your father's house to a land that I will show you" (Gen. 12:1). There are countless reasons for Abraham to decline this request. To leave his land and his relatives is to leave behind not only familiarity but also the security and safety that one's clan would bring. Abraham is also seventy-five years old, and it would not be surprising if Abraham told God that he was just too worn out at this point in his life to begin such an adventure. But he responds in freedom to God's request and trusts that somehow God will bring about the promises that God makes: "I will make of you a great nation, and I will bless you: I will make your name great, so that you will be a blessing" (12:2). Thus God makes a covenant with Abraham, promising him that his offspring will be as numerous as the stars in the sky (15:5) and that his descendants will be given the land of Canaan (15:18-21). And in the midst of all these events we are told, "Abram put his faith in the Lord" (15:6).

As the story of Abraham continues, it is difficult to figure out how God will be able to successfully fulfill God's promises to Abraham. After all, Abraham and his wife, Sarah, are very old and they still do not have a son. How can Abraham be the father of a great nation without any children in his advanced years? There is a marvelous story about the extent to which Abraham and Sarah will need to trust in God's promises—promises that seem too outlandish. They are visited by three strangers—who unbeknownst to Abraham are really God and two angels—by the oak of Mamre. Pleased with the wonderful hospitality that Abraham and Sarah have displayed, the mysterious stranger promises that when he returns about this time in the next year, Sarah will be with child. Sarah, hearing this from the tent, and realizing how old she is, begins to laugh. But the Lord says to Abraham: "Why did Sarah laugh and say, 'Will I really bear a child, old as I am?'" (Gen. 18:13). And then the Lord adds another thought—one that cuts to the heart of the matter—when he asks, "Is there anything too marvelous for the Lord to do?" (18:14). This is what Abraham must trust in—the marvelous power of God who is worthy of trust when trust seems foolish.

We are told that the Lord does for Abraham and Sarah what has been promised: "Sarah became pregnant and bore Abraham a son in his old age, at the set time that God had stated" (Gen. 21:2). But Abraham's faith in God and God's ways is put further to the test when he is asked by God to sacrifice the very son upon whom Abraham thought all the future rested. Yet Abraham follows God's commands and saddles his donkey and sets out with Isaac to the place of which God has told him. When they reach the place, Abraham builds an altar, arranges the wood on it, binds his son Isaac, and puts him on top of the wood of the altar. As Abraham takes the knife to slaughter his son, the angel of the Lord appears and stays his hand, saying, "Do not lay your hand on the boy. Do not do the least thing to him. For now I know that you fear God, since you did not withhold from me your son, your only one" (22:11–12).

As we saw in chapter 9, it is difficult to let go of our own plans and to trust in God's plan. No doubt, Abraham probably figured that God's promise of "descendants as countless as the stars of the sky and sands of the seashore" (Gen. 22:17) rested upon his son Isaac. And yet God now directs Abraham to offer up his only son. We could imagine Abraham asking himself, "What kind of plan is this?" It would make no sense to him, and we would not be surprised if Abraham were to cling to his own plan in the face of the crazy plan that God proposes. But Abraham is willing to let go of his own plan and embrace God's plan, willing to trust even though he cannot see evidence of it making sense.[2] This is why Abraham is called the "Father of Faith," for he puts his trust completely in God. As we will see again in the second part of this chapter when Jesus trusts completely in God as he dies on the cross, Abraham's trust in God proves to be warranted, for God is able to bring the future of Israel out of the near death of Isaac.[3]

Because Abraham is ready to hand over his son to God, he is able to receive him back from God. But this means, at the same time, that Isaac has seen his father's faith and thus has learned what it is to trust in God. This points to what is central to the story of Abraham: its effect upon his descendants, the Israelites.[4] Through Abraham, God gathers a people who trust freely in God and who begin to see as God sees. Through Abraham and his descendants, Israel, God is able to begin to bring about God's plan by bringing salvation to the entire world. In Israel, we might say, God's sal-

2. It is worth mentioning that Abraham does not have what might be termed "blind faith." His faith is founded on the assurances of God.

3. Given the widely attested practice of child sacrifice at the time of Abraham, this story could be understood as God asking Abraham to trust, not in the practice of his day, but in God who abhors this practice and desires that Abraham abandon it if he is to walk in the ways of God. In this case, Abraham would have had to place his trust in a God who has a different vision of what should happen to the firstborn son.

4. Lohfink, *Does God Need the Church?*, 63.

vation is made visible, for God finds in Israel a people who will freely enter into relationship with God so as to carry out God's plan. We have seen in chapter 11, however, that the partnership that God has with Israel is hindered by its mistrust and even rebellion toward God. Lohfink appropriately sums up the balance of God's steadfast love in the midst of Israel's infidelity:

> Israel is a society arising out of constantly renewed leading by God. Throughout its existence it is continually in danger; its faith is often sustained by only a few, and those few are frequently outsiders. God's cause always hangs by a thin thread. But the thread does not break. God's fidelity is equal to the weight of infidelity. God remains in the midst of the people.[5]

God's fidelity to Israel, and thus to the entire world to whom Israel is called to be a light,[6] is fulfilled in Jesus, the Word made flesh. He embodies the attitudes and actions of the "suffering servant" of Isaiah, placing his complete trust in God. This complete trust in God makes possible nothing less than the salvation of the entire cosmos so that God's plan for us can be brought to fruition.

Suffering Servant

There are four passages—often called the suffering servant songs—in Isaiah that deal with one who suffers greatly and is vindicated by God. The first passage (Isa. 42:1-4) describes the servant as God's "chosen one with whom I am well pleased." God has placed God's spirit upon him so that he will bring forth justice to the nations. He will faithfully bring about this justice, not by crying out or by shouting, but through the gentle persuasion of his own life. In the second passage (49:1-6), the servant reveals that he thought he was toiling in vain, but realizes that his trust in God continues to be his source of strength. He also comes to the realization that God will work through his lack of strength so that Israel will become a light to the nations in order that God's salvation will reach to the ends of the earth. The third song (50:4-9)

---

5. Lohfink, *Does God Need the Church?*, 106.

6. "It is too little, he says, for you to be my servant, to raise up the tribes of Jacob, and restore the survivors of Israel. I will make you a light to the nations, that my salvation may reach to the ends of the earth" (Isa. 49:6).

announces the suffering and rejection that the servant has had to endure from those who declare his guilt, but he continues to place his trust in God who affirms his innocence. The fourth passage (52:13–53:12) is the longest of the four songs. The song notes that the servant was spurned and avoided by all, a man of suffering, who knew pain. He was "like one from whom you turn your face, spurned" and held in no esteem (53:3). Yet his pain and suffering were borne for the guilty.

> Yet it was our pain that he bore, our sufferings he endured.
> We thought of him as stricken, struck down by God and afflicted.
> But he was pierced for our sins, crushed for our iniquity.
> He bore the punishment that makes us whole, by his wounds we were
>   healed.
> We had all gone astray like sheep, all following our own way;
> but the Lord laid upon him the guilt of us all. (53:4–6)

Although God's servant is treated harshly, he submits to his suffering "like a lamb led to slaughter" (Isa. 53:7). Even though this just and innocent person has had to endure such hardship, God's will is accomplished through him, bringing about the justification of the many. The song also declares that the servant, himself, will not be forgotten: "Because of his anguish he shall see the light; because of his knowledge, he shall be content" (53:11). Indeed, because he was willing to surrender himself to death, God will "give him his portion among the many" (53:12).

The New Testament sees the trials and vindication of the "suffering servant" of Isaiah fulfilled in Jesus. For the New Testament authors, the same God who acted to redeem the nations through the suffering servant has now acted to complete redemption through the suffering of Jesus in fulfillment of what Israel had already done in part.[7] We see, for instance, in Mark's gospel that Jesus, in a prophetic gesture that points to his imminent death, "took bread, said the blessing, broke it, and gave it to them and said, 'Take it; this is my body'" (Mark 14:22). Likewise, "He took a cup, gave thanks, and gave it to them, and they all drank from it. He said to them, 'This is my blood of the covenant, which will be shed for many'" (14:23–24). Both images of "breaking" and "shedding" point to Jesus's death, which is offered for the many. As Lohfink succinctly summarizes:

7. Lawrence Boadt, *Reading the Old Testament: An Introduction* (New York: Paulist Press, 1984), 428.

Thus we can say that according to Mark Jesus, during the ritual of the Passover meal, interpreted the broken bread and the red wine to the twelve disciples in terms of his imminent death. And when he handed the bread and wine to the twelve disciples he gave them, and Israel through them, a share in the power of his death. For this death is interpreted simultaneously as atonement for Israel, which had succumbed to sin and guilt, and as a renewal of the covenant of Sinai. But through this eschatological Israel the new salvation now definitively is to extend to the nations.[8]

What does this new salvation, offered for all nations, involve? First, we may point out that salvation has been part of God's plan from the beginning. Paul, in his Letter to the Ephesians, describes God's plan of salvation as something that God has freely chosen "before the foundation of the world" (Eph. 1:4). This plan originates "in love," because God "destined us for adoption to himself through Jesus Christ, in accord with the favor of his will" (1:5). At the heart of this plan is God becoming human in Jesus, for "in him we have redemption by his blood, the forgiveness of transgressions" (1:7). Through Jesus, God has made known to us the mystery of God's will, which is "to sum up all things in Christ, in heaven and on earth" (1:9-10).

Second, the Letter to the Ephesians points out that the culmination of this plan concerns "all things." This phrase "all things" (*panta* in Greek) suggests that salvation includes more than our souls,[9] and even more than just humanity. God's plan of salvation embraces all that has been created, the entire cosmos. One of the earliest texts in the New Testament is the Christological hymn about Christ, found in Paul's Letter to the Colossians. The hymn takes its texture, shape, and meaning from the Old Testament texts of wisdom literature. The hymn professes that Jesus, as the image (or icon) of the invisible God, is "the firstborn of all creation, for in him were created *all things* in heaven and on earth, the visible and the invisible, whether thrones or dominions or principalities or powers; *all things* were created through him and for him" (Col. 1:15-16). Further, Jesus "is before *all things*, and in him *all things* hold together" (1:17). As head of the body, the church, Jesus is the firstborn from the dead, and through him the fullness of grace dwells; it is through Jesus that God is able "to reconcile *all things* for him" (1:18-20).

---

8. Lohfink, *Does God Need the Church?*, 193.

9. Christians believe in an immortal soul, but also in the resurrection of the body. See 1 Corinthians 15:1-58.

In relation to all creation, this Christological hymn professes that Jesus is Lord of the cosmos: all things come about through him, all things cohere in him, and all things are reconciled in him. He is the beginning and the end, the Alpha and the Omega. He is the agent of both creation and redemption (re-creation). Just as Wisdom is described in the Old Testament, Christ is the artificer of all creation,[10] and he continues to be ever present to it, in ways that continue to permeate, penetrate, and pervade it.[11] The fullness of God (as the Wisdom of God) dwells in Christ, and Christ now dwells in the church as its head.[12]

A third implication of God's salvation through Jesus is that, while we still must live out the struggles—individual, social, and global—of life, ultimately we do not have to be afraid! Paul, in his Letter to the Romans, reminds us that all creation groans, as in labor pains, to be completed, and like all creation, we too "groan within ourselves as we wait for adoption [and] the redemption of our bodies" (Rom. 8:22-23). However, we know that the victory has been won over sin and death. Preface I of Easter in the Eucharistic liturgy reminds us that "by dying he destroyed our death, and by rising, restored our life."[13] So, Christians can live life with a certain freedom,

---

10. See, for instance, Proverbs 8:22-31, where Wisdom is present, accompanying God in all creation: "When he fixed the foundations of earth, then was I beside him as artisan" (8:29).

11. See, for instance, Sirach 24:1-31, where Wisdom is compared to trees and flowers and cinnamon that provide fragrances that permeate; to water that moves through the land, overflowing and channeling, seeping and penetrating; to mist that overlays everything; to a terebinth whose branches cover everything; and to a vine that twists and turns its way around all things. See also Wisdom 7:21-26, where Wisdom is described as "mobile beyond all motion," and as the breath of the power of God, the pure emanation of the glory of the Almighty, the aura of the might of God, the reflection of the eternal light, the spotless mirror of the power of God, and the image of God's goodness.

12. See, for instance, Sirach 24:7-8, where Wisdom seeks a dwelling place among Israel as the Law, the Torah. The Gospel of John reminds us that "The Word became flesh and made his dwelling among us" (John 1:14).

13. *The Roman Missal*, renewed by decree of the Most Holy Second Ecumenical Council of the Vatican, promulgated with the authority of Pope Paul VI and revised at the direction of Pope John Paul II, English translation according to the third typical edition, for use in Dioceses of the United States of America, approved by the United States Conference of Catholic Bishops and confirmed by the Holy See (Totowa, NJ: Catholic Book Publishing Co., 2011), 410. Preface I of Easter reads: "It is truly right and just, our duty and our salvation, at all times to acclaim you, O Lord, but at this time above all to laud you yet more gloriously, when Christ our Passover has been sacrificed. For he is the true Lamb who has taken away the sins of the world; by dying he destroyed our death, and by rising, restored our life. Therefore, overcome with paschal joy, every land, every people exults in your praise."

knowing that they have been redeemed by the God who created them out of love and who continues to draw "all things" to God in love.

Yet we know that our lives can be consumed with fear and anxiety about the future. This fear may come as a result of the awareness of our sinfulness—raising questions about our worthiness. But fear and anxiety about the future also can come about through a type of "cosmic anxiety," wherein we wonder about our significance—or insignificance—in the face of the billions of people who have lived throughout the centuries and the pure immensity of the universe that is so far beyond our understanding. In other words, is it audacious to believe that I matter within the vastness of the cosmos? Interestingly, Paul in his letters addressed a similar anxiety that his fellow Christians experienced. We mentioned one of these texts earlier but did not draw attention to this concern. The ancient hymn to Christ that Paul includes in his letter addressed to the people of Colossae makes reference to thrones, dominions, principalities, and powers (Col. 1:16). These are sometimes referred to as "elemental powers" or as celestial beings that were thought in pagan cultures to control the world.[14] The hymn proclaims that even these beings "were created through him and for him" (1:16). Paul notes later in this letter that Christ in "despoiling the principalities and the powers . . . made a public spectacle of them, leading them away in triumph by [the cross]" (2:15). This image of the elemental powers being defeated is likened to the public spectacle and triumph of a Roman emperor's victory parade where defeated enemies were displayed before the Roman people.[15] In other words, Paul is encouraging his fellow Christians to not be afraid of these elemental powers, for they no longer hold sway in their defeat.

There are other references to the fear that people had in the face of these elemental powers, but none more striking than in another ancient Christological hymn that Paul includes in his Letter to the Philippians. The context for the inclusion of this text is Paul's plea to the Philippians that they "do nothing out of selfishness or out of vainglory; rather humbly regard others as more important than yourselves" (Phil. 2:3). Paul encourages the Philippians to have the same mindset among themselves as Christ Jesus, "Who, though he was in the form of God, did not regard equality with God as something to be grasped. Rather he emptied himself, taking the form of a slave . . . becoming obedient to death, death on a cross" (2:6–8). In other words, the Philippians should embrace the humility of Christ and not be

14. *Catholic Study Bible*, footnote on Galatians 4:3, 1650.
15. *Catholic Study Bible*, footnote on Colossians 2:15, 1673.

thinking of their own greatness in relation to others.[16] As it continues, the hymn indicates that the trust Jesus has put in God will be rewarded—as we saw in the Suffering Servant of Isaiah—and God will greatly exalt him and "bestow upon him the name that is above every other name" (2:9). According to the hymn, this name has cosmic repercussions because now at the name of Jesus "every knee should bend, of those in heaven and on earth and under the earth, and every tongue confess that Jesus Christ is Lord, to the glory of God the Father" (2:10-11). This verse presupposes a three-tiered cosmos inhabited by elemental powers. But, rather than controlling the world, these elemental powers have been defeated and they are now paying homage to Jesus as Cosmic Lord, bending their knees before him and proclaiming with their tongues that he is Lord.

Conclusion

How might these ancient Christological hymns be relevant to us today? Surely, we do not think that we live in a three-tiered cosmos. We are aware that heaven does not exist above the clouds and that there is not a "world" within or under the earth. We also do not believe in elemental powers that control our lives.[17] But one thing we do have in common with people of ancient times is a certain "cosmic anxiety." While we may not be afraid of elemental powers, we might have questions about the meaningfulness of life, and we might be afraid about many things, such as terrorism, global warming, germs, political unrest, global instability, world hunger, etc. These fears can be crippling because we often feel so helpless to do anything that will eliminate them or keep them under control. In the face of these fears, the ancient Christological hymns can speak a word of hope to us: do not be afraid! Although we need to continue to live out our personal response to God's plan, this plan has been brought to completion through Christ. The victory over sin and death has been won. There is no clearer text that summarizes the confidence that people

16. It is noteworthy that in contrast to Adam who is tempted by the serpent "to be like God," Christ Jesus, the new Adam, does not regard equality with God as something to be grasped. Not willing to trust, Adam in Genesis wants to "grasp" what God is willing to give freely, while Christ Jesus is willing to empty himself to the point of death on a cross because he puts his total and absolute trust in God.

17. There are people, however, who take more seriously than others the reading of horoscopes, which use the positions of the sun, moon, and planets—which were thought to be gods in ancient times—to ascertain certain relationships and events in life.

should have in this victory than these words of Paul when he writes about the indomitable love of Christ:

> What then shall we say to this? If God is for us, who can be against us? He who did not spare his own Son but handed him over for us all, how will he not also give us everything else along with him? Who will bring a charge against God's chosen ones? It is God who acquits us. Who will condemn? It is Christ Jesus who died, rather, was raised, who also is at the right hand of God, who indeed intercedes for us. What will separate us from the love of Christ? Will anguish, or distress, or persecution, or famine, or nakedness, or peril, or the sword? . . . No, in all these things we conquer overwhelmingly through him who loved us. For I am convinced that neither death, nor life, nor angels, nor principalities, nor present things, nor future things, nor powers, nor height, nor depth, nor any other creature will be able to separate us from the love of God in Christ Jesus our Lord. (Rom. 8:31-39)

God's plan for us existed "before the foundation of the world." As a plan that is directed toward our welfare, not our woe, it has been brought to fruition through the suffering, death, and resurrection of Jesus, who willingly trusted in God's plan like the "suffering servant" of Isaiah. This plan still calls for our personal response because God will never coerce or force us; rather, God is always looking for partners who will freely fall in love with God and will freely embrace seeing as God sees. This might seem to be an insurmountable challenge if we were to try to accomplish this alone. However, God has given us another advocate, the Holy Spirit, who lives within us, enabling us within the church and within our own personal call and response to God's plan.

For Reflection and Further Study

1. God's plan revisited
Many, including some great medieval theologians such as Thomas Aquinas, think of the incarnation, God's plan for salvation in Christ, as a result of the fall of our first parents. If Adam and Eve had not sinned, then the incarnation would not have had to be. As an aside, this idea that the incarnation is a

response to the fall avoids a "Plan B" status because of God's foreknowledge. The incarnation is not needed to complete God's perfection of creation. Yet, even though it is a remedy for sin, the incarnation is part of the plan from the beginning. In short, the incarnation is necessitated by sin. However, this view is not unanimous. Others, especially most contemporary theologians but also the likes of St. Albert Magnus (Thomas Aquinas's teacher), think differently. The incarnation has been part of God's plan from the beginning and would have happened even without the fall. No doubt the incarnation is a remedy for the intrusion of sin into creation, but it also reveals to us what it is to be God and what it is to be human. That is, God in Jesus Christ unifies the divine and human; he embodies in himself and shares with us the fulfillment of human life in partnership with God.

This disagreement is a matter of theological speculation; it does not have to be settled. But the second view, we think, is preferable because (1) it offers an important insight about the incarnate unity of God in human life and (2) it provides this insight while including the idea that the incarnation is also a response to sin. In any case, consider how Thomas Aquinas deals with the question in the *Summa theologica* III, "Whether, if man had not sinned, God would have become incarnate?"[18]

2. Cosmic anxiety

Years ago, each of us would conjure up cosmic anxiety among our students during the first class period in moral theology. (We have since given up the habit.) We would ask, "Why are you here?" Someone would respond, "To fulfill a requirement." Sometimes, answers would take a more noble turn: "To learn something." In either case, we would follow up every answer with another question.

Why do you have to fulfill a requirement?
To graduate.
Why do you need to graduate?
To get a job.
Why do you need a job? Why do you need a house and car? Why do you need a family?

---

18. *Summa theologica* III, question 1, article 3. This section of the *Summa* can be found at http://www.newadvent.org/summa/4001.htm.

Eventually questions would get to a "meaning of life" level, and answers would cease. We caused cosmic anxiety because few of us today are able to articulate how our everyday matters of life are connected to the meaning of things. If you are interested in this disconnection as a sociological problem, we recommend Douglas Porpora's *Landscapes of the Soul: The Loss of Moral Meaning in American Life*.[19] We mention Porpora's work to underline a point. Lurking behind our busyness with social media and our sometimes frantic efforts to make something of ourselves, there is a cosmic anxiety that, in the big picture, who we are and what we do does not matter to anyone.

That said, take another look at Colossians 1:15-20 and Philippians 2:5-11. As you think of life, what fears or anxieties occupy your thoughts or consume you? Are these fears about personal unworthiness? About meaningfulness in life? About problems and issues facing the world? How might the ancient Christological hymns respond to these fears and anxieties?

3. The victory is won, but . . .

Consider Romans 8:22-24 (preceding the portion of Romans 8 cited at the end of the chapter):

> We know that all creation is groaning in labor pains even until now; and not only that, but we ourselves, who have the firstfruits of the Spirit, we also groan within ourselves as we wait for adoption, the redemption of our bodies. For in hope we were saved. Now hope that sees for itself is not hope. For who hopes for what one sees?

Through his suffering, death, and resurrection, Jesus has conquered sin and death. However, we still encounter the effects of sin and death in our lives, and we ourselves still need to live in a way that responds to God's call. How do you reconcile the experience that God's reign "has come near" but is "not yet"?

19. Douglas Porpora, *Landscapes of the Soul: The Loss of Moral Meaning in American Life* (New York: Oxford University Press, 2001).

CHAPTER 13

Church

W hen I (Jim) was young, if someone had asked me to draw "the church," I would have drawn a building. Today, most people would draw a group of people. The Second Vatican Council (1962-65) was at the heart of this changed perception and identification of the church as the people of God.[1] Gathered by God, inaugurated and equipped with the gifts of Jesus, and sanctified and guided by the Holy Spirit, the church has received the mission of proclaiming and establishing the kingdom of God among all peoples, and it is, on earth, the seed and beginning of that kingdom (*Lumen gentium*, nos. 4 and 5). *Lumen gentium* (no. 6) describes the church as a sheepfold that acts as the entrance to Christ, as a flock that is led and brought to pasture by Christ the Good Shepherd, as a farm or field that has been planted by God and whose lifeline is Christ the true vine, as God's building that is built upon the apostles, as a holy temple that is the dwelling place of God, as the New Jerusalem of which we are a part like living stones, as our mother who produces numerous offspring, and as the spotless spouse whom "Christ loved . . . and for whom he delivered himself up that he might sanctify her" (Eph. 5:26).

To complement all these rich and varied images of the church, *Lumen gentium* reminds us that the church is on a pilgrimage as in a foreign land, journeying as in exile as it seeks and is concerned about "those things that are above" (no. 7). Rather than understanding this last phrase as something abstract and otherworldly, *Lumen gentium* states that Christ was sent by the Father "to bring good news to the poor," "to seek and to save what was lost" (Luke 4:18; 19:10) and, similarly, the church "encompasses with its love all

---

1. See *Dogmatic Constitution on the Church* (*Lumen gentium*), in *The Documents of Vatican II*, ed. Walter M. Abbott, trans. Joseph Gallagher (Piscataway, NJ: America Press, 1966).

those who are afflicted by human infirmity and it recognizes in those who are poor and who suffer, the likeness of its poor and suffering founder" (no. 8). These brief references to the opening articles of *Lumen gentium* remind us that the church has been gathered by God and that it continues to journey in this earthly life toward the end of time, when the mysteries of the Lord, which it now bears, will be revealed in the fullness of light. This chapter will focus on three aspects of the church: it is gathered to be *one* and to be *holy* as it journeys in its *missionary service*.

The Church Is One

The New Testament contains many stories that illustrate that the church is called to be one people, especially in relation to two situations: the relationship between Jews and Gentiles, and the relationship between the rich and the poor. Stories about the relationship between Jews and Gentiles permeate the entire New Testament. Simply put, all the early disciples of Jesus were Jews, including St. Paul who became the "Apostle to the Gentiles." A question arose about what should happen with those Gentiles who wanted to become followers of Jesus: Should they have to become Jews first? After all, Gentiles, as non-Jews, were considered to be unclean, and association with them would render a Jew ritually unclean. We might think, for instance, of the tax collectors and how they were shunned in Jesus's day in Jewish society. While they may have been ruthless in their ways of collecting taxes, the chief problem was that they worked for and associated with the Romans, who were Gentiles. This is why so many Jews were outraged that Jesus would eat with these tax collectors! Of course, one solution, advocated by some, was to make the Gentiles become Jews, but this would entail circumcision for males and the need to follow the Mosaic practices of food laws and ablutions. What to do?

The Acts of the Apostles gives us an account of the decision made at the Council of Jerusalem (Acts 15:1-35). The need for this council arose because some of the Jewish Christian brothers had come from Jerusalem to Antioch and had begun to preach that "unless you are circumcised according to the Mosaic practice, you cannot be saved" (15:1). Paul and Barnabas debated the brothers on this point, and it was decided that they, with some others, would travel to Jerusalem to talk with the apostles and presbyters about this question. Once in Jerusalem, some from the party of the Pharisees who had become believers said, "It is necessary to circumcise them and direct them to observe the Mosaic Law" (15:5). However, after much debate, Peter spoke:

> My brothers, you are well aware that from early days God made his choice among you that through my mouth the Gentiles would hear the word of the gospel and believe. And God, who knows the heart, bore witness by granting them the Holy Spirit just as he did us. He made no distinction between us and them, for by faith he purified their hearts. Why, then, are you now putting God to the test by placing on the shoulders of the disciples a yoke that neither our ancestors nor we have been able to bear? On the contrary, we believe that we are saved through the grace of the Lord Jesus, in the same way as they. (15:7-11)

One might think that a council such as this would have ended the debate, but we have evidence in the New Testament that the issue continued to bedevil the early church. Mark, writing some thirty-five years after the Council of Jerusalem, is still dealing with the question about the integration of Jews and Gentiles. He is writing in Rome for a community composed of a majority of Gentile Christians, but with a smaller number of conservative Jewish Christians. Eating together becomes a huge problem when the conservative Jewish Christian members of the community insist on seeing the Gentile Christians as "unclean" and claim that they must follow the Mosaic practices of diet and ablutions. Mark, in his gospel, deals with this problem in several ways. One way is to remind the community—both Jews and Gentiles—of the words that Jesus had spoken to his disciples: "Do you not realize that everything that goes into a person from outside cannot defile, since it enters not the heart but the stomach and passes out into the latrine?" (Mark 7:18-19). Interestingly, Mark—to make his point—punctuates the words of Jesus with his own editorial comment when he adds: "Thus Jesus declared all foods clean" (15:19)!

In addition to using the words of Jesus to address this problem, Mark also organizes stories in his gospel so that the arrangement of the stories also tells a story, one that is more encompassing than any individual story on its own. We turn to the two stories of the multiplication of the loaves and fish in Mark's gospel as an illustration of how he arranges his stories to address the continued tension between Jews and Gentiles in his community. If we were to look at a map, we would see that the first story of the multiplication of the loaves and fish (Mark 6:34-44) occurs in Jewish territory near the Sea of

Galilee and that the second story of the multiplication of the loaves and fish (Mark 8:1-9) occurs in Gentile territory near the Sea of Galilee. We could also point to the differences in the stories. In the first story (Jewish side), there are five loaves and two fish, 5,000 men fed, and twelve wicker baskets full of fragments. In addition, the people are organized to sit in groups of 100s and 50s on the green grass. In the second story (Gentile side), there are seven loaves and a few fish, 4,000 people fed, and seven baskets full of fragments. Further, we are told that the people have come from a great distance and have been there for three days.

The numbers in the first story are numbers that we would associate with Jews: five alludes to the Pentateuch (the five Books of the Law at the beginning of the Bible) and twelve alludes to the twelve sons of Jacob and the twelve tribes of Israel (and even the twelve apostles, the new Israel).[2] In addition, the reference to the groups organized in 100s and 50s recalls when Moses chose officers to rule the people by thousands, hundreds, fifties, and tens (Exod. 18:21, 25). The green grass is an allusion to, among many Old Testament passages, Psalm 23:1-2: "The Lord is my shepherd . . . in green pastures he makes me lie down." Other details in the (Jewish) multiplication story include the reference to men (*andres*), because only men were counted in the Jewish assemblies, and the description of the basket as a *wicker* basket, which was a basket unique to the Jews.

For the second story, in Gentile territory near the Sea of Galilee,[3] four alludes to the four corners of the world, and seven is an allusion to the seventy nations that make up the entire world. It also alludes to the situation described in the Acts of the Apostles (6:1-7) when the apostles settled the problem of fair distribution of food to the Gentile Christian widows and orphans by appointing seven deacons, all of whom were Gentiles (Stephen, Philip, Prochorus, etc.). The mention of being there for three days recalls a rather obscure story from the Book of Joshua (9:3-27), when Joshua is charged with wiping out the inhabitants of the land of Canaan. The Gibeonites, realizing that they will be killed, pack up their belongings and move away to a far distance. At the appropriate time they approach Joshua and the Israelites and are not killed because Joshua is fooled into

2. The setting for this story is clearly in Jewish territory near the Sea of Galilee, where Jesus has just healed a woman who has been hemorrhaging for *twelve* years, and where he has just raised the *twelve*-year-old daughter of a *synagogue official*.

3. The setting for this story is clearly in Gentile territory near the Sea of Galilee because Jesus has moved from Tyre, where he healed the daughter of a Syrophoenician woman, and went by way of Sidon into the district of the Decapolis—Greek for "the ten cities."

believing that they are not inhabitants of this land, but wayfarers who have come from a great distance. They feast together for three days and make a treaty. At this point the Gibeonites reveal their true identity, but Joshua cannot kill them because he has just made the treaty—so he takes them as slaves! Other details in the (Gentile) multiplication story include the reference to counting people (*anthrōpoi*), rather than the Jewish way of just counting men (*andres*), and there is no mention of the basket unique to Jewish people.

Is it just a coincidence that there are two similar stories with some differences? Or did Mark arrange these stories with a purpose in mind? If so, what might this all mean? What might he be trying to teach his Christian community that lived in the midst of the Jewish-Gentile tension? We could look at the concluding biblical passage of this arrangement of stories for an answer that indicates that Mark did have a purpose in mind.

> [The disciples] had forgotten to bring bread, and they had only one loaf with them in the boat. He enjoined them, "Watch out, guard against the leaven of the Pharisees and the leaven of Herod." They concluded among themselves that it was because they had no bread. When he became aware of this he said to them, "Why do you conclude that it is because you have no bread? Do you not yet understand or comprehend? Are your hearts hardened? Do you have eyes and not see, ears and not hear? And do you not remember, when I broke the five loaves for the five thousand, how many wicker baskets full of fragments you picked up?" They answered him, "Twelve." "When I broke the seven loaves for the four thousand, how many full baskets of fragments did you pick up?" They answered him, "Seven." He said to them, "Do you not understand?" (Mark 8:14-21)

It is interesting that the very next story that Mark includes is the story of the healing of a blind man (8:22-26)! What is it that Mark wanted his community "to see"? Well, Mark's community would not have been large, and, with the divisions in his community, we surmise that the Jewish Christians would not eat with the Gentile Christians. This is extremely problematic when we realize that, in the early church, the Eucharist was celebrated as part of the meal. This meant that Mark's community was not united around the Eucharist, but was divided. In this story, the disciples are befuddled because they have only one loaf. But that is exactly the point that Mark is trying to make to his divided community: we need only one loaf for the one Eucharist because we are one Body in Christ. Mark makes this point to his community through his arrangement of stories in the genre of gospel writing. Paul, on the other hand, in the genre of letter writing, made the same point decades earlier—perhaps more clearly—when he wrote: "There is neither Jew nor Greek, there is neither slave nor free person, there is not male and female; for you are all one in Christ Jesus" (Gal. 3:28).[4] Both of them—Mark the evangelist and Paul the apostle—were concerned about one thing: the unity of the one Body in Christ.

The New Testament is concerned not only with the divisions in the church that come about through the dichotomy between Jews and Gentiles, males and females, and slaves and free persons but also with the injustices that are caused because of the disparity of wealth in the community. In his first letter to the people of Corinth, Paul begins a section of his letter by addressing such a concern. He has heard that when the Corinthians meet as a church, divisions exist among them. He declares from the very introduction of this issue that he does "not praise the fact that your meetings are doing more harm than good" (1 Cor. 11:17-18). Paul describes what he has heard: when people gather, each carries on with his or her own supper. The result is that "one goes hungry while another gets drunk" (11:21). Remember that, in the early church, Christians—in places like Corinth—would gather together in "house churches," where they would share a meal in a manner that we might liken to "potluck dinners." During the course of the meal, the Eucharist would be celebrated by offering and sharing bread and wine transformed into Christ's body and blood.

Paul is disappointed because the self-centered actions of the richer members of the community exclude the poor, treating them with contempt and making them feel ashamed that they have so little (1 Cor. 11:22). This happens even in the face of going through the Eucharistic actions. Paul's judgment on this type of gathering is that "when you meet in one place, then, it is not to eat the Lord's supper" (11:20). Why does Paul write this? In his view, the richer members, through their neglect of the poorer members, are

4. See also Romans 10:12—"For there is no distinction between Jew and Greek; the same Lord is Lord of all, enriching all through him"; 1 Corinthians 12:13—"For in one Spirit we were all baptized into one body, whether Jews or Greeks, slaves or free persons, and we were given to drink of one Spirit"; and Colossians 3:11—"Here there is not Greek and Jew, circumcision and uncircumcision, barbarian, Scythian, slave, free; but Christ is all in all." (While the focus in this section of the chapter has been on the relations between Jews and Gentiles, notice that these passages in Mark and Paul are directed also against divisions between male and female, and slaves and free persons.)

being selfish. This is, of course, the exact opposite of what is at the heart of the Eucharist, which is the selfless offering of Christ for others. Indeed, Paul recounts this very act of Christ's sacrifice as a justification for his judgment on the rich people of Corinth:

> For I received from the Lord what I also handed on to you, that the Lord Jesus, on the night he was handed over, took bread, and after he had given thanks, broke it and said, "This is my body that is for you. Do this in remembrance of me." In the same way also the cup, after supper, saying, "This cup is the new covenant of my blood. Do this, as often as you drink it, in remembrance of me." For as often as you eat this bread and drink this cup, you proclaim the death of the Lord until he comes. (11:23–26)

Paul understands that Jesus's body is broken for us and his blood is poured out for us, an embodiment of the loving sacrifice he makes for us: "No one has greater love than this, to lay down one's life for one's friends" (John 15:13). Following the example of Christ, the Corinthians are called to be of service to those in need; they are called to "proclaim the death of the Lord" through their sacrifice for others. In doing so, they will embrace the paschal mystery of dying to themselves and uniting themselves to Christ's sufferings through their service in order to rise with him to new life.

Today, parish communities might not struggle to unite Jews and Gentiles, but they continue to be challenged to include rather than to exclude those on the margins: the economically poor, immigrants and refugees, those who are physically and mentally challenged or diminished, those who feel excluded because of divorce, people of different sexual orientations, those in assisted-living situations and nursing homes, and even those who live farther away, such as needier people in a particular diocese or another part of our country or our world. Parishes have risen to the challenge: by building ramps and elevators to provide easier access to worship spaces; by joining with poorer "sister parishes" in other parts of their diocese and world; by sponsoring and assisting immigrants and refugees; by providing winter shelters for the homeless; by organizing rides for the sick and elderly who might not have other means to attend the Eucharist, the sacrament of reconciliation, and communal celebrations of anointing of the sick; by hosting divorced and remarried groups; and by outreach programs for those who have drifted away from the church. All of these efforts—significant, but seemingly insufficient given the needs of our world—bear witness to the importance of working continually in service so that our voices will be joined to Jesus's prayer "that they may all be one, as you, Father, are in me and I in you" (John 17:21).

The Church Is Holy

The many and varied actions of the people of God that promote unity are closely connected to the church's call to be holy. St. Teresa of Avila reminds us of the connection between action and holiness when she says that there is no better crucible for testing holiness than compassion. Rightly so, we often associate holiness with people like the apostles St. Peter, St. Paul, and St. Mary Magdalene, early church fathers such as St. John Chrysostom, St. Augustine, and St. Jerome, saints of the Middle Ages such as St. Teresa of Avila, St. Francis of Assisi, St. Ignatius of Loyola, and St. Thomas Aquinas, and more modern saints such as St. John XXIII and St. John Paul II. It is easy to see them as examples of what it is to be holy and saintly.

Here in Emmitsburg, Maryland, we are fortunate to have an example of "saintly" holiness in the first American-born saint, St. Elizabeth Ann Seton (1774–1821), who was canonized on September 14, 1975. She founded the first American congregation of sisters, the Sisters of Charity of St. Joseph, and began St. Joseph Academy and Free School, the beginning of Catholic education in the United States. More recently, we are blessed to be touched by another inspiring person who walked this ground of Emmitsburg in the person of Fr. Stanley Rother, who is the first United States martyr. He was beatified[5] at a Mass on September 23, 2017, in Oklahoma City. Father Rother studied at Mount St. Mary's Seminary and was ordained a priest in 1963. After serving in parishes in his home diocese for five years, Father Rother traveled to Oklahoma City's mission in Santiago Atitlán, Guatemala, to serve the Tzutuhil people. Because he grew up in farming country, he was able to be of assistance to the poor people who tried to scrape a living from the land. Interestingly, although he struggled to master Latin in the seminary, Father Rother translated the New Testament into the Tzutuhil dialect, which is known to be one of the most difficult languages to learn.[6]

---

5. Beatification is the step before canonization. Beatification is conducted under the authority of the Pope, which allows the person to be publicly venerated, usually at the local or regional level.

6. Tom Gallagher, "A Story of What It Means to Be a Pastor," *National Catholic Reporter*, August 9, 2010.

Father Rother served in Guatemala at a difficult time of political turmoil when people were being kidnapped, tortured, and murdered. After witnessing a kidnapping, he wrote,

> I realized that I had just witnessed a kidnapping of someone that we had gotten to know and love and were unable to do anything about it. They had his mouth covered, but I can still hear his muffled screams for help. As I got back to the rectory I got a cramp in my back from the anger I felt that this friend was being taken off to be tortured for a day or two and then brutally murdered for wanting a better life and more justice for his pueblo.[7]

Seven months later (July 28, 1981), Father Rother was shot to death in the rectory of his mission church. At his friends' insistence, he had briefly returned to the United States when his name appeared on the death list, but after a week of prayer and contemplation at Mount St. Mary's he decided to return to his flock. As he told the rector of that time, Fr. Harry Flynn (who is now the archbishop emeritus of St. Paul-Minneapolis), "If I speak out, they will kill me. If I remain silent, what kind of pastor would I be?"[8] Day after day, Father Rother had celebrated the Eucharist, raising the chalice and saying, "Take this, all of you, and drink from it, for this is the chalice of blood . . . which will be poured out for you." In his martyrdom, he conformed himself completely to Christ, willing to lay down his life for his friends.[9]

In addition to the story of this priest-martyr, the church is also filled with examples of holiness among its most unknown and unheralded members. I am most inspired and encouraged to strive for holiness in my own life when at St. Bernadette Parish, during the first Sunday of the month, married couple after married couple stand up and announce the date of their anniversary and the number of years that they have been married. The announcements of "Two years on the fifteenth of the month!" and "Five years on the third of the month!" are met with applause for these married couples who have only begun their journey of becoming one. There is greater applause for those who announce, "Twenty-five years on the thirti-

7. Stanley Rother, "Letter from a Priest," made available by William L. Wipfler, Director of the Office of Human Rights, National Council of Churches (January 5, 1981).

8. Gallagher, "A Story of What It Means to Be a Pastor."

9. John Rosengren, "Father Stan Rother: A Martyr's Courage," *U.S. Catholic*, August 2006, 47.

eth!" and "Thirty years on the twelfth!" for we know that they have learned what it means to be together "in good times and in bad times, in sickness and in health." But there is a sense of reverence and awe when more elderly couples stand and—with justifiable pride—announce "Fifty years on the sixth!" and "Sixty-two years on the eighteenth!" We recognize that their holiness is radiated through a commitment over time of mutual service and sacrifice for each other and for their children and grandchildren, their friends and neighbors, their fellow parishioners and those in need. Their lives tell the stories of people who have, over the years, been shaped by God's Word, the liturgical action of the sacraments, and the service that they have provided for those in need. Although they are still flawed and sinful people, these experiences have conformed them to be more Christlike, helping them to see as God sees. Most likely, they will not be canonized as official saints in the church, but their lives provide us with concrete examples of charity and justice.

I (Jim) think of my father as an example of one who will never be canonized but who served as an illustration of what it is to be holy. He and my mother were married for fifty-four years. They both, of course, had their faults, but they were good people. My dad prided himself in looking younger than his years, and this occasionally got him into trouble. Once when he had taken my mother to a doctor's visit, he was chatting with the two receptionists while my mother was meeting with the doctor. They told him that they had been talking about him and noticed how much care he took of his *mother*. My dad responded, "Well, you do what you can do." Unfortunately for my dad, my mother was coming around the corner in her wheelchair and had overheard both the receptionists' comments and his reply!

This type of slip-up, however, does not count much within the larger context of things. Over the last seven years of her life, my mother was unable to walk. With assistance, she was able to transfer from her wheelchair to a chair in the living room, to the toilet in the bathroom, and to the seat in the car. She needed assistance about five times a night to use the toilet, and my father dutifully helped her day after day, week after week, month after month, year after year. And then he went to work, putting in a full day after having to wake up five times each night. One time when I was home for a visit, after my father had helped my mother get into bed, we were sitting in the living room together. I looked at him and asked him how he managed to keep doing all this. He said, "Well, what can you do?" Because I know him, I understand that he did not mean, "Hey, what can you do? I'm trapped." Rather, he meant, "What else can you do when you have been married to someone for over fifty years, and over all these years we have become one?" This is holiness in the concrete; it is love and compassion that passes the crucible for testing holiness.

The Church Is Missionary

The Second Vatican Council reminded us that, as the people of God, we are each called to a life of holiness.[10] As a people who have been gathered by God to be the Body of Christ, the church, we continue to be on a missionary journey. We have been conformed to Christ in baptism, and on our life journey as Christians we are called to become ever more closely conformed to him so that, in the world, we can be Christ—salt for the earth and light for the world. As we continue on this journey, we can learn to see with new eyes, recognizing the presence of Jesus in new and surprising ways.

Think, for instance, of the story of the disciples on the road to Emmaus (Luke 24:13-35) and how they learn to "recognize" Jesus in different ways. Certainly, the story indicates some more "traditional" ways in which we come to see Jesus on our journey: the Word ("Were not our hearts burning within us while he spoke to us on the way and opened the scriptures to us?"); the Eucharistic bread and wine ("While he was with them at table, he took bread, said the blessing, broke it, and gave it to them. With that their eyes were opened and they recognized him"); and the community ("Where two or more are gathered together in my name, there am I in the midst of them"). This makes sense to us, because we would expect to find Christ in his Word, in the Eucharist under the form of bread and wine, and in his Body, the church. But this story also contains a "nontraditional" way for us to come to encounter and recognize Jesus.

It is clear that the two disciples on the road to Emmaus would never have "seen" Jesus if they had not done something else: they welcomed the stranger. This gesture of hospitality is what made the recognition of Jesus possible. Along similar lines, Matthew's gospel reminds us that we can come to "see" Jesus in the hungry, the thirsty, the naked, the ill, and the imprisoned: "Whatever you did for one of these least brothers and sisters of mine, you did for me" (Matt. 25:40). Journeying with the one in whom we have

---

10. "Strengthened by so many and such great means of salvation, all the faithful, whatever their condition of state, are called by the Lord—each in his own or her own way—to that perfect holiness by which the Father himself is perfect" (*Lumen gentium*, article 11).

been baptized continues to give us new sight so that we can complete our mission in the church and world.

The Second Vatican Council continually speaks of baptism as the source of all Christian service. It is the source of all Christians' participation in the threefold mission of Christ as priest, prophet, and king. To reinforce the idea that this is not a call reserved only for priests and religious, *Lumen gentium* reiterates this teaching specifically in relation to laity, stating that, by baptism, laity are in their own way made sharers in priestly, prophetic, and kingly functions of Christ, carrying out their own part in the mission of the whole Christian people with respect to the church and the world (nos. 10–13). While distinguishing between the common priesthood of the faithful and the ministerial or hierarchal priesthood (no. 10), *Lumen gentium* states that all the faithful, whatever their condition or state, are called by the Lord, each in his or her own way, to a life of perfect holiness (no. 11).

Dedicated to Christ and anointed by the Spirit, the baptized exercise their priestly ministry in their particular way by offering all their work as a spiritual sacrifice: their prayer and apostolic works, their married and family life, their daily work, their mental and physical recreation, and even life's troubles as they are patiently borne (no. 34). In the prophetic office, the baptized members of the common priesthood exercise their ministry with the testimony of their daily social and family life. This work is understood as evangelization, for the laity carry forth the message of Christ through their words and the witness of their lives in the ordinary worldly situations of life. They are called to let the power of the gospel shine through their daily social and family life (no. 35). In the kingly office, the baptized members of the common priesthood are called to spread the kingdom of God, particularly in the secular world, "so that the world may be penetrated with the Spirit of Christ" (no. 35). This is the principal role of the laity: penetrating the world with the spirit of Christ so that the world will more effectively attain its purpose in justice, in love, and in peace. Specifically, this will entail such efforts as working for a more equitable distribution of the world's goods and improving secular structures and conditions that are sinful and unjust. Through the activities of those baptized into Christ, the whole of human society will be enlightened by the saving light of Christ (no. 35).

Conclusion

The people of God are gathered in the Eucharist so that they may conform themselves more deeply to Christ, in whom they have been baptized. Not only are the gifts of bread and wine changed into the Body of Christ, but those who are gathered are transformed more closely to Christ so that they can be Christ in the world. It should come as no surprise, then, for Christians to hear words to this effect as the Eucharist concludes.

> O God, who have willed us that we be partakers in the one Bread and the one Chalice, grant us, we pray, so to live that, made one in Christ, we may joyfully bear fruit for the salvation of the world. (Prayer after Communion, Fifth Sunday in Ordinary Time)[11]

Having become Christ, they are to be Christ, sent on mission: "Go in peace, glorifying the Lord by your life."

For Reflection and Further Study

1. The church is one

The Decree on Ecumenism (*Unitatis redintegratio*) of Vatican II begins by stating that a divided church "contradicts the will of Christ, scandalizes the world, and damages the holy cause of preaching the Gospel to every creature."[12] This chapter also gave examples of divisions within the early church—specifically the divisions between Jewish Christians and Gentile Christians and between the rich and the poor—and ways that the church worked to overcome this disunity. Consider the problem of church division on two levels. First, consider the variety of documents and a variety of churches on the United States Conference of Catholic Bishops website under

11. *The Roman Missal*, renewed by decree of the Most Holy Second Ecumenical Council of the Vatican, promulgated with the authority of Pope Paul VI and revised at the direction of Pope John Paul II, English translation according to the third typical edition, for use in Dioceses of the United States of America, approved by the United States Conference of Catholic Bishops and confirmed by the Holy See (Totowa, NJ: Catholic Book Publishing Co., 2011).

12. Vatican II, *Unitatis redintegratio* (Vatican City: Libreria Editrice Vaticana, 1964), no. 1, www.vatican.va/archive/hist_councils/ii_vatican_council/documents/vat-ii_decree_19641121 _unitatis-redintegratio_en.html.

"Ecumenical and Interreligious Affairs."[13] Second, think of something that your local parish or church can do or has done to become more hospitable or welcoming to some group of people. What group might you identify that may feel alienated by or isolated from the church today? What steps might a local parish or diocese take to overcome this disunity?

2. The church is holy

The chapter claims that everyone is called to a life of holiness and that holiness is best measured by compassion. One common problem when thinking about "holiness" is that, in our modern world, we tend to emphasize only personal or private matters—like purity of heart. Do you think holiness is something that is interior, or should it have an outward manifestation? Do you think holiness is a characteristic of a select few in the church or the call that should be embraced by everyone? How, concretely, do you think that you are called to a life of holiness? Can you think of people you know or are familiar with who demonstrate holiness (measured by compassion)?

In discussions on this topic, over the years, we have tumbled into some pitfalls. Conversations tend toward thinking about only individuals. Name a holy person? The answers go straight to extraordinary people like Mother Teresa or Bishop Desmond Tutu. But is holiness that scarce? Isn't everyone called to holiness? With this question the answers often shift to how we as individuals can be nice to people in our school, neighborhood, or workplace. Here, we don't do anything different, but do things in a different, more affable way. Niceness and random acts of kindness are wonderful, but in associating these with holiness we are stretching the idea of sanctity pretty thin. Consider approaching the question in a different framework—different but no less difficult to achieve. Holiness in the church is supposed to be shared. This is why ordinary people gather to worship—to be gathered by God to be made into a holy people and to be sent forth from worship to "Go in peace, glorifying the Lord by your life." So here are some new questions: By what means can communities as a whole be holy? Or better, how can each of us—in ways appropriate to our own gifts—contribute to the holiness of a faith community?

13. See http://www.usccb.org/beliefs-and-teachings/ecumenical-and-interreligious /ecumenical/index.cfm.

2. Priest, prophet, king

Gathered by Christ, the church is called to be on mission. Recall the discussion of the offices of priest, prophet, and king at the end of the chapter. Following a deep and long tradition, *Lumen gentium* (Vatican II) explains that the laity "are by baptism made one body with Christ and are constituted among the People of God; they are in their own way made sharers in the priestly, prophetical, and kingly functions of Christ; and they carry out for their own part the mission of the whole Christian people in the Church and in the world."[14] Consider chapter 4 (nos. 30–38) of *Lumen gentium*. Each of us fulfills the priestly function when we live out our day-to-day lives "to the glory of God and the salvation of men" (no. 34). The description of prophetic office emphasizes our witness to God in how we live (no. 35). The kingly office is one of service, humility, and patience—as Christ's kingship comes through his self-giving to the world (no. 36).

14. *Lumen gentium*, no. 31, http://www.vatican.va/archive/hist_councils/ii_vatican _council/documents/vat-ii_const_19641121_lumen-gentium_en.html.

CHAPTER 14

A Life of Prayer

The God who is beyond all, the one of whom we speak with the limitation of puny human words, created the entire cosmos and everything within it. Within the vast universe of creation, God made human beings in God's own image and likeness (Gen. 1:27), endowing us with a special gift—to be open to receiving God. God could have created human beings so that we enjoyed natural happiness, without ever knowing the existence of our Creator. But God made us so that we can hear and respond to God's voice (prayer) and be filled with God's very life (grace).[1] This radical openness to God is concretized in certain practices called prayer that enable us to be transformed over time so that we can see the world as God sees it and so that we can act in the world as God would act. This transformation, through practices of prayer, enables us to discover and explore our personal gifts and to discern our personal callings so that we can live the fullness of life in service to others in our church and world. This chapter will explore the source of all prayer in the liturgy as the common work of the people of God—as "all Christian prayer finds its source and goal" in the liturgy.[2] We will conclude with a discussion of the liturgy in relationship to personal prayer.

1. Karl Rahner refers to this as the "supernatural existential," wherein grace is a permanent modification of human nature, orienting the fulfillment of humanity to receiving grace—the gift of God's very life in this life and in the next.

2. *Catechism of the Catholic Church*, with modifications from the *Editio Typica* (New York: Doubleday, 1995), no. 1073. The Second Vatican Council's *Constitution on the Sacred Liturgy* (*Sacrosanctum concilium*) phrased it this way: "Nevertheless, the liturgy is the summit toward which the activity of the Church is directed; at the same time it is the fountain from which all her power flows" (no. 10). *The Documents of Vatican II*, ed. Walter M. Abbott, trans. Joseph Gallagher (Piscataway, NJ: America Press, 1966).

Sacramental Life

Although there is a wide array of liturgical prayer, we might narrow the discussion by focusing on sacramental liturgies. It is important to note that our contemporary understanding of sacraments was influenced by the understanding of the human nature of Jesus Christ as a sacrament of God's own nature (presented by Edward Schillebeeckx in 1960), the exposition of the church as the original sacrament (presented by Otto Semmelroth in 1960, and then in a more developed way by Karl Rahner in 1961), and the position of the church as the basic sacrament that is found in the documents of Vatican II.[3] In this light, Jesus Christ is the fundamental sacrament of God—making the invisible God visible—and the primary sacrament of making the Risen Lord present in the world in his Body, the church.

The individual sacraments, then, are the ways that people continue to encounter the Risen Lord, in particular moments of life, so that they can be more deeply conformed to Christ in the paschal mystery (Christ's saving suffering, death, and resurrection), transforming them ever more deeply into his Body, the church. In this sense, we understand baptism as the sacrament that initiates us into the pascal mystery of Christ and his Body, the church, wherein we die with Christ so that we will be raised to new life with him. As St. Paul wrote, "Are you not aware that we who were baptized into Christ Jesus were baptized into his death? Through baptism into his death we were buried with him, so that, just as Christ was raised from the dead by the glory of the Father, we too might live a new life" (Rom. 6:3-4). Every other sacrament, in turn, continues to join us to the redemptive activity of Christ's dying and rising: conforming us more deeply to Christ in confirmation; teaching us his pattern of loving and dying in our vocations of marriage and holy orders; restoring us to his friendship and making us ambassadors of forgiveness and new life in the sacrament of reconciliation; and joining us to his redemptive sufferings in anointing of the sick and viaticum.[4]

Among the church's many liturgies, the Eucharistic liturgy is the preeminent gateway to see ourselves in the paradoxes of who we are: isolated among others, yet gathered together into Christ's Body; formed into our own stories, yet welcomed into God's story; selfish and self-centered, yet

---

3. See Kenan B. Osborne, OFM, *Sacramental Theology: 50 Years after Vatican II* (Hobe Sound, FL: Lectio Publishing, LLC, 2014), 2-15.

4. Kathleen Hughes, *Saying Amen: A Mystagogy of Sacraments* (Chicago: Liturgy Training Publications, 1999), 181.

moved to offer ourselves in thanksgiving as a living sacrifice; filled up with the consumption of many things, yet emptied to be consumed; set in our ways, yet transformed and sent out to be salt for the earth and light for the world. These are some of the ways that the Eucharistic liturgy will shape our sight and form us into becoming a certain kind of human being. Given the predominant influences that most of us face, however, this shaping might be minimal; but for those who are open, it can be a "dangerous activity." As Rodica Stoicoiu notes, "Celebrating the Eucharist is dangerous. We put ourselves at risk because each time we celebrate the Eucharist we are changed."[5] An overview of the different actions of the Eucharist—gathering, listening, preparing, thanking, asking, communing, and being sent—will illustrate how these practices will change us: helping us to see differently and to become a certain kind of person and to be gathered as a people so that we can act purposefully in our world as part of Christ's Body, the church.

Gathering, Listening, and Preparing

Over forty years ago, Henri Nouwen wrote *Reaching Out*, a book that traces three movements of the spiritual life. It is striking how this book still resonates with people today. There is something in each of the movements he identifies that speaks to the importance of being gathered in liturgy so that we can see differently. In his first movement, from loneliness to solitude, Nouwen notes that the roots of people's loneliness are very deep and cannot be touched by optimistic advertising, substitute love images, or social togetherness.[6] He recognizes that it is the experience of most people that "there is no one who cares and offers love without conditions, and no place where we can be vulnerable without being used" (16). Nouwen understands that the second movement, the movement from hostility to hospitality, is equally hard and full of difficulties, for "our society seems to be increasingly full of fearful, defensive, aggressive people anxiously clinging to their property and inclined to look at their surrounding world with suspicion, always expecting an enemy to suddenly appear, intrude, and do harm" (46). In the third movement, from illusion to prayer, Nouwen notes that "our human relationships

---

5. Rodica Stoicoiu, "Eucharist and Hope," *Today's Liturgy* 4 (2010): 10.

6. Henri Nouwen, *Reaching Out: The Three Movements of the Spiritual Life* (Garden City, NY: Doubleday, 1975), 16. In this section, we will give the page numbers from Nouwen's book in parentheses in the text.

easily become subject to violence and destruction when we treat our own and other people's lives as properties to be defended or conquered and not as gifts to be received" (84). He thinks that "the idols of our dreams"—especially our illusion of immortality—are much greater temptations than we tend to believe, reminding us that "we still have a long way to go before we are ready to meet our God, not the God created by our own hands or mind, but the uncreated God out of whose loving hands we are born" (85).

As we speak of Christians gathering—or better still, of being gathered—we are reminded of a clarification that Nouwen makes at the beginning of the third movement, where he explains his ordering of the movements. He notes that the first two—from loneliness to solitude and from hostility to hospitality—are "first" "only in the sense that they are more quickly recognizable and easier to identify with. Not because they are more important" (80). Nouwen well understands that the movement from illusion to prayer "undergirds and makes possible the movement from loneliness to solitude and from hostility to hospitality and leads us to the core of the spiritual life" (80).

Marked by the sign of the cross under which they were baptized, welcomed into the grace and peace of the Father, Son, and Holy Spirit, and joined together in the opening "collect," Christians engage in the introductory or gathering rite of Eucharist, which acts as a doorway to a different way of seeing themselves, each other, and God. Loneliness, hostility, and illusion—three words that capture our common experience—do not have to be denied or avoided because Christians are gathered in a space where they can courageously understand and confess them, in the hope that they can slowly be converted into solitude, hospitality, and prayer. Because we are gathered by a loving God, we begin to see the ways in which God calls us to reach out to our innermost self so that we will be open to a deeper compassionate engagement in the burning issues of our time (43). Because we are gathered by a loving God, we begin to see the ways in which God calls us to reach out to others, to become less and less fearful and defensive and more and more open to the other and his or her world, even when it leads to suffering and death (78). Because we are gathered by a loving God, we begin to see the ways in which God calls us to cast off illusions that hold us captive, entering into intimate union, while still awaiting the day of his final return (114).

We all remember the little rhyme we sang when we were kids: "Sticks and stones may break my bones, but words will never harm me!" Most of us, as adults, regard this more as bravado than as truth. We have come to learn that words are important and they have power. In the liturgy we listen to God's words; they seem strange and out of tune with the words that most often fill our ears. The words come in stories that capture our imagination as we enter into the worlds of Abraham and Sarah, Joseph and Moses, and prophets such as Elijah and Jeremiah. They are words about compassion and forgiveness, about justice and love, about peace and reconciliation. The words come in the form of paradoxes, such as "Whoever wishes to save his life will lose it, but whoever loses his life for my sake and that of the gospel will save it" (Mark 8:35). The words come in parables that use ordinary images such as a field, a coin, a sheep, and two brothers. Like a good book or a good movie, they invite us into another world where we come to see with new eyes and return to our own world transformed, for we are not the same now as we look at things from a different perspective.

Consider, for instance, the parable of the vineyard (Matt. 20:1-16). We know the story well. A landowner goes out at dawn to hire workers to labor in his vineyard. He goes out several more times during the day, hiring laborers even at the last hour. When it comes time to pay the laborers, those who have worked for only an hour are paid the full daily wage. Those who have worked the whole day receive the same—and they are angry. Who wouldn't be angry? Years ago, when studying the Gospel of Luke, I (David) was struck by the Eucharistic themes that are woven throughout the gospel and started to see the parable in a different way. I realized that I would be angry if I had worked all day, unless "one of the workers who labored for an hour was a dear friend."[7]

> I would have been worrying about him all day. Is he still in town waiting to be hired? He needs work desperately. I know his situation; he must be pacing nervously, eager to take any kind of work. Finally, when I see that he has arrived at the vineyard, even at the last hour, I am happy. When he receives a full day's wage, I am overjoyed. I love him as a brother, and I would gladly work all day so that each of us can put food on the table. The owner of the vineyard commits no injustice, and those who had labored all day would see the good of his actions if the last workers were their friends.[8]

If we see from the point of view of friendship and family, "we would see that they have been waiting anxiously and hoping against hope to be hired. Imag-

---

7. David Matzko McCarthy, *The Good Life: Genuine Christianity for the Middle Class* (Grand Rapids: Brazos, 2004), 45.
8. McCarthy, *The Good Life*, 45.

ine their joy when they were hired as the sun was beginning to set. Imagine their joy at a day's wage. God's justice is strange to the world because we are asked not only to give others what they deserve but also to see them as our friends because they are friends of God."[9]

Therese Lysaught provides an important insight regarding how God's stories open up new ways of seeing, becoming, and doing. She notes that we may have to struggle to learn and understand these stories because we are so deeply shaped by a world of stories that are very different, such as the survival of the fittest, life as a zero-sum game, and an eye for an eye.[10] Lysaught insists not only that God's stories are different, but that they are the truest version of reality: "People often say that ethics need to be 'realistic'—that Christians have to navigate in the 'real' world and therefore make all kinds of compromises. But Christians proclaim that the world described in Scripture is the 'real' world—that through Jesus' incarnation, cross, and resurrection God initiated a new reality. . . . By hearing this story in worship, we come to see differently—to see all the world differently, to see the world truthfully."[11]

Bread and wine, as well as other gifts for the poor or the church, are presented. *The General Instruction of the Roman Missal* notes that even though the faithful no longer bring from their own possessions the bread and wine intended for the liturgy as in the past, "nevertheless the rite of carrying up the offerings still retains its force and its spiritual significance" (§73).[12] Edward Foley's commentary on the *General Instruction* notes that "its force and spiritual significance" can be realized, however, only if the worshiping community has "a sustained and recognizable commitment to the poor and oppressed that both extends outside of worship and also has explicitly been brought to prayer in the liturgy."[13] A community engaged in works of charity

---

9. McCarthy, *The Good Life*, 45.

10. M. Therese Lysaught, "Love and Liturgy," in *Gathered for the Journey: Moral Theology in Catholic Perspective*, ed. David Matzko McCarthy and M. Therese Lysaught (Grand Rapids: Eerdmans, 2007), 33.

11. Lysaught, "Love and Liturgy," 33.

12. United States Conference of Catholic Bishops, *The General Instruction of the Roman Missal*, including Adaptations for the Diocese of the United States of America (Washington, DC: United States Catholic Conference, 2003), http://www.usccb.org/liturgy/current/chapter 2.shtml#sect3c.

13. Edward Foley, "The Structure of the Mass, Its Elements and Its Parts," in *A Commentary on the General Instruction of the Roman Missal*, developed under the Auspices of the Catholic Academy of Liturgy and Cosponsored by the Federation of Diocesan Liturgical Commissions, ed. Edward Foley, Nathan D. Mitchell, and Joanne M. Pierce (Collegeville, MN: Liturgical Press, 2008), 166.

and justice, expressing the prayer for those in need in the general interces-
sions, will enable its members to see these gifts as a spiritual donation that
symbolically expresses the personal surrender of one's life within Christ's
unique sacrifice.[14]

Another challenge rests in understanding the presentation of the gifts
of bread and wine as the generous and frequent giving of things needed for
one's own sustenance that are instead given as the fruits of one's labor, as a
"sacrifice."[15] William T. Cavanaugh maintains that the changes in our econ-
omy and society have detached us from the material production, producers,
and even the products that we buy.[16] Our consumer culture makes it difficult
to "see" that the bread is that which "the earth has given and human hands
have made" and that the wine is "the fruit of the vine and work of human
hands." Although it may seem insignificant to many, the practice of preparing bread for the Eucharistic liturgy can retard our tendency to become
more and more detached from the creation of things and from the earth that
discloses "the Creator's presence by visible and tangible signs."[17]

Giving Thanks, Asking for New Vision, Sharing in Communion

The faithful now gather around the one table in thanksgiving and respond
with one voice as they signify their unity as the Body of Christ and their solidarity with all God's people and creation. As the Eucharistic Prayer is prayed,
the community remembers the loving sacrifice of Christ, whose body was
broken and whose blood was poured out for the life of the world, especially
the poor and the wounded, the oppressed and the neglected. Through this
great prayer, the community sees who it is becoming. In the famous words of
Augustine, "It is your own mystery that is placed on the Lord's table. . . . Be

14. Johannes H. Emminghaus, *The Eucharist: Essence, Form, Celebration*, rev. and ed.
Theodor Maas-Ewerd, trans. Linda M. Maloney (Collegeville, MN: Liturgical Press, 1997), 158.
15. Emminghaus, *The Eucharist*, 158.
16. William T. Cavanaugh, "Consumer Culture," in *Gathered for the Journey: Moral Theology in Catholic Perspective*, ed. McCarthy and Lysaught, 243.
17. United States Conference of Catholic Bishops, *Renewing the Earth: An Invitation to
Reflection and Action on the Environment in Light of Catholic Teaching*, A Pastoral Statement of
the United States Catholic Conference (Washington, DC: United States Catholic Conference,
November 14, 1991), http://www.usccb.org/issues-and-action/human-life-and-dignity/environ
ment/renewing-the-earth.cfm. The practice of using consecrated hosts from a previous Mass
is another practice that detaches people from the gifts that are presented at Eucharist.

what you see; receive what you are."[18] The gifts are transformed, but so are the gathered people at the Eucharist. Robert J. Daly notes this, when he writes:

> Two interrelated transformations, both brought about by the power of the Holy Spirit, can be identified as taking place during the Eucharistic celebration. The more important of these, for this is the whole goal and purpose of the Eucharistic celebration, is the ongoing, deepening transformation of the worshipping assembly into the Body of Christ. Subordinate to that transformation, and for the purpose of more effectively achieving it, is the transformation of the bread and wine into the body and blood of Christ for the spiritual nourishment of the assembly in the Holy Communion. In other words, the transformation of the elements does not take place simply to have Christ become present upon the altar but rather, first and foremost, to have Christ and his virtuous dispositions become present in the hearts, minds, wills, and lives of members of the Eucharistic assembly.[19]

Renewed as the new creation that Christians became at baptism, they must now act like Christ and so they pray, asking God to give them continued new sight so that they can become Christ in the world. Having prayed that they will grow in "perfect charity" with their pope, their local bishop, and the entire people whom God has made as God's own people, they further pray that God will:

> Open our eyes to the needs of our brothers and sisters;
> inspire in us words and deeds to comfort those who labor and are
>   burdened.
> Make us serve them truly, after the example of Christ and at his
>   command.
> And may your Church stand as a living witness
> to truth and freedom, to justice and peace,
> that all people may be raised up to a new hope.[20]

18. Augustine, Sermon 272. The Latin text reads: "*Mysterium vestrum in mensa Dominica positum est . . . Estote quod videtis, et accipite quod estis.*" http://www.earlychurchtexts.com /main/augustine/sermon_272_eucharist.shtml.

19. Robert J. Daly, *Sacrifice Unveiled: The True Meaning of Christian Sacrifice* (New York: T&T Clark, 2009), 22. I am indebted for this source to Gerard Austin's "Theosis and Eschatology," *Liturgical Ministry* 19 (Winter 2010): 6-7.

20. "Eucharist Prayer IV: Jesus, the Compassion of God," *Eucharist Prayer for Masses for*

Remembering the actions of Jesus, the community pledges itself again to do likewise in memory of him, to be bread for the world, nourishment for the poor and the hungry.[21]

Writing about the Eucharist, Kathleen Hughes remarks that Jesus's ministry of table fellowship was a scandal throughout his life. His welcome extended to the most disreputable types, such as outcasts, tax collectors, sinners, and the marginalized.[22] And still, today, Christians are welcomed to this table. Perhaps the contemporary challenge for first-world Christians is to not approach this table as another commodity that will enrich our lives. William Cavanaugh clarifies that the practice of the Eucharist is resistant to such tendencies because the consumer of the Eucharist is taken up into the larger body, the Body of Christ.[23] As he notes, "the act of consumption is thereby turned inside out; instead of simply consuming the body of Christ, we are consumed by it."[24] Cavanaugh sees this communing as the decentering and repositioning of the small individual self into "the context of a much wider community of participation with others in the divine life."[25] He uses words spoken by God to Augustine to illustrate this view: "I am food of the fully grown; grow and you will feed on me. And you will not change me into you like the food your flesh eats, but you will be changed into me."[26]

Being Sent Out

In his article "Theosis and Eschatology," Gerard Austin reviews the work of Daniel A. Keating, who writes about the three stages of deification: "It begins in us in a particular moment, it grows and progresses through the entirety of our earthly life, and it is completed in the life of the age to

Various Needs and Occasions, approved for use in the Dioceses of the United States of America by the United States Conference of Catholic Bishops and confirmed by the Apostolic See, English translation according to the Third Typical Edition (Totowa, NJ: Catholic Book Publishing Co., 2011).

21. James Donohue, "The Liturgy as a Source of Formation in Catholic Social Teaching," in *The Heart of Catholic Social Teaching: Its Origins and Contemporary Significance*, ed. David Matzko McCarthy (Grand Rapids: Brazos, 2009), 40.

22. Hughes, *Saying Amen*, 197.

23. Cavanaugh, "Consumer Culture," 256.

24. Cavanaugh, "Consumer Culture," 256.

25. Cavanaugh, "Consumer Culture," 256.

26. Augustine, *Confessions*, trans. Henry Chadwick (Oxford: Oxford University Press, 1991), 7.16, 124. Taken from Cavanaugh, "Consumer Culture," 256.

come."[27] As Austin notes, the second of these three stages constitutes our entire lifetime. If Christian lives can be viewed as "Eucharistic," then we must keep in mind not only how deification—becoming more God-like—is ritually celebrated, but also how it is lived out in ordinary life, for this is the "stuff" or "matter" of one's spiritual sacrifice offered not only at Mass on Sunday, but daily in the world.[28]

In his encyclical letter *Redemptoris missio*, Pope John Paul II outlines some contemporary challenges for "being sent" into the global world. He likens the role of the Christian to St. Paul as he arrived in Athens and spoke at the Areopagus, proclaiming the gospel in language appropriate to and understandable in those surroundings (Acts 17:22-31); he sees this as a symbol of the new sectors in which the gospel must be proclaimed.[29] John Paul II identifies the world of communication—in particular mass media—as the first Areopagus of the modern age. Here he is proposing the use of media not merely to strengthen the spread of the gospel but to integrate the gospel into the "new culture" created by modern communication.[30] In addition to the world of communication, John Paul II finds other forms of "Areopagus" in the modern world toward which the Christian's mission should be directed: commitment to peace; development and liberation of peoples; the rights of individuals and people, especially those of minorities; the advancement of women and children; safeguarding the created world; as well as the immense "Areopagus" of culture, scientific research, and international relations that promote dialogue and open up new possibilities.[31]

These are great challenges to meet as Christians work to faithfully fulfill their "Eucharistic" mission in the world. David Power indicates that there is a continued need for a better theological, practical, and canonical integra-

27. Daniel A. Keating, *Deification and Grace* (Naples, FL: Sapientia Press of Ave Maria University, 2007), 40. Taken from Gerard Austin, "Theosis and Eschatology," *Liturgical Ministry* 19 (Winter 2010): 4.

28. Austin, "Theosis and Eschatology," 5.

29. John Paul II, *Redemptoris missio* (On the Permanent Validity of the Church's Missionary Mandate), December 7, 1990, in *The Encyclicals of John Paul II*, ed. Michael Miller, CSB (Huntington, IN: Our Sunday Visitor Publishing, 1996), 525.

30. John Paul II, *Redemptoris missio*, 526. Pope John Paul II recognizes that this is a complex issue and that this "new culture" originates not just from whatever content is eventually expressed, but from the very fact that there exist "new ways of communicating, with new languages, new techniques and a new psychology." He quotes Pope Paul VI, who wrote that "the split between the Gospel and culture is undoubtedly the tragedy of our time."

31. John Paul II, *Redemptoris missio*, 526.

tion of the baptized into mission in and to the world.[32] Power also suggests that different parts of the world will fulfill this mission in particular ways. Generally, he remarks that "the South is marked by the continued urgency of mission to the poor, a mission for justice, peace, and reconciliation, and a mission of dialogue with persons of other living faiths," while in "the North, especially in Europe, it is a matter of spelling out the presence and mission of the church in secularized cultures, with the realization that ecclesial presence in the development of society is guaranteed by the laity."[33] As Power's observations point out, the needs of the world continue to cry out for the faithful to fulfill their mission, but each in their own "Eucharistic" manner.

Discipleship demands that Christians act justly, have compassion for the poor and the needy, and be people of forgiveness, peace, and reconciliation in a troubled world. Gathering, listening, preparing, thanking, asking, communing, and being sent are liturgical practices that change our mode of interpreting life. As a gateway, the liturgy reveals a truth that challenges us to test the accuracy of the world's claims by seeing differently and by becoming "Eucharistic" people, who live in a certain way and who discover the new life that this way of living offers.

Conclusion

The Holy Trinity, who is responsible for the "work" of the liturgy,[34] sustains that work in our personal prayer. Just as the Father is present in the liturgy, blessing us with God's many gifts—creation, life, incarnation, church, sacraments—God the Father continues to bless us with love and life each moment of our graced lives. Just as Jesus Christ is present in the liturgy—in the person of the minister, in his word, in the community, and under the form of bread and wine—Jesus Christ continues to be present in life "as we live and move and have our being" (Acts 17:28). Just as the Holy Spirit works in the liturgy—to prepare our reception of Christ, to recall and make present the mystery of Christ, and to form us into communion with Christ so that we will always bear fruit beyond the Eucharistic celebration—the Holy Spirit continues to inspire and lead us so that our prayer and our Christian

---

32. David Noel Power, *Mission, Ministry, Order: Reading the Tradition in the Present Context* (New York: Continuum, 2008), 62.

33. Power, *Mission, Ministry, Order*, 62.

34. *The Catechism of the Catholic Church* begins its treatment on sacraments with no. 1: "The Liturgy—Work of the Holy Trinity." See nos. 1077-1109.

life will be inseparable. This is important because our prayer and our life "concern the same love and the same renunciation, proceeding from the same love; the same filial and loving conformity with the Father's plan of love; the same transforming union in the Holy Spirit who conforms us more and more to Christ Jesus; the same love for all men, the love with which Jesus has loved us."[35]

Our personal prayer, originated and sustained by liturgical prayer, is the space within our life journey where we seek to hear God's voice so that we might be of service with the gifts that God has given us. This journey in prayer is often marked by a sense of unworthiness because of our sinfulness and brokenness, by uncertainty and confusion about clarity and task, and by hesitation and worry because of fear and lack of trust; but it is grounded and sustained by the belief that "we love because God first loved us" (1 John 4:19).[36]

For Reflection and Further Study

1. Seeing and praying
There are many influences upon us in life: family and friends, education in school, media (advertisements, social media, television, movies, etc.), our home environment (the city, state, country that we live in), and our family and national heritage, to name a few. How might our prayer—liturgical and personal—act in relation to these other influences? In our prayer life, where might we find support within these other areas? Where might we find conflicting worldviews and values?

2. A Eucharistic life
A key purpose of the Eucharist is to gather us together and to nourish us with the Body of Christ so that we can become Christ in the world. What are the challenges to this process of being gathered, and how—concretely—might the Eucharist shape us to carry on Christ's mission in the world?

---

35. *The Catechism of the Catholic Church*, no. 2745.
36. See also John 3:16: "For God so loved the world that he gave his only son, so that everyone who believes in him might not perish but might have eternal life"; and Romans 5:8: "But God proves his love for us in that while we were still sinners Christ died for us."

3. Getting in the way

This chapter reminds us that liturgical and personal prayer begins with God's work: God the Father blesses us; Jesus Christ is present to us; and the Holy Spirit prepares us for Jesus's presence, recalls and makes Jesus Christ present, and draws us into communion with one another so that we can produce good fruit. What kind of obstacles do we place before God in order to block this work in liturgical prayer? What kind of obstacles do we place before God in our personal prayer?

Conclusion

We hope that the treatment of Scripture in the second part of the book has enlivened your imagination and has given you new ways to see God in the world. In our treatment of prudence in chapter 8, we noted the role of memory in putting our lives in proper perspective and making wise judgments. Consider Scripture as a groundwork of common memory. By reading and reflecting on Israel and the church's memory of God's work in human life, we become part of that work and see ourselves as participants in God's redemptive ways in the world. Notice that we matched thematic concerns, such as prudence and faith, with biblical stories. The Bible is primarily a record and interpretation of events in the life of people as they respond (well or poorly) to God's call. It is story rather than specific principles that shapes our vision and shows us how to respond to the gifts and challenges, joys and sorrows of life. We noted in chapter 7 that the moral law also plays an important role in shaping moral vision. Too often, however, we narrow the moral guidance of Scripture to passages that offer sets of rules. Take some time and place yourselves within the drama/s of Scripture.

We encourage you—moving forward—to read and pray upon Scripture in relationship to the key narratives in the life of Israel and the church. Rather than asking, "What does this passage mean?," ask questions in relationship to character and story: In what ways am I like Mary? In what ways like Martha? What is God calling me to be or do during my "Martha" moments of life? In what ways are we like the people of Israel, who complain in the wilderness that they would prefer to go back to enslavement in Egypt? What do the little people of the gospels, like blind Bartimaeus (Mark 10:46-52), have to tell us about what it means to be open to God in Jesus Christ? How are we like the disciples—willing to follow but often unable to let go of our presumptions about what we think God ought to do? We ought to encounter Scripture as an artist or artisan, willing and open to criticism, in order to perfect her art or craft (chapter 6). It is this kind of reflection and study that cultivates in us what Iris Murdoch calls the "discipline" of a "just and loving gaze."

The discipline of moral vision is the foundation of the moral life. Our inquiry into Scripture and the theological topics of Part 2 follow from the philosophical investigations in Part 1. According to Iris Murdoch, "I can only choose within the world I can see, in the moral sense of 'see' which implies that clear vision is a result of moral imagination and moral effort."[1] We have attempted a defense of this claim by engaging standard figures in moral philosophy, such as Aristotle, Thomas Aquinas, David Hume, Immanuel Kant, and John Stuart Mill. Along with moral vision, Part 1 has also taken an initial step in a treatment of virtue and the connection between vision and virtue. In our treatment, however, we have barely crossed the threshold of richly furnished rooms in moral theology. In our questions for reflection and discussion, we have indicated ways to delve more deeply into a long and interesting tradition of moral philosophy and theology. We have imagined this book as the kind you can go through again and again, drawing on different questions and topics for reflection each time.

We recommend that the interested reader go more deeply into study and reflection. As noted, the questions for reflection offer suggestions on key texts, such as Aristotle's *Nicomachean Ethics*, book 1, or Thomas Aquinas's treatise on happiness, *Summa theologica* II-I, questions 1–5 (see our chapter 4). Beyond a discussion of happiness and the purposes of life, good next steps are inquiry into the cardinal and theological virtues—prudence, justice, fortitude, and temperance, faith, hope, and love. As might be expected, the vices and deadly sins might be the most interesting approach, books such as Henry Fairlie's *Seven Deadly Sins Today* (University of Notre Dame Press) or Rebecca K. DeYoung's *Glittering Vices: A New Look at the Seven Deadly Sins and Their Remedies* (Brazos). Finally, vision and virtue should be put together as a whole along with treatment of principles and norms. We have depended upon two different texts, and we recommend them to you: William Mattison's *Introducing Moral Theology* (Brazos) and David McCarthy and Therese Lysaught's *Gathered for the Journey: Moral Theology in Catholic Perspective* (Eerdmans). In other words, we hope that this book has provided a good look at the moral life amid the lifelong endeavor of learning to develop a "just and loving gaze" upon reality—in terms of moral theology, seeing the world as God's and imbued with divine love and justice.

---

1. Iris Murdoch, *The Sovereignty of Good* (New York: Routledge & Kegan Paul, 1986), 37.

Bibliography

Aquinas, Thomas. *Summa Theologica*. Translated by Fathers of the English Dominican Province. New York: Benziger Brothers, 1948.

Aristotle. *Nicomachean Ethics*. Translated by Martin Ostwald. New York: Macmillan, 1962.

Augustine. *Confessions*. Translated by Henry Chadwick. Oxford: Oxford University Press, 1991.

Benedict XVI. *Caritas in veritate*. Vatican City: Libreria Editrice Vaticana, 2009.

Birge, Mary Katherine, SSJ. "Genesis." In *Genesis: Evolution and the Search for a Reasoned Faith*. Winona, MN: Anselm Academic, 2011.

Catechism of the Catholic Church. Vatican City: Libreria Editrice Vaticana, 1993.

Catholic Study Bible, New American Bible Revised Edition. Edited by Donald Senior, John J. Collins, and Mary Ann Getty. New York: Oxford University Press, 2011.

Chesterton, G. K. *Favorite Father Brown Stories*. New York: Dover, 1993.

Conradi, Peter J. *Iris Murdoch: A Life*. New York: W. W. Norton, 2001.

Covey, Stephen. *The 7 Habits of Highly Effective People: Restoring the Character Ethic*. New York: Simon & Schuster, 1989.

Daly, Robert J. *Sacrifice Unveiled: The True Meaning of Christian Sacrifice*. New York: T&T Clark, 2009.

The Documents of Vatican II. Edited by Walter M. Abbott. Translated by Joseph Gallagher. Piscataway, NJ: America Press, 1966.

Donohue, James, CR. "The Liturgy as a Source of Formation in Catholic Social Teaching." In *The Heart of Catholic Social Teaching: Its Origins and*

Contemporary Significance, edited by David Matzko McCarthy. Grand Rapids: Brazos, 2009.

Emminghaus, Johannes H. *The Eucharist: Essence, Form, Celebration*. Revised and edited by Theodor Maas-Ewerd. Translated by Linda M. Maloney. Collegeville, MN: Liturgical Press, 1997.

Foley, Edward, Nathan D. Mitchell, and Joanne M. Pierce, editors. *A Commentary on the General Instruction of the Roman Missal*. Developed under the Auspices of the Catholic Academy of Liturgy and Cosponsored by the Federation of Diocesan Liturgical Commissions. Collegeville, MN: Liturgical Press, 2008.

Hughes, Kathleen. *Saying Amen: A Mystagogy of Sacraments*. Chicago: Liturgy Training Publications, 1999.

Hume, David. *A Treatise of Human Nature*. Edited by Ernest C. Mossner. New York: Penguin, 1969.

John Paul II. *Redemptoris missio*. On the Permanent Validity of the Church's Missionary Mandate. In *The Encyclicals of John Paul II*, edited by Michael Miller, CSB. Huntington, IN: Our Sunday Visitor Publishing, 1996.

John XXIII. *Pacem in terris*. Vatican City: Libreria Editrice Vaticana, 1963.

Kant, Immanuel. *Critique of Pure Reason*. Translated by Paul Guyer. New York: Cambridge University Press, 1999.

Kant, Immanuel. *Foundations of the Metaphysics of Morals*. Translated by Lewis White Beck. New York: Macmillan, 1959.

Kovesi, Julius. *Moral Notions*. London: Routledge & Kegan Paul, 1967.

Lohfink, Gerhard. *Does God Need the Church? Toward a Theology of the People of God*. Translated by Linda Maloney. Collegeville, MN: Liturgical Press, 1999.

MacIntyre, Alasdair. *After Virtue*. 2nd edition. Notre Dame: University of Notre Dame Press, 1984.

———. *A Short History of Ethics*. Notre Dame: University of Notre Dame Press, 1988.

Mattison, William C., III. *Introducing Moral Theology*. Grand Rapids: Brazos, 2008.

McCabe, Herbert. *What Is Ethics All About?* Washington, DC: Corpus Books, 1969.

McCarthy, David Matzko. *The Good Life: Genuine Christianity for the Middle Class*. Grand Rapids: Brazos, 2004.

McCarthy, David Matzko, and M. Therese Lysaught, editors. *Gathered for the Journey: Moral Theology in Catholic Perspective*. Grand Rapids: Eerdmans, 2007.

Metzger, Bruce M. *A Textual Commentary on the Greek New Testament.* 3rd edition. Stuttgart: United Bible Societies, 1971.

Mill, John Stuart. *Utilitarianism.* 2nd edition. Edited by George Sher. Indianapolis: Hackett, 2002.

Moloney, Francis J. *The Gospel of John.* Sacra Pagina 4. Collegeville, MN: Liturgical Press, 1998.

Murdoch, Iris. *The Sovereignty of Good.* New York: Routledge & Kegan Paul, 1986.

Nouwen, Henri. *Reaching Out: The Three Movements of the Spiritual Life.* Garden City, NY: Doubleday, 1975.

Plato. *The Republic.* Translated by Robin Waterfield. New York: Oxford University Press, 1993.

Porpora, Douglas. *Landscapes of the Soul: The Loss of Moral Meaning in American Life.* New York: Oxford University Press, 2001.

Power, David Noel. *Mission, Ministry, Order: Reading the Tradition in the Present Context.* New York: Continuum, 2008.

Taylor, Charles. *A Secular Age.* Cambridge, MA: Belknap, 2007.

United States Conference of Catholic Bishops. *Renewing the Earth: An Invitation to Reflection and Action on the Environment in Light of Catholic Teaching.* A Pastoral Statement of the United States Catholic Conference. Washington, DC: United States Catholic Conference, 1991.

United States Conference of Catholic Bishops. *The General Instruction of the Roman Missal.* Including Adaptations for the Diocese of the United States of America. Washington, DC: United States Catholic Conference, 2003. http://www.usccb.org/liturgy/current/chapter2.shtml#sect3c.

United States Conference of Catholic Bishops. *The Roman Missal.* Renewed by decree of the Most Holy Second Ecumenical Council of the Vatican. Promulgated by authority of Pope Paul VI and revised at the direction of Pope John Paul II. English translation according to the third typical edition. Approved by the United States Conference of Catholic Bishops and confirmed by the Holy See. Totowa, NJ: Catholic Book Publishing Co., 2011.

Vatican II. *Gaudium et spes: Pastoral Constitution of the Church in the Modern World.* Vatican City: Libreria Editrice Vaticana, 1965.

Vatican II. *Lumen gentium: Dogmatic Constitution on the Church.* Vatican City: Libreria Editrice Vaticana, 1964.

Weil, Simone. *Waiting for God.* Translated by Emma Craufurd. New York: Putnam, 1951.

Index

Abraham, 147-49

Aquinas, Thomas, 46-47, 52-53, 65, 67, 71-73, 80, 85-86, 93-94, 109-10, 114, 121, 131, 156-57, 166

Aristotle, 14-15, 17, 42-43, 45-48, 51-53, 55, 63, 65, 71, 73, 85, 108

Augustine, 38, 144-45, 166, 180-82

baptism, 169-70, 173, 175, 181

beauty, 18, 23, 26, 36-37, 88, 135

Bible. *See* gospels; New Testament letters; Old Testament

Chesterton, G. K., 83-86, 92-93

church, 156, 159-73; communion of, 180-81; as holy, 166-69, 172; as living/ spiritual sacrifice, 168, 170, 176, 183; in *Lumen gentium*, 159-60, 170, 173; as missionary, 169-70; mission of priest, prophet, king, 170, 173; New Testament/early, 113, 124, 130, 153-54, 171; as one, 160-66, 171-72; sacramental life of, 175-76; as sent out, 182-84

compassion, 7, 13, 58-59, 112-13, 118, 128, 172, 177-78, 184

conscience, 50, 103-4, 109

covenant, 134, 140, 142, 146, 148, 151-52, 165

Covey, Stephen, 105-7

creation, 112, 120, 123, 125, 134-38, 143-46, 152-53, 157-58, 180-81; in Genesis, 135-37, 143, 145

disciples/discipleship, 117-19, 123-30, 152, 160-61, 163, 169, 184, 187-88; and the way of God, 123-24, 126-29

Eucharist, 135, 153, 163-65, 169, 171, 175-78, 180-85; and the paschal mystery, 165, 175

evil, 67, 95, 102-3, 136-37, 143-46

exodus, the, 138-40

faith, 48-49, 111-22, 123-24, 127, 129, 139, 148-49

forgiveness, 124-25, 152, 175, 178, 184

fortitude, 48, 88-90, 109, 131

Francis, Pope, 26, 29

friendship, 9-10, 14, 24-25, 37-39, 45-46, 175, 179

God, 46, 48-50, 95-96, 102-5, 111-17, 120-22, 123-27, 129-31, 134-46, 147-57, 159-61, 168-71, 177-84, 187-88; the Father, 175, 184-86; the Trinity, 49, 143, 184. *See also* Holy Spirit; Jesus Christ

good/goodness, 16-18, 21-22, 24-28,

193

CPSIA information can be obtained
at www.ICGtesting.com
Printed in the USA
JSHW011326230123
36620JS00001B/64

9 780802 874870